KATHERINE MANSFIELD
AND
VIRGINIA WOOLF

KATHERINE MANSFIELD
AND
VIRGINIA WOOLF

A PUBLIC OF TWO

ANGELA SMITH

CLARENDON PRESS · OXFORD
1999

Oxford University Press, Great Clarendon Street, Oxford OX2 6DP
Oxford New York
Athens Auckland Bangkok Bogotá Buenos Aires Calcutta
Cape Town Chennai Dar es Salaam Delhi Florence Hong Kong Istanbul
Karachi Kuala Lumpur Madrid Melbourne Mexico City Mumbai
Nairobi Paris São Paolo Singapore Taipei Tokyo Toronto Warsaw
and associated companies in
Berlin Ibadan

Oxford is a registered trade mark of Oxford University Press

Published in the United States
by Oxford University Press Inc., New York

British Library Cataloguing in Publication Data
Data available

Library of Congress Cataloging in Publication Data
ISBN-0-19-818398-4
Data available

1 3 5 7 9 10 8 6 4 2

Typeset by Graphicraft Limited, Hong Kong
Printed in Great Britain
on acid-free paper by
Bookcraft Ltd,
Midsomer Norton, Somerset

FOR

DAN SMITH

Preface

THIS book began when I first read C. K. Stead's Penguin sel-
ection of Katherine Mansfield's letters and journals and was
dazzled by their mixture of wit, intensity, and insight into
modernity. Her anxiety about reviewing Virginia Woolf's *Night
and Day* produced a brilliant, oblique comment about her own
fiction, and about her peculiar position as both an insider and
an outsider in London's literary world. When the volumes of
the Clarendon edition of Mansfield's letters appeared, from 1984,
contextualized with scholarly care by Vincent O'Sullivan and
Margaret Scott, the rapport and intimacy as well as the jealousy
and malice of Mansfield's relationship with Virginia Woolf intrigued me and I began to read their fictions in conjunction with
their personal writings to try to understand what Woolf's professional reasons were for persisting with what was evidently,
in many ways, a prickly and difficult friendship.

I propose an explanation for their affinity in the first chapter
on liminality. The following two chapters are biographical in
that they trace liminal experience through the personal writings
of the two women, revealing similarities that mould their fiction:
attitudes to time and memory; to childlessness and loss; to life-
threatening disease; to sexuality; to being married to editors, and
to artistic experiment. The main focus of the book is then on
aspects of their fiction and on the two writers' particular inflection
of modernism, considering how they embodied in their fictional
techniques their own responses to the impact on their imagina-
tions of their creative context, particularly Post-Impressionism
in painting, and the cinema.

The quality and quantity of critical writing on Katherine Mansfield is significantly lower than that on Virginia Woolf, though
there are notable exceptions, such as the essays in two fairly
recent collections, *Katherine Mansfield: In from the Margin*, edited
by Roger Robinson, and *The Critical Response to Katherine*

Mansfield, edited by Jan Pilditch, as well as *Illness, Gender, and Writing* by Mary Burgan. In order to avoid an imbalance in my treatment of the two writers, I have included details of valuable critical assessments principally in the notes rather than in the main text. As I was concluding the book I obtained a copy of Nóra Séllei's *Katherine Mansfield and Virginia Woolf: A Personal and Professional Bond*; like mine, its approach is through the personal writings to the fiction, but it suggests that Woolf, for instance, influenced the transformation of *The Aloe* into 'Prelude', whereas I try to explore a less tangible reciprocity. I was also able to read Patricia Moran's *Word of Mouth*, a fine comparative study of Mansfield and Woolf that focuses on their attitudes to their own bodies. Like me, she uses the writings of Julia Kristeva in her readings of the texts.

I should like to acknowledge the stimulus and help provided by colleagues at Stirling and elsewhere, friends, and family. Felicity Riddy and Andrew Gurr introduced me to the range and diversity of New Zealand writing in general, and to Mansfield in particular; teaching Woolf with Neil Keeble changed my view of her writing. Nick Royle's insight and encouragement were invaluable, and the vigorous scholarship of both Mary Maaga and Kerryn Goldsworthy provided impetus at key moments. The work and interest of past and current postgraduates and colleagues, particularly Stephanie Newell, Jane Stewart, and Renata Casertano, have provided a congenial context for thinking and talking about Woolf and Mansfield. The OUP readers and Sally Stopford offered constructive comments for which I am grateful. The most significant debt is to my family, particularly to my husband and colleague, Grahame, for his thoughtful reading of various drafts, to Matthew, to Helena for her revisions, and to the dedicatee, whose incisive, detailed, and sympathetic responses to my work and to Woolf's and Mansfield's writing have been as irreplaceable to me as his computing skills and his patience in using them on my behalf.

I should like also gratefully to acknowledge the grant awarded to me by the Carnegie Trust for the Universities of Scotland to visit the Katherine Mansfield Archive at the Turnbull Library in Wellington, and to acknowledge the kindness and co-operation of the librarians at the Turnbull Library. Tony Bradshaw at the Bloomsbury Workshop has been generous in offering me advice and help. I was able to write this book only because of the University of Stirling's policy of providing sabbatical leave to support research, for which I am grateful.

A. S.

Stirling
6 December 1997

Acknowledgements

The author wishes to thank the following copyright holders for permission to use material:

The estate of Virginia Woolf, the editors, the title, and Hogarth Press as publisher for extracts from *The Diary of Virginia Woolf* and *The Letters of Virginia Woolf*

The Society of Authors as the Literary Representative of the Estate of Virginia Woolf for extracts from *Mrs Dalloway, To the Lighthouse, Jacob's Room, The Voyage Out* and *The Complete Shorter Fiction of Virginia Woolf*

Harcourt Brace and Company for extracts from *Mrs Dalloway, To the Lighthouse, Jacob's Room, The Complete Shorter Fiction of Virginia Woolf, The Diary of Virginia Woolf* and *The Letters of Virginia Woolf*

The Society of Authors as the Literary Representative of the Estate of Katherine Mansfield for extracts from *The Journal of Katherine Mansfield* and *The Letters of Katherine Mansfield*

Alfred A Knopf Inc for extracts from *The Short Stories of Katherine Mansfield*

Extracts from *The Collected Letters of Katherine Mansfield*, 4 vols, (Oxford: Clarendon Press, 1984–96) are reprinted by permission of Oxford University Press

Henrietta Garnett for Vanessa Bell's woodcut 'A Society' in Virginia Woolf's *Monday or Tuesday* (Hogarth Press)

Contents

Abbreviations

CS   Katherine Mansfield, *The Collected Short Stories* (Harmondsworth: Penguin, 1981)

CSF   *The Complete Shorter Fiction of Virginia Woolf*, ed. Susan Dick (London: Hogarth, 1989)

KMCL   *The Collected Letters of Katherine Mansfield*, ed. Vincent O'Sullivan and Margaret Scott, 4 vols. (Oxford: Clarendon Press, 1984–96)

KMJ   *The Journal of Katherine Mansfield*, ed. J. M. Murry, Definitive Edition (London: Constable, 1954)

KML   *The Letters of Katherine Mansfield*, ed. J. M. Murry, 2 vols. (London: Constable, 1928)

KMMML *Letters Between Katherine Mansfield and John Middleton Murry*, ed. Cherry A. Hankin (London: Virago, 1988)

VWD   *The Diary of Virginia Woolf*, ed. Anne Olivier Bell and Andrew McNeillie, 5 vols. (Harmondsworth: Penguin, 1979–85)

VWL   *The Letters of Virginia Woolf*, ed. Nigel Nicolson and Joanne Trautmann, 6 vols. (London: Chatto & Windus, 1980–3)

Strictly speaking, 'Katherine Mansfield' is a pseudonym and should be used in its entirety throughout the text, but I abbreviate it to 'Mansfield'.

What a queer fate it is—always to be the spectator of the public, never part of it. This is part of the reason why I go weekly to see K. M. up at Hampstead, for there at any rate we make a public of two.

Virginia Woolf's diary, 30 November 1918

I

Liminal Experience

> [T]his part of Hampstead recalls Katherine to me—that faint
> ghost, with the steady eyes, the mocking lips, &, at the
> end, the wreath set on her hair.[1]

THE haunting presence of Katherine Mansfield recurs in
Virginia Woolf's personal writing throughout her life, often as
a slightly challenging phantom. Mansfield was a foreigner for
Woolf; she came from a distant colony and had travelled from
the Antipodes twice and returned there once by the time she
was 20. Woolf was awed by the wildness of both her colonial
and her bohemian life. At the same time Mansfield was deeply
familiar, as Woolf recognized and their writing reveals. They
mirror each other constantly, in spite of their evident differences.
In 1920, for instance, each describes a moment of suspension
which is at once a response to the natural world and an impression of their experience of writing. For both writers the site where
the moment occurs is significant: for Mansfield it is the sea's edge,
and for Woolf the Sussex downs. For Mansfield 'that moment
of suspension' is like the movement of the waves, when one 'is
flung up—out of life—one is "held", and then,—down, bright,
broken, glittering on to the rocks, tossed back, part of the ebb
and flow.'[2] Woolf's story about writing describes the narrator's
experience as that of 'the hawk over the down—alone, or what
were the worth of life? To rise; hang still in the evening, in
the midday; hang still over the down . . . Oh, but I drop to the
turf!'[3] Mansfield's account is, characteristically, more violent and
physically traumatic than Woolf's, but the moment of intense
perception comes 'while one hangs, suspended in the air'.[4]

---

[1] VWD iii. 50, 7 Dec. 1925. The punctuation and spelling in both writers' diaries
and letters are erratic; I quote them as they are in the originals.
[2] KMJ 203, Feb. 1920.   [3] CSF 117.   [4] KMJ 203.

The moment of isolated suspension is for both writers fleeting, but revealing of schism. This is manifest in the passage in Mansfield's journal. Suspended, Mansfield sees the seascape but also 'a huge cavern where my selves (who were like ancient sea-weed gatherers) mumbled, indifferent and intimate . . . and this other self apart in the carriage, grasping the cold knob of her umbrella, thinking of a ship, of ropes stiffened with white paint and the wet, flapping oilskins of sailors'.[5] The moment is gendered in contradictory ways. The huge cavern is womb-like, occupied by undifferentiated multiple selves whose language, a semiotic babble, is in touch with the instinctual maternal body and with the sea, perhaps a version of amniotic fluidity. The other self is defined through phallic imagery, stiffened ropes and the umbrella knob, and is preoccupied with control of the heaving water. The 'glimpse' in which 'the whole life of the soul is contained' is an in-between moment, the wave caught in the air before it falls, the writer caught between femininity and masculinity, in a liminal space.

In a wide-ranging exploration of the cultural significance of borders, *Strangers to Ourselves*, Julia Kristeva identifies the shift in which the stranger, the foreigner, is acknowledged to be within and not a hostile presence outside the self: Kristeva argues that, after centuries in which the self was defined by identifying others as foreign through their nationality, religion, or culture, human consciousness changed. With the advent of the Freudian concept of the unconscious 'foreignness is within us: we are our own foreigners, we are divided.'[6] Kristeva focuses particularly on Freud's essay *Das Unheimliche*, published in 1919, just after the end of the First World War. The date is significant since the war itself both exacerbated and problematized boundaries and definitions of foreignness; large numbers of troops from all over the empire, including Mansfield's brother among the Anzacs, arrived to fight and die in a remote European war. Wilfred Owen's poem 'Strange Meeting' indicates the difficulty of defining the enemy as other when the poet dreams that he encounters the German he had bayoneted to death the day before. The man

[5] KMJ 203.
[6] Julia Kristeva, *Strangers to Ourselves*, trans. Leon S. Roudiez (London: Harvester Wheatsheaf, 1991), 181.

says: ' "I am the enemy you killed, my friend." '[7] In the same year that *Das Unheimliche* was published, Woolf and Mansfield were in close touch with one another, and discussing how to construct subjectivity in fiction, to acknowledge the strange within the self, the masculine within the feminine. The crossover in Freud's essay, the point at which the familiar becomes the unfamiliar and consequently frightening, uncanny, is constantly enacted in Woolf's and Mansfield's fiction, when Kezia is terrified by the well-known house in 'Prelude', for instance, or when Mrs Ramsay has to wrap the sheep's head in a shawl to pacify Cam in *To the Lighthouse*. In Freud's terms, the fear which has been repressed, which ought to have remained secret, comes to light. As Kristeva interprets this: 'The foreigner is within us. And when we flee from or struggle against the foreigner, we are fighting our unconscious—that "improper" facet of our impossible "own and proper." '[8]

Freud theorizes, and Woolf and Mansfield depict these moments of encountering the foreigner within, as ordinary experiences of the extraordinary, but in *Powers of Horror* Kristeva pursues the idea of the unconscious further and discusses a foreigner that cannot be accommodated within the self. In abjection, a horror that fascinates but repels is 'ejected beyond the scope of the possible, the tolerable, the thinkable. It lies there, quite close, but it cannot be assimilated.'[9] Though they seem not to have acknowledged it directly to each other, both Mansfield and Woolf experienced abjection. This is discussed in an analysis of their personal writings in the second and third chapters, but Kristeva's account of abjection's effect on narrative applies to their fiction: 'when even the limit between inside and outside becomes uncertain, the narrative is what is challenged first. If it continues nevertheless, its makeup changes; its linearity is shattered, it proceeds by flashes, enigmas, short cuts, incompletion, tangles and cuts.'[10] Fictional borders are erased in Woolf's and Mansfield's entries into their characters' abjection, for instance in the horrors revealed through Septimus Warren-Smith in *Mrs Dalloway* or through Linda in 'Prelude', but the two authors' personal writings indicate that their own experience of

---

[7] Wilfred Owen, *Collected Poems* (London: Chatto & Windus, 1963), 36.

[8] Kristeva, *Strangers to Ourselves*, 191.

[9] Julia Kristeva, *Powers of Horror*, trans. Leon S. Roudiez (New York: Columbia University Press, 1982), 1.　　　　　　　　　　　　　[10] Ibid. 141.

abjection made them aware of the inadequacy of the fictional modes that they inherited from the nineteenth century. The two chapters on abjection as it is explored in the personal writings lead into chapters that focus exclusively on its effect on the fiction, within the wider context of an interpretation of liminality in their work.

The word 'liminality' derives from the Latin *limen* meaning boundary or threshold. Limits and borders fascinate Woolf and Mansfield, though their familiarity with in-between places is often a source of pleasure rather than horror:

Don't you think the stairs are a good place for reading letters? I do. One is somehow suspended. One is on neutral ground—not in ones own world nor in a strange one. They are an almost perfect meeting place. Oh Heavens! How stairs do fascinate me when I think of it. Waiting for people—sitting on strange stairs—hearing steps far above, watching the light *playing* by itself—hearing—far below a door, looking down into a kind of dim brightness, watching someone come up ... *Must* put them in a story though! People come out of themselves on stairs—they issue forth, unprotected. And then the window on a *landing*. Why is it so different to all other windows?[11]

In this letter, written in 1921, Mansfield expresses her fascination with the transitional, an in-between place, which was a preoccupation and sometimes a place of habitation that she shared with Woolf. At the time that she wrote the letter her friendship with Woolf was effectively over as Mansfield, who died in January 1923 at the age of 34, was too ill with tuberculosis to live in London after September 1920; following what proved to be their final meeting, though they did not realize it at the time, Woolf records in her diary how 'of a sudden comes the blankness of not having her to talk to.'[12] The tantalizing suggestion and playfulness of the letter about the staircase help to indicate why Woolf was persistently haunted by the 'faint ghost' of Mansfield.

In the passage, stairs and letters are brought together, as means of communication between one place and another: letters a meeting-place for people who are parted, stairs a link between floors but also, like letters, another point of suspension. Letters bring the past of the writer into the present of the reader, so

[11] KMCL iv. 256, 29 July 1921.   [12] VWD ii. 61, 25 Aug. 1920.

the reader is suspended in time, 'not in ones own world nor in a strange one'. This position of unobserved watcher, as well as reader yearning for the pleasure of the letter, suggests the writer who longs to put all this into a story, a kind of suspended letter to her own reader. The immanence and strangeness of the familiar scene stem from the evocation of light: the oxymoron 'dim brightness' and the joyful image of 'the light *playing* by itself'. This is what Woolf describes as 'that direct flick at the thing seen which was her gift',[13] a moment of ordinary bliss, of domestic revelation, in which people on stairs, not knowing that they are seen, appear without masks. The roots of the humdrum word 'landing' are revealed and made strange; it is the point of rest on a voyage, with, for Mansfield, a special window as a point of perspective.

This study will explore the personal, critical, and fictional writing of Katherine Mansfield and Virginia Woolf, tracing through the personal writings the private experiences which cemented the strange and, in many ways, unlikely affinity between them, pivoting particularly on liminality in their life and writing. The focus as far as Woolf is concerned will be on her writing up to *To the Lighthouse* (1927), the period in which her interaction with Mansfield's ideas and writing is most intense. In a little pamphlet published in 1972, Ronald Hayman drew attention to the effect of Mansfield's writing on her contemporaries, and specifically on Woolf:

Together with James Joyce and the novelist Dorothy Richardson, Virginia Woolf is usually given far more credit than Katherine Mansfield for introducing the 'stream of consciousness' to swing the novel's pendulum in the other direction. Katherine has even been accused (by V. S. Pritchett) of imitating Virginia. Virginia's earliest use of the technique was in her short stories *Monday or Tuesday* which were written between 1917 and 1921 . . . But Katherine started to use the technique in her short story *Feuille d'album*, which was published in 1917, so if Virginia was imitating anyone, it was Katherine. 'And I was jealous of her writing,' she wrote when Katherine died, '— the only writing I have ever been jealous of.'[14]

---

[13] VWD iv. 315, 26 May 1935.
[14] Ronald Hayman, *Literature and Living: A Consideration of Katherine Mansfield & Virginia Woolf*, Covent Garden Essays, 3 (London: Covent Garden 1972), 16.

Without subscribing to the notion that a critical gold medal can be awarded to the winner of the stream of consciousness race, one can concur with Hayman's general argument, as Clare Hanson does: 'Just as Mansfield's work has been devalued because she worked in the short story form, so the substantial amount of work she produced in her letters and journals has been consistently undervalued.'[15]

Katherine Mansfield was until recently disregarded in studies of modernism. Hanson suggests that 'there is a clear connection between Mansfield's choice of the short story form and her marginal position' because the 'short story is a genre which, both formally and in terms of its traditional content, has always been marginal, fragmented.'[16] The situation changed with the publication of Sydney Janet Kaplan's *Katherine Mansfield and the Origins of Modernist Fiction*, which explores Mansfield's experimental fictional techniques in relation to the writing of her contemporaries, particularly Woolf. In her brief study, Nóra Séllei discusses the 'complementarity of Woolf's and Mansfield's versions of female modernism'.[17] In a major book on matrophobia in the work of Woolf and Mansfield, Patricia Moran affirms that '[j]uxtaposing their work in this way allows me both to decenter Woolf and, at the same time, to restore Mansfield to her position as a key figure in the development of British women's modernism.'[18] Her argument is that, for Mansfield, creativity becomes 'a search for principles of boundedness that would defend against feminine materiality.'[19] This study is equally concerned with boundaries, but with an exploration of the transitional zone that Woolf and Mansfield were both threatened and excited by when they were producing their finest fiction. The liminal place inflects their version of modernism, and affects their perception of the boundaries between different art forms; Chapter 6 has a particular focus on Post-Impressionist painting, and Chapter 7 on early cinema. As Kaplan indicates, 'women are at the center

[15] Bonnie Kime Scott (ed.), *The Gender of Modernism: A Critical Anthology* (Bloomington, Ind.: Indiana University Press, 1990), 300.   [16] Ibid.
[17] Nóra Séllei, *Katherine Mansfield and Virginia Woolf: A Personal and Professional Bond* (Frankfurt: Peter Lang, 1996), 111.
[18] Patricia Moran, *Word of Mouth: Body Language in Katherine Mansfield and Virginia Woolf* (London: University Press of Virginia, 1996), 15.
[19] Ibid. 89.

rather than the margins of British modernism, and this is no less the case with Katherine Mansfield than it is with Virginia Woolf.'[20] Later chapters will suggest that the formal and thematic pre-occupations of their fictions intersect, and that close attention to their personal writings as well as their fiction and criticism shows that their experience gave them a particular insight into the uncertainties and dilemmas of the early twentieth century from the perspective of women on the cusp, trying to negotiate a pro-fessional and personal stance within patriarchy. This introduct-ory chapter discusses interpretations of liminality, in an attempt to explain why Woolf was haunted by Mansfield, 'that faint ghost'. It moves from apparently accidental similarities in their perception of non-chronological time, to psychic experiences in which a more significant resemblance is perceptible. In confronting their own demons, arising from their late-Victorian childhoods and the constructions of gender they were offered as a norm, both writers become familiar with liminal sexual territory. Their precarious health makes them seem to fit the mould of the help-lessly dependent woman while their drive to write and to control their professional lives is seen by both writers as masculine, and also by Woolf as androgynous. The encoding of the conflict, its transposition into fiction, is welcomed by both of them as a refuge from total disintegration.

Margins and boundaries, traditionally sites of dispute and dis-tress, are the stuff of post-structuralist interrogation; in 'From Work to Text' Roland Barthes expresses it like this: 'The Text is not a co-existence of meanings but a passage, an overcrossing; thus it answers not to an interpretation, even a liberal one, but to an explosion, a dissemination.'[21] The personal writings, the texts, of Katherine Mansfield and Virginia Woolf, particularly of Mansfield, reveal a constant questioning of conventional lim-its in social behaviour and in fictional modes, but they also show an intimate knowledge of overcrossing, being suspended, sitting on strange stairs, inhabiting an in-between place, a state of lim-inality, a crossing-place from one state of being to another. In antiquity such boundaries were revered and represented: on

[20] Sydney Janet Kaplan, *Katherine Mansfield and the Origins of Modernist Fiction* (Ithaca, NY: Cornell University Press, 1991), 6.
[21] Roland Barthes, *Image-Music-Text*, ed. Stephen Heath (London: Fontana, 1977), 159.

Etruscan sarcophaguses from the third and fourth centuries BC, grieving relatives are shown grouped at the boundary beyond which they cannot follow the dead person into the afterlife, with husband and wife sometimes holding hands across the divide at the moment of parting. This transitional zone has been mythologized, for instance in the story of Orpheus and Eurydice; it is when they are leaving the underworld and approaching the world of the living, after Orpheus has braved the terrors of Hades, that he looks back and the potential danger is realized. In the ancient world, places of transition were haunted and perilous; Hecate, an attendant on Persephone, and so in a sense a ruler over the living and the dead, was worshipped at crossroads, where dishes of food were left for her. Ancient statues of Hecate show her in triple form, perhaps looking along three roads, again an indication of potential confusion and danger for humans with only one pair of literal and metaphorical eyes; in transitional places humans cannot see clearly enough. The Roman god Janus was also represented as a double-faced head, though the word means 'gate'; the *janus* was usually a free-standing gate or arch, not attached to a city wall, used for the formal setting out of an army. There was a right and a wrong way to march out, emphasizing the significance attached to the place of transition; Janus also became the god of the doorway of a Roman house, and prayers were offered to him as the god of beginnings. Until fairly recently in Britain, crossroads, traditionally the burial place for suicides who could not be interred in sanctified ground because they had committed self-murder, were liminal territory, out of holy bounds but not exactly damned.

Julia Kristeva interprets classical thresholds in relation to writing. She instances James Joyce when she suggests in an interview with Susan Sellers that the language of male writers has 'recourse to the semiotic, the inscription of the archaic relation to the mother in language—it isn't the monopoly of women . . . Any creator necessarily moves through an identification with the maternal, which is why the resurgence of this semiotic dynamic is important in every act of creation.'[22] The selves as ancient seaweed gatherers, mumbling and intimate, in Mansfield's

---

[22] Philip Rice and Patricia Waugh (eds.), *Modern Literary Theory*, 3rd edn. (London: Edward Arnold, 1996), 135–6.

moment of suspension by the waves, seem to represent the semiotic, but this identification with the maternal holds a particular danger for women. Because the woman writer and her mother are both female, the woman writer may lose her identity in that of the archaic mother, the semiotic, whereas the male writer can differentiate himself from the other. Kristeva interprets the myth of Eurydice's failure to escape from Hades in this context: she reads the descent into hell as the resurgence of the semiotic: 'This explains perhaps why it's more difficult for women to get out of hell, this descent: Orpheus manages it but Eurydice doesn't.'[23] This is the anxiety explored in Moran's book; she suggests that Woolf's and Mansfield's painful separation from the mother was effected, partially at least, through their fiction, but that their writing is also permeated by revulsion and self-loathing. The fear in matrophobia is the fear of becoming the mother; in the terms of Mansfield's moment of suspension, it is a fear of remaining in the sea-cave or womb, and not attaining the independent stance, gendered as masculine, of the self that sits in the carriage thinking of a ship.

Mary Burgan rightly rejects the proposition that Mansfield indicates resistance to patriarchal constraints by consistently adopting the language of the sea-cave dwellers: 'I cannot make a case for her writing as inspired dictation taken from the imaginary realm of maternal, pre-Oedipal silence . . . Mansfield's writing is a willed resistance to the chaos of hallucinatory dementia.'[24] The question of pre-Oedipal communication is addressed in *Gender Trouble*, where Judith Butler summarizes Kristeva's position in relation to the irruption of the semiotic in poetic language: 'Her strategic task, then, is neither to replace the Symbolic with the semiotic nor to establish the semiotic as a rival cultural possibility, but rather to validate those experiences within the Symbolic that permit a manifestation of the borders which divide the Symbolic from the semiotic.'[25] Butler's critique of Kristeva's position is grounded in her interrogation of the heterosexual norm posited by Freud and accepted by

[23] Ibid. 136.
[24] Mary Burgan, *Illness, Gender, and Writing* (London: Johns Hopkins University Press, 1994), 91–3.
[25] Judith Butler, *Gender Trouble: Feminism and the Subversion of Identity* (London: Routledge, 1990), 85.

Lacan and Kristeva; she asks whether 'we read the desire for the father as evidence of a feminine disposition only because we begin, despite the postulation of primary bisexuality, with a heterosexual matrix for desire'.[26] Her argument is persuasive in suggesting that the assumption that a child must repress its desire for the parent of the other sex is evidence of acculturation in what is defined as a primal moment before acculturation takes place. Because Kristeva does not challenge this, she sees psychotic dangers in a female writer's sustained entry into the semiotic. However, both Woolf and Mansfield align themselves with a position that posits heterosexuality as a norm, although they also defy it; in the writing of both there is anxiety about deferring to the Father's Law and an implicit acknowledgement of its power. Both cross its boundaries, and assert the semiotic, but the incursions are fleeting raids rather than anything sustained. Because their view of gender is congruous with Kristeva's, her reading of gender and of abjection is used to interpret liminality in their work.

The root of 'liminal' recurs in the word 'limbo', from *limbus* in Latin, meaning edge or border. Limbo, originally the zone outside hell where the spirits of the just who died before Christ, and of unbaptized babies, awaited the Last Judgement, subsequently came to mean a general condition of neglect or oblivion. This is again undefined space which can be turned into a site of resistance and even celebration, as in the slaves' limbo dance when they were on the Middle Passage between the old world in Africa and the new world of the plantations; the dance required extreme agility in an almost impossibly cramped and confined space. However, limbo is more often associated, as the Middle Passage must have been for most of the slaves, with negation of a coherent sense of self and identity, like the gateway from Hades for Kristeva's Eurydice.

In the late nineteenth century the word 'liminality' began to be used in psychology to mean the threshold of sensation, but it is in twentieth-century anthropology that its resonance as a concept is explored most fully. Victor Turner and Edith Turner developed the early work of Arnold van Gennep, the French ethnographer who, in 1908, isolated and named 'rites of passage'

---

[26] Butler, *Gender Trouble: Feminism and the Subversion of Identity*, 60.

as a crucial part of ritual in tribal societies. In the first phase the ritual subjects are detached and separated from their habitual place in their society; they are then 'liminars'; finally they are re-aggregated, inwardly and outwardly changed, into their society. Victor and Edith Turner define the ritual subjects in the liminal phase as 'ambiguous, for they pass through a cultural realm that has few or none of the attributes of the past or coming state. Liminars are betwixt and between. The liminal state has frequently been likened to death; to being in the womb; to invisibility, darkness, bisexuality, and the wilderness.'[27] Though Mansfield and Woolf were both bisexual, other liminal experience is even more significant for them: for instance, that their childlessness left them feeling ambivalent but sometimes uncreated as women, and Woolf's mental illness and Mansfield's tuberculosis left them betwixt and between either sanity and derangement, or life and death. Victor Turner's powerful phrase 'threshold people'[28] evokes a significant aspect of their lives. This is not the rather romantic twilight zone of the intellectual *émigré* described by Homi Bhabha, 'gathering at the frontiers; gatherings in the ghettos or cafés of city centres; gathering in the half-life, half-light of foreign tongues'[29] but a psychological site that claims threshold people whether they like it or not. As Mary Douglas says, 'all margins are dangerous.'[30] Liminars are often traditionally regarded as polluting, taboo, or inauspicious to other people because their in-between state can be experienced as threatening or anarchic in relation to an established order, be it social, political, or artistic. This has a bearing on Mansfield and Woolf, in that tuberculosis, suicide, and insanity were all regarded in the nineteenth and early twentieth centuries as shameful and therefore taboo; respectable working-class families often concealed the presence of their consumptives, just as people of a range of social classes were secretive about attempted or actual familial suicide because it could lead to social ostracism, and relatives classified as mad were locked away.

[27] Victor Turner and Edith Turner, *Image and Pilgrimage in Christian Culture* (Oxford: Basil Blackwell, 1978), 249.

[28] Victor Turner, *The Ritual Process* (New York: Aldine de Gruyter, 1995 (1969)), 95.

[29] Homi Bhabha, *The Location of Culture* (London: Routledge, 1994), 139.

[30] Mary Douglas, *Purity and Danger: An Analysis of Concepts of Pollution and Taboo* (London: Routledge & Kegan Paul, 1966), 121.

The Turners' exploration of the liminal makes clear that it can be a transitional state, as it is in rites of passage or in pilgrimage in what they call 'historical' as opposed to 'tribal' religions, but it can also be a place of spiritual and physical habitation. The religious who has renounced the world and home, becoming a mendicant who depends on charity, inhabits liminality. Without suggesting that what Woolf and Mansfield experienced was in any way perceived by them as religious, I hope to identify both dimensions of liminality in their work, the rite of passage and the place of habitation. Mansfield's ceaseless physical journeys in search of a climate that would allow her to breathe more easily and so to work were repeated rites of passage in that the journeys sharpened her already acute senses: 'Every tiny flower seems to shine with a new radiance. That queer chain of modern life seems to be unknown.'[31] Similarly Woolf, after a phase of intense anxiety which was for her a symptom of the beginning of a phase of mental illness, writes in her diary that 'at one's lowest ebb one is nearest a true vision.'[32] As the Turners say of the defamiliarizing effect of travelling, when pilgrims at the end of their pilgrimage encounter what are essentially well-known images and icons, they are made strange, a positive version of the uncanny: 'The innocence of the eye is the whole point here, the "cleansing of the doors of perception".'[33] While this is a personal happening and is concerned with the effects of transition, though for the pilgrims it may take place in the company of others, dwelling in a liminal space may also open the liminar to unpredictable experiences: 'Communitas breaks into society through the interstices of structure, in liminality'.[34] Victor Turner asserts that liminality generates works of art; he refers to Henri Bergson, whose philosophy was part of the context in which Mansfield and Woolf came to maturity:

Bergson saw in the words and writings of prophets and great artists the creation of an 'open morality,' which was itself an expression of what he called the *élan vital*, or evolutionary 'life-force.' Prophets and artists tend to be liminal and marginal people, 'edgemen,' who strive with a passionate sincerity to rid themselves of the clichés associated

[31] KMCL iv. 254, 25 July 1921.   [32] VWD i. 298, 13 Sept. 1919.
[33] Turner and Turner, *Image and Pilgrimage in Christian Culture*, 11.
[34] Ibid. 251.

with status incumbency and role-playing and to enter into vital relations with other men in fact or imagination.[35]

The suggestion is that the liminar may be surprised by *communitas*, that is, one dweller in the in-between zone may recognize
another because '[t]he bonds of communitas are undifferentiated,
egalitarian, direct, extant, nonrational, existential'.[36] Liminars
'are neither here nor there', partly because they develop a
heightened faculty of memory, a crucial aspect of both Woolf's
and Mansfield's creativity. Turner comments that liminars 'tend
to develop an intense comradeship'.[37] In Woolf's words this might
be described as the 'queer sense of being "like" '[38] that she had
about Mansfield; she writes flippantly but tellingly to a friend
about the spiritual dimension of her relationship with Mansfield:

Katherine Murry is, poor woman, very ill; she has been all the winter,
and gets no better. Probably she will go to San Remo; but I feel rather
dismal about her. You thought her too painted and posed for your more
spartan taste I think. But she is all kinds of interesting things underneath, and has a passion for writing, so that we hold religious meetings
together praising Shakespeare.[39]

Liminality is used in this study as a state of transition but
also as a trope to suggest a place of erratic and sometimes erotic
habitation for Woolf and Mansfield in their lives and in their
fiction, relating that to the imperatives of modernism as they
perceived and formulated them. The in-between place could
be pleasurable, like the stairs, but was frequently experienced
by both writers as what Woolf calls the dark underworld, the
gateway between life and death. What Susan Gubar writes of
Mansfield's protagonists obtains also for Mansfield and Woolf
themselves, and is a description of the abjection portrayed by
Kristeva: Gubar suggests that they 'dread that they are contaminating creatures, neither healthily animal nor fully human,
inhabiting a frightening liminal zone where even the boundaries
of the body refuse to function predictably.'[40]

---

[35] Turner, *The Ritual Process*, 128.
[36] Turner and Turner, *Image and Pilgrimage in Christian Culture*, 250.
[37] Turner, *The Ritual Process*, 95.   [38] VWD ii. 45, 31 May 1920.
[39] VWL ii. 382–3, 12 Aug. 1919.
[40] Susan Gubar, 'The Birth of the Artist as Heroine', in Carolyn G. Heilbrun and
Margaret R. Higonnet (eds.), *The Representation of Women in Fiction* (Baltimore:
Johns Hopkins University Press, 1983), 32.

Virginia Woolf had seen Mansfield in this in-between state[41] and remembered it. When Mansfield died in 1923 at the age of 34, Woolf wrote both to their mutual friend Dorothy Brett and to Mansfield's husband, John Middleton Murry, to ask for a photograph of her, and in 1932 she responded positively to the suggestion that there should be a picture of Mansfield in the National Portrait Gallery as 'there is always something in a picture that a photograph cannot give.'[42] What the painter might have seen is clear in Woolf's own vignette recalling visits to Mansfield in 1920, written a week after Mansfield's death in 1923. The phrase 'neither healthily animal nor fully human' is prefigured in her comment that Mansfield 'looked very ill—very drawn, & moved languidly, drawing herself across the room, like some suffering animal.' The diary entry, looking back two and a half years, moves in and out of the present tense as if the writer is reliving the experience:

I go up. She gets up, very slowly, from her writing table . . . She had her look of a Japanese doll, with the fringe combed quite straight across her forehead. Sometimes we looked very steadfastly at each other, as though we had reached some durable relationship, independent of the changes of the body, through the eyes. Hers were beautiful eyes—rather doglike, brown, very wide apart, with a steady slow rather faithful & sad expression. Her nose was sharp, & a little vulgar. Her lips thin & hard. She wore short skirts & liked 'to have a line round her' she said.[43]

The provocative suggestion that the durable relationship is independent of the body, reached through the eyes, perhaps refers obliquely to a homoerotic attraction between the two women which is rejected in favour of a writerly rapport. Woolf's description of Mansfield also implies that she sees her as a series of lines, with her straight fringe, short skirts, sharp nose and thin, hard lips. Woolf seems to construe these lines as expressing boundaries; Mansfield liked to have a limit around her. Only the expression of the eyes crosses these barriers, an observation that can be read in a variety of ways. Mansfield felt that her

---

[41] Moran interprets Gubar to refer the secret liminal presence here to the engulfing femininity of the pre-Oedipal mother. I accept this, but my own use of liminality has a wider application.　　[42] VWL v. 135, 11 Dec. 1932.
[43] VWD ii. 226, 16 Jan. 1923.

territory was constantly invaded by domestic demands at this time, and by the disease invading her body and consuming her lungs: 'The house is full of women, today. The peevish old lying cook in the kitchen who says it is I who make all the work; L. M. bringing my lunch with a "take, eat, this is my body" air; an old 'un sweeping the stairs away & down in the studio a little dwarf sewing buttons'.[44]

The steadfast gaze exchanged between Woolf and Mansfield indicates Mansfield's relief at escaping, in conversation with Woolf, what she describes dismissively as a 'house full of women' carping about their domestic tasks, and in Patricia Moran's reading, attempting to engulf her in 'excessive maternal generosity'.[45] 'L. M.', Mansfield's companion Ida Baker, offers herself as the means by which Mansfield can live, a version of feeding off the maternal, self-sacrificing body but also of being encompassed by it. Mansfield's loathing of the relationship is evident; Moran demonstrates a similar resistance in Woolf, much later when she was within weeks of her death, because her doctor, Olivia Wilberforce, had offered her quasi-maternal food, milk and cream, when she was in a state of torment about her capacity for creative writing.

Woolf's description of Mansfield obviously says as much of Woolf herself as of Mansfield: about the sense that she betrayed the friend who had kissed her, and who had promised a relationship that would not allow interference from gossip and malice. There is an awareness that her own snobbery and jealousy had warped her perception of Mansfield: 'Still there are things about writing I think of & want to tell Katherine . . . I have the feeling that I shall think of her at intervals all through life. Probably we had something in common which I shall never find in anyone else.'[46] That this was a unique friendship is borne out by Woolf's subsequent writing; in 1931 she tells Vita Sackville-West that Mansfield 'had a quality I adored, and needed . . . I dream of her often—now thats an odd reflection—how one's relation with a person seems to be continued after death in dreams, and with some odd reality too.'[47] The language here, in a letter to her living lover, emphasizes unresolved desire for a ghostly lover,

[44] KMCL ii. 334, 27 June 1919.   [45] Moran, *Word of Mouth*, 39.
[46] VWD ii. 227, 16 Jan. 1923.   [47] VWL iv. 366, 8 Aug. 1931.

tantalizing because it can never be even temporarily fulfilled. In her journal she recounts a dream of Mansfield eight years after her death, saying that 'we met, beyond death, & shook hands; saying something by way of explanation, & friendship: yet I knew she was dead.'[48]

The dreams perhaps reveal that Woolf did not need the photograph she had asked Murry to supply; certainly the visual image that she conjures up is as potent as any of the surviving photographs or portraits of Mansfield. The nature of the rapport between the two women, and the significance of their friendship in terms of their writing, is implicit in Murry's comment on Woolf and her sister, Vanessa Bell. It is included in a letter to Mansfield when she was dangerously ill and wintering in the Mediterranean, as she had to do for several years, this time at Ospedaletti, on the Italian Riviera. It anticipates Woolf's memory that Mansfield liked to have a line round her:

I suppose it's because they are . . . sincere & devoted artists. They don't make that continual, ghastly, enervating *personal* claim on your attention that other women do. If you disagree with them, they don't visibly hasten to agree with you. There's something hard & definite & self-contained about them . . . I realised how much she liked you. I think her affection for you is quite genuine & real.[49]

The affinity between Woolf and Mansfield will be fully explored in subsequent chapters, tracing the liminal in their experience and its expression in their writing; this affinity is suggested by what appears to be the physical accident of the form that Mansfield's journals take. They are not in any obvious chronological sequence, prefiguring the form of Woolf's later novels. One of Mansfield's early mentors, Arthur Symons, whose *Studies in Prose and Verse* she quotes from in her early notebooks, writes that 'human life and human manners are too various, too moving, to be brought into the fixity of a quite formal order.'[50] This seems to chime with Mansfield's experience as it is represented in her journals. Murry published a version of Mansfield's journal first in 1927, with a scrapbook in 1940 and what he called a definitive edition of the journal in 1954. Rather than the fixity

[48] VWD iv. 29, 8 June 1931.
[49] C. A. Hankin (ed.), *The Letters of John Middleton Murry to Katherine Mansfield* (London: Constable, 1983), 223–4.
[50] Arthur Symons, *Studies in Prose and Verse* (London: J. M. Dent, 1904), 18.

of the formal order of a journal, however, the sources for the volumes edited by Murry are a series of notebooks oddly anti- cipating Doris Lessing's *The Golden Notebook* in that they are concurrent, not chronological, and contain a variety of material: unposted letters, drafts of letters, self-analysis, ideas for stories, fragments of stories, the final version of stories, reminiscences, comments on and quotations from the books she was reading, and a medical record of her various treatments and encounters with doctors.[51] Many of the notebooks seem to have belonged to her in childhood but to have been used throughout her life; often the adult notebooks have a slightly adolescent opening, as if the writer is remembering the role of the diary as a confidante and confessional for a girl at odds with her family. Mansfield begins the fourth notebook in the Turnbull Archive, dated 1915 when she was 27: 'I shall be obliged if the contents of this book are regarded as my private property.' The twenty-fourth note- book, from 1917, begins: 'In these notes—so help me Lord, I I shall be open and above board.'[52] Fiction and autobiography blur in the notebooks; shopping lists, and quotations from writers such as Shakespeare and Dickens jostle each other; little drawings and squiggles ornament the pages; Mansfield tries dif- ferent signatures and different names. The intrusive reader of these private records can often only guess at the dates of entries, judging by handwriting or knowledge of Mansfield's biography. Past and present interact physically; moods swing. In May 1921 the seventh notebook contains a joking unposted letter from the editor of the *Tig Courier*; Tig and Wig were the nicknames she and Murry used. It gives her address, invalid as she is, as 'Tig, Stillin, Bedfordshire',[53] but this is followed by a serious statement of intent, identifying herself with her mother: 'One thing I am determined upon. And that is *to leave no sign*. There was a time— it is not so long ago—when I should have written *all* that has happened since I left France. But now I deliberately choose to tell no living soul. I keep silence as Mother kept silence.'[54] The fact that her private space has been posthumously invaded makes this discomforting reading.

[51] Ian Gordon gives an accurate and detailed description of this in 'The Editing of Katherine Mansfield's Journal and Scrapbook', repr. in Jan Pilditch (ed.), *The Critical Response to Katherine Mansfield* (Westport, Conn.: Greenwood, 1996), 77–82.
[52] KMJ 119.   [53] Ibid. 248, May 1921.   [54] Ibid. 254, July 1921.

The link between this representation of her own experience through the notebooks, which Mansfield used as a source for her fiction, and Woolf's interest in evoking 'an ordinary mind on an ordinary day' is obvious; Woolf wrote 'Modern Fiction' at the time when she was closest to Mansfield, was liking 'her more & more' and thinking 'we have reached some kind of durable foundation.'[55] The resistance to chronological development, and to the assumption 'that life exists more fully in what is commonly thought big than in what is commonly thought small' is embodied in the form of Mansfield's notebooks, though the specific reference in 'Modern Fiction' is to Joyce's *A Portrait of the Artist as a Young Man*:

The mind receives a myriad impressions—trivial, fantastic, evanescent, or engraved with the sharpness of steel. From all sides they come, an incessant shower of innumerable atoms; and as they fall, as they shape themselves into the life of Monday or Tuesday, the accent falls differently from of old; the moment of importance came not here but there . . . Life is not a series of gig lamps symmetrically arranged; life is a luminous halo, a semi-transparent envelope surrounding us from the beginning of consciousness to the end . . . Let us record the atoms as they fall upon the mind in the order in which they fall.[56]

Reviewing the first published version of Mansfield's journal after her death, Woolf comments on the way in which Mansfield recorded the atoms as they fell and shows how the process acquires its own pattern and significance:

But then as the scraps accumulate we find ourselves giving them, or more probably receiving from Katherine Mansfield herself, a direction. From what point of view is she looking at life as she sits there, terribly sensitive, registering one after another such diverse impressions? She is a writer; a born writer. Everything she feels and hears and sees is not fragmentary and separate; it belongs together as writing.[57]

Despite the touch of irony in the repetition in the essay of the phrase 'terribly sensitive', it is clear that Woolf admires and understands, possibly with the jealousy she admits to elsewhere, Mansfield's ability to create a coherence out of apparently random

[55] VWD i. 291, 12 July 1919.
[56] Virginia Woolf, *The Common Reader* (London: Hogarth, 1962), i. 189–90.
[57] Pilditch (ed.), *Critical Response to Katherine Mansfield*, 16.

jottings, though the full diversity of the notebooks would not have been evident from the printed and edited version.

In the same review Woolf recognizes a division in the self that writes the journal; though she does not acknowledge it here, her own diaries are evidence that she was aware of her role as the writer of the diary. Woolf comments in 1924: 'It strikes me that in this book I *practise* writing; do my scales; yes & work at certain effects.'[58] In the review of the journal, Woolf describes Mansfield's diary as her 'mystical companion', thinking perhaps of such passages as the one in which Mansfield addresses a new journal with the words: 'Come, my unseen, my unknown, let us talk together.'[59] Woolf respects the intimacy of the journal:

We feel that we are watching a mind which is alone with itself; a mind which has so little thought of an audience that it will make use of a shorthand of its own now and then, or, as the mind in its loneliness tends to do, divide into two and talk to itself . . . But then the diary is so private and so instinctive that it allows another self to break off from the self that writes and to stand a little apart watching it write.[60]

This passage perceives intuitively a process that Mansfield describes in a letter she wrote, shortly before she died, to Koteliansky, a Ukrainian Jew who settled in England in about 1911 and was a friend of both Mansfield and Woolf: 'I am a divided being with a bias towards what I want to be, but no more. And this it seems I cannot improve . . . If you knew how many note books there are of these trials, but they never succeed. So I am always conscious of this secret disruption in me'.[61]

It could be argued that awareness of the divided self is a central concern of modernism and has no essential relationship with liminality or with women's experience; 'The Love Song of J. Alfred Prufrock', *The Waste Land*, *A Portrait of the Artist as a Young Man*, *Women in Love*, *The Secret Sharer*, and *Heart of Darkness*, for instance, are clearly preoccupied by the divided if not the fragmented self, and Woolf and Mansfield knew Conrad's, Joyce's, Lawrence's, and Eliot's work. But the particular demons of division that Mansfield and Woolf wrestled

[58] VWD ii. 319, 17 Oct. 1924.   [59] KMJ 270, 13 Nov. 1921.
[60] Pilditch (ed.), *Critical Response to Katherine Mansfield*, 16.
[61] KML ii. 260, 19 Oct. 1922.

with arose partly from the female condition of their class and generation, and were given spectral forms in two defining late Victorian familiars, the apparently undemonic Angel in the House, and the vampire. The struggle was exacerbated by the precarious health of the two writers; unlike Janus or Hecate, they could not look two or three ways simultaneously. Both found the gendered behaviour expected of them by the societies into which they were born incompatible with their sense of themselves as writers; both were the daughters of fathers with strongly developed notions of respectability and of the dignity of their high bourgeois status. The Victorian ideal of woman-hood is wittily evoked by Virginia Woolf in a speech, 'Professions for Women', given to the Women's Service League in 1931, that parodies Sarah Stickney Ellis's *The Women of England: Their Social Duties and Domestic Habits* (1839) in which Ellis asks 'what man is there in existence who would not rather his wife should be free from selfishness, than be able to read Virgil without the use of a dictionary?'[62] The unselfish model wife encapsulates the qualities of the Angel in the House, according to Woolf; the phrase is taken from Coventry Patmore's four-part poem of that name. She assumes that her audience belong to 'a younger and happier generation' than hers and need to be introduced to the Angel, though she is still quite a familiar familiar at the end of the twentieth century:

She was intensely sympathetic. She was immensely charming. She was utterly unselfish. She excelled in the difficult arts of family life. She sacrificed herself daily. If there was a chicken, she took the leg; if there was a draught she sat in it—in short she was so constituted that she never had a mind or a wish of her own, but preferred to sympathize always with the minds and wishes of others. Above all—I need not say it —she was pure.[63]

Ironically enough, this is an accurate summary of the character of Woolf's beloved mother, Julia Stephen, which gives a particular dimension to Woolf's triumph in murdering the Angel and invites a matrophobic interpretation; the matricidal impulse

[62] Quoted in M. H. Abrams (ed.), *The Norton Anthology of English Literature*, 6th edn. (New York: W. W. Norton, 1993), ii. 1599.
[63] Virginia Woolf, *The Death of the Moth and Other Essays* (London: Hogarth, 1942), 150.

could be applied to the brutal attack on the Angel and to the death of Mrs Ramsay in *To the Lighthouse*.[64] Woolf only hints at the impossibility of killing a phantom, but it undermines the apparent confidence in the passage and relates to the division in the self that both she and Mansfield were aware of. Her justification for the slaughter was that it was either the Angel or her, a claim that will be examined more fully in the second and third chapters which concern Woolf's relationship with her parents.

Early in Woolf's writing career the Angel had intervened decorously but insistently whenever she was about to review a novel by a male writer, whispering that she should ' "be tender; flatter; deceive; use all the arts and wiles of our sex. Never let anybody guess that you have a mind of your own." '[65] She is of course in the process of using some of those beguiling arts in her speech, charming her audience, though she has triumphantly a mind as well as a room of her own. The significant shift is that her version of Patmore's Angel uses her wiles to beguile men, whereas for Woolf they are ways of communicating with other women. Woolf's analysis of the Angel's death focuses sharply on the power of a fiction, a myth, a cultural construction, to control behaviour, and to waste the time and emotional energy of women with purpose and ambition. The Angel had to be wiped out by the emblem of Woolf's profession, an inkpot:

Thus, whenever I felt the shadow of her wing or the radiance of her halo upon my page, I took up the inkpot and flung it at her. She died hard. Her fictitious nature was of great assistance to her. It is far harder to kill a phantom than a reality. She was always creeping back when I thought I had despatched her. Though I flatter myself that I killed her in the end, the struggle was severe; it took much time that had better have been spent upon learning Greek grammar; or in roaming the world in search of adventures. But it was a real experience; it was an experience that was bound to befall all women writers at that time.[66]

Woolf's defiant act is not just murder but sacrilege, the profanation of the mother's law of self-sacrifice in defence of Woolf's intellectual identity; the phantom survives and haunts Woolf's text.

---

[64] Patricia Moran provides a detailed and incisive account of this reading in *Word of Mouth*, ch. 5.

[65] Woolf, *The Death of the Moth and Other Essays*, 150.   [66] Ibid. 151.

The fact that the Angel is gendered as female in Woolf's battle with patriarchy suggests the power of female complicity with patriarchal values, and that Woolf found it harder to resist the role model of the sympathetic woman than the more obvious injustices of paternal phallocentrism. The physicality of her description of a fight with an abstraction endorses her assertion that it was 'a real experience', as demanding as, though less fulfilling than, learning Greek, putting her and all those women who had to attempt to kill their *alter ego* in this way, as she ironically suggests, at a disadvantage in terms of education and range of fictional material.

Mansfield initially seemed much more resilient, bohemian, and in control of her destiny than Woolf; the Angel does not haunt her early personal writing. It was she who invited Murry to become her tenant and then her lover, just as she got her own way with her family in New Zealand. When she was ill and lonely in Ospedaletti in 1919, however, she reverted to the wistful role of the child bride, dependent and frightened. Murry remained in London to edit the *Athenaeum*; when he failed to respond adequately to her desperate need for comfort and sympathy she sent him the poem called 'The New Husband' which begins:

> Some one came to me and said
> Forget, forget that you've been wed
> Who's your man to leave you be
> Ill and cold in a far country
> Whos the husband—who's the stone
> Could leave a child like you alone.[67]

Murry's understandable response to this was that it seemed 'more like a snake with a terrible sting'[68] than a poem, and he complains that he is not made of steel but will try to carry Mansfield's burden as well as his own. In analysing her reaction to Murry's letter in one of her notebooks, she traces her own decline from being an independent woman into one that resembles a Victorian ideal of womanhood, the sentimental ballad form confirming the lapse. While the Angel was tough though she pretended not to be, the clinging dependent woman drained a man who was himself rather dependent:

[67] KMCL iii. 136, 4 Dec. 1919.   [68] KMMML 236, 8 Dec. 1919.

Before that I had been the man and he had been the woman and he had been called upon to make no real efforts. He'd never really 'supported' me. When we first met, in fact, it was I who kept him, and afterwards we'd always acted (more or less) like men-friends. Then this illness—getting worse and worse, and turning me into a woman and asking him to put himself away and to *bear* things for me . . . I *clung* to him still—still the child.[69]

The dismissive equating of femininity with helplessness is linked to the burden of the female body as it is in Mansfield's 'Prelude' where Linda, trapped by the beginning of another feared pregnancy, imagines herself as captain of a ship sailing away from domestic bondage. In her letters Mansfield uses a significant metaphor of herself; in her helpless femininity, as she sees it, she has become a haunting and predatory presence to Murry: 'I wont be such a vampire again'[70] and 'You make me out so cruel that—I feel you cant love me in the least—a vampire—I am not.'[71] She constructs herself as the sinister angel/vampire because she has had to take on the role of dependent and frail, even predatory, femininity; the divided self, the dual personality looking at itself which Woolf commented on in her review of the journal is clear in all its complexity here.

The horror of the vampire myth obviously derives, as it is presented in *Dracula* for instance, from the state of being undead, neither decaying decently in the coffin nor fully alive, encapsulated in the fact that Dracula's image does not appear in Jonathan Harker's shaving mirror. Like Woolf's Angel in the House, the vampire 'was always creeping back when I thought I had despatched her' as Mansfield feels that she herself does with Murry, the alien otherness of the vampire terrifying those who want to shut out what they cannot cope with, which Murry admitted he did with Mansfield's disease. In the darkest disintegration of the self, both Mansfield and Woolf had experience of liminality, inhabiting as a constant rather than transitional state a limbo between life and death. In her phases of incipient insanity, Woolf tried to take her own life, and eventually succeeded because she feared that she would prey on Leonard: 'I cant fight it any longer, I know that I am spoiling your life, that

---

[69] KMCL iii. 159, 15 Dec. 1919.   [70] Ibid. 150, 9 Dec. 1919.
[71] Ibid. 156, 12 Dec. 1919.

without me you could work. And you will I know.'[72] What she feared most, as she explained in a farewell note to her sister, was the 'undead' state of being alive but insane: 'I feel that I have gone too far this time to come back again. I am certain now that I am going mad again. It is just as it was the first time, I am always hearing voices, and I know I shant get over it now.'[73] This is not a divided self caught between social expectations and inner impulses but a terrible liminal place, looking both ways, not mad but not confident of sanity. In a parallel passage in her journal Mansfield sums up her undead situation, reminding the reader of Keats's last letter to Charles Brown in which he writes: 'I have an habitual feeling of my real life having past, and that I am leading a posthumous existence.'[74] Mansfield, separated from Murry, wonders whether to enter the Gurdjieff Institute for the Harmonious Development of Man in Fontainebleau, a commune which claimed to restore the harmony between the physical, emotional, and intellectual which civilization had destroyed:

My spirit is nearly dead. My spring of life is so starved that it's just not dry. Nearly all my improved health is pretence—acting. What does it amount to? Can I walk? Only creep. Can I do anything with my hands or body? Nothing at all. I am an absolutely hopeless invalid. What is my life? It is the existence of a parasite. And five years have passed now, and I am in straiter bonds than ever.[75]

The fear of being predatory, a parasite and abject, makes her decide to keep apart from Murry because '[l]ife together, with me ill, is simply torture with happy moments. But it's not life.'[76] The spectre of contamination had arisen on their wedding day, when Mansfield saw Murry surreptitiously wipe his lips after they had kissed. Both writers in fact dread that they are, in Gubar's phrase quoted earlier, abjects, 'contaminating creatures, neither healthily animal nor fully human'.[77] Though there is no Gothic element to their creative writing, their experience of what Kristeva calls 'the strange within us' leads to fascination with mapping psychic borders. Both are familiar with their own ghosts;

---

[72] VWL vi. 481, 18? Mar. 1941.   [73] Ibid. 485, 23? Mar. 1941.
[74] Maurice Buxton Forman, (ed.), *The Letters of John Keats* (London: Oxford University Press, 1952), 529.   [75] KMJ 332, 14 Oct. 1922.
[76] Ibid. 333.   [77] Gubar, 'Birth of Artist as Heroine', 32.

Kristeva links the uncanny with the foreigner, enabling a reading of Woolf's and Mansfield's fear of the liminal within:

The uncanny would thus be the royal way . . . by means of which Freud introduced the fascinated rejection of the other at the heart of that 'our self,' so poised and dense, which precisely no longer exists ever since Freud and shows itself to be a strange land of borders and othernesses ceaselessly constructed and deconstructed . . . The foreigner is within us.[78]

For both Mansfield and Woolf writing itself was a way of exploring the ambiguous liminal state, of mapping it and so of relieving their fear of it; Mansfield exclaims in her journal, a few months before her death: 'Ah, I feel a little calmer already to be writing. Thank God for writing!'[79] Writing is the means of investigating what Woolf describes as 'the dark underworld' which 'has its fascinations as well as its terrors'.[80] In 1982, Vincent O'Sullivan expressed this view about them:

With Katherine Mansfield, as with her friend and competitor Virginia Woolf, the strands of fiction and biography are not easily unwound. They *may* be, of course, and for literary assessment must be. Yet for most readers, an interest in one usually takes with it a curiosity about the other. Few of us read so purely that the author quite drops away, as theory frequently recommends.[81]

The final comment may refer to the critical anxiety arising from Barthes's essay 'The Death of the Author'; for Barthes, however, personal writings are as much texts as fictions. Without a preoccupation with biography, it is possible to recognize, for instance, that the interaction between the fiction, the critical, and the personal writings of Woolf and Mansfield expresses their conviction that life, critical response, and writing cannot be divided into tidy parcels. As Mansfield says to the novelist William Gerhardi of Laura in 'The Garden Party':

That is bewildering for a person of Laura's age. She feels things ought to happen differently. First one and then another. But life isn't like that. We haven't the ordering of it. Laura says, 'But all these things must

[78] Kristeva, *Strangers to Ourselves*, 191.   [79] KMJ 332, 14 Oct. 1922.
[80] VWD ii. 126, 8 Aug. 1921.
[81] Katherine Mansfield, *The Aloe with Prelude* (Wellington: Port Nicholson, 1982), 7.

not happen at once.' And Life answers, 'Why not? How are they divided from each other.' And they *do* all happen, it is inevitable.[82]

The phrase 'life isn't like that' echoes Woolf's question in 'Modern Fiction', 'is life like this?' Woolf and Mansfield emphasize the constant unravelling of myths and cultural constructions of femininity and masculinity in life, and in every kind of writing. Just as, in 'The Garden Party' and in *Mrs Dalloway*, death and the party are elements of the same experience for Laura and Clarissa, so the fictions and the critical and personal writings open up a shared experience for the reader. To privilege the fiction over the personal writing would be to mirror the veneration for masculine discourse that Woolf attacks in *A Room of One's Own*:

And since the novel has this correspondence to real life, its values are to some extent those of real life. But it is obvious that the values of women differ very often from the values which have been made by the other sex; naturally, this is so. Yet it is the masculine values that prevail. Speaking crudely, football and sport are 'important'; the wor-ship of fashion, the buying of clothes 'trivial'. And these values are inevitably transferred from life to fiction. This is an important book, the critic assumes, because it deals with war. This is an insignificant book because it deals with the feelings of women in a drawing-room. A scene in a battle-field is more important than a scene in a shop— everywhere and much more subtly the difference of value persists.[83]

This book will maintain a comparative focus. It begins with a close examination of the personal writings of Mansfield and Woolf, exploring their experience of liminality, and their refusal of masculine hieratic value. It then moves on to trace the ways in which the pleasures, desires, and terrors of lives shadowed by death and insanity are expressed in fiction. Woolf's attraction to Mansfield began with Mansfield's story 'Prelude', which was first published by the Woolfs' Hogarth Press. The story hints at an awareness of the Angel in the House, in Kezia's resistance to play-ing with dolls; of the vampire, in Linda's physical dependence and dreams of escape; and of matrophobia (fear of becoming the mother) in Linda's attraction to her mother combined with her resolute rejection of the maternal role. Woolf shows, in a diary entry in 1928, five years after Mansfield's death, that she is still

---

[82] KML ii. 196, 13 Mar. 1922.
[83] Virginia Woolf, *A Room of One's Own* (London: Hogarth, 1929), 110–11.

haunted by her unique friendship with her. Though she was at the time writing *Orlando*, partly in celebration of another writer, Vita Sackville-West, her dream of Mansfield reveals that her intense feeling about Mansfield is central to her writing, and to her insight into the nature of women's experience as the 'sad faced women' suggest:

All last night I dreamt of Katherine Mansfield & wonder what dreams are; often evoke so much more emotion, than thinking does—almost as if she came back in person & was outside one, actively making one feel; instead of a figment called up & recollected, as she is, now, if I think of her. Yet some emotion lingers on the day after a dream; even though I've now almost forgotten what happened in the dream, except that she was lying on a sofa in a room high up, & a great many sad faced women were round her. Yet somehow I got the feel of her, & of her as if alive again, more than by day.[84]

The relation between Woolf and Mansfield, as it is reflected in their fiction and personal writing, reveals doublings in unexpected places, and Woolf, as she shows in this passage, retained a sense of Mansfield as instigator, 'actively making one feel', after Mansfield's death. Mansfield's entourage of 'many sad faced women' in Woolf's dream also hints at Woolf's perception of Mansfield's capacity to interpret female experience in her fiction. In Woolf's dreams, memory, and imagination Mansfield is often pictured in limbo, in the liminal space between one world and another, no man's land in every sense, but territory made familiar to both these women through their experience of the Angel in the House, of the vampire and of disease, the foreigners within. The wreath Mansfield wears in Woolf's image of her a week after her death links love with writing and death; a white wreath has bridal connotations, but the fact that she seems to have attained the wearing of the wreath reminds the reader of Woolf's jealousy of Mansfield. She may be crowned with the poet's garland of laurels, as well as with an ice-cold symbol of death. Woolf's yearning for her dead friend is unmistakable: '[W]here is she, who could do what I can't! Then, as usual with me, visual impressions kept coming & coming before me—always of Katherine putting on a white wreath, & leaving us, called away; made dignified, chosen. And then one pitied her. And one felt her reluctant to wear that wreath, which was an ice cold one.'[85]

Julia Kristeva's exploration of women's writing in 'Women's Time'[86] provides a framework for interpreting what I have described as liminality in relation to Woolf and Mansfield. Kristeva links 'guiltless maternity' with literary creation. Creativity in motherhood consists in the ability to succeed 'without masochism and without annihilating one's affective, intellectual and professional personality'.[87] Similarly she sees, in the identification with the imaginary, a desire in women's writing to 'lift the weight of what is sacrificial in the social contract from their shoulders, to nourish our societies with a more flexible and free discourse, one able to name what has thus far never been an object of circulation in the community: the enigmas of the body, the dreams, secret joys, shames, hatreds of the second sex'.[88] The putative connection between childlessness and writing will be addressed in the second chapter, but it is the intention of this book to argue that Mansfield and Woolf are preoccupied by finding formal equivalents that enable them to inscribe women's dreams, joys, shames, and hatreds. In this search they are anticipating an over-crossing which Kristeva defines as a signifying space where the binary oppositions of the Father's Law are disintegrated rather than challenged:

In this third attitude, which I strongly advocate—which I imagine?—the very dichotomy man/woman as an opposition between two rival entities may be understood as belonging to *metaphysics*. What can 'identity', even 'sexual identity', mean in a new theoretical and scientific space where the very notion of identity is challenged? . . . What I mean is, first of all, the demassification of the problem of *difference*, which would imply, in a first phase, an apparent de-dramatization of the 'fight to the death' between rival groups and thus between the sexes. And this not in the name of some reconciliation—feminism has at least had the merit of showing what is irreducible and even deadly in the social contract—but in order that the struggle, the implacable difference, the violence be conceived in the very place where it operates with the maximum intransigence, in other words, in personal and sexual identity itself, so as to make it disintegrate in its very nucleus.[89]

[85] VWD ii. 226, 16 Jan. 1923.
[86] Julia Kristeva, *The Kristeva Reader* (Oxford: Basil Blackwell, 1986), 187–213.
[87] Ibid. 206.   [88] Ibid. 207.   [89] Ibid. 209.

Toril Moi applies this passage effectively to Lily Briscoe in *To the Lighthouse*, but it might equally be used to describe the narrative voice in many, though not all, of Mansfield's and Woolf's fictions where the voice is not gendered, and moves flexibly between gendered consciousnesses. While the inner monologues reflect the gendering process that results from the enforcement of the Father's Law, the narrative voice plays by itself, like the light on the landing, denying essentialism and fixed identity, inhabiting the in-between place. What Moi writes of Woolf applies equally to Mansfield:

[W]e can read Woolf's playful shifts and changes of perspective, in both her fiction and in *Room [of One's Own]*, as something rather more than a wilful desire to irritate the serious-minded feminist critic. Through her conscious exploitation of the sportive, sensual nature of language, Woolf rejects the metaphysical essentialism underlying patriarchal ideology . . . She also reveals a deeply sceptical attitude to the male-humanist concept of an essential human identity. For what can this self-identical identity be if all meaning is a ceaseless play of difference, if *absence* as much as presence is the foundation of meaning?[90]

While both Woolf and Mansfield were literally foreign to each other, in terms of nationality and upbringing, they were also familiar; in recognizing the affinity between themselves they were also recognizing the foreigner within, and acknowledging a kind of doubling. In the movement between the mumbling seaweed gatherers and the self in the carriage Mansfield shows the apprehension of absence and presence that Moi attributes to Woolf. The next two chapters focus on the personal writings, to indicate why Mansfield remained for Woolf a presence in absence, a faint ghost, throughout the years she survived her.

[90] Toril Moi, 'Who's Afraid of Virginia Woolf? Feminist Readings of Woolf', 87–8, in Su Reid (ed.), *New Casebooks: Mrs Dalloway and To the Lighthouse* (London: Macmillan, 1993).

2

A Common Certain Understanding

> I feel a common certain understanding between us—a queer
> sense of being 'like'—not only about literature—& I think
> it's independent of gratified vanity. I can talk straight out
> to her.[1]

IN spite of Virginia Woolf's insistence in her personal writing on
the significance of her relationship with Katherine Mansfield,
some of her biographers pay scant attention to it, though this
is not true of Mansfield's major biographers, Antony Alpers and
Claire Tomalin, who each include a chapter on the friendship.
Recommending Tomalin's account, Lyndall Gordon comments
astutely that in 'the case of Katherine Mansfield's relation to
VW, less is to be gained from those biographies which dwell on
spite rather than discern points of contact in their writing.'[2] Phyllis
Rose in her biography of Woolf, *Woman of Letters*,[3] mentions
Mansfield twice in passing, and yet her emphasis is on the way in
which Woolf shaped her own career as a writer; John Mepham,
in *Virginia Woolf: A Literary Life*,[4] also refers only casually to
Mansfield, though he comments that Mansfield was Woolf's clos-
est rival. Mansfield does not appear at all in Jane Dunn's *A Very
Close Conspiracy: Vanessa Bell and Virginia Woolf*,[5] nor in Roger
Poole's *The Unknown Virginia Woolf*.[6] However, Hermione Lee's
biography of Woolf devotes a chapter to the relationship with

---

[1] VWD ii. 45, 31 May 1920.

[2] Lyndall Gordon, *Virginia Woolf: A Writer's Life* (Oxford: Oxford University
Press, 1986), 329.

[3] Phyllis Rose, *Woman of Letters: A Life of Virginia Woolf* (London: Pandora,
1986).

[4] John Mepham, *Virginia Woolf: A Literary Life* (London: Macmillan, 1991).

[5] Jane Dunn, *A Very Close Conspiracy: Vanessa Bell and Virginia Woolf* (London: Jonathan Cape, 1990).

[6] Roger Poole, *The Unknown Virginia Woolf*, 4th edn. (Cambridge: Cambridge
University Press, 1995).

Mansfield, describing their friendship as 'intimate but guarded, mutually inspiring but competitive'.[7] Lee interprets this as crucial to Woolf's development as a writer because she and Mansfield were similar in their investigation of modernist initiatives: 'Both she and Katherine wanted to work through intense short pieces, not on the scale of *Pilgrimage* or *Ulysses*, and to explore consciousness in a more fluid impersonal way than May Sinclair or Dorothy Richardson.'[8] Lyndall Gordon, in her brief but incisive account of the relationship, observes that under their malicious comments about each other, 'their work was all the time converging on similar positions'.[9] In a series of emphatic statements Woolf herself highlights her relationship with Mansfield; she describes Mansfield as 'the very best of women writers'[10] in a letter to Duncan Grant (an opinion she certainly modified in other places), and visits her because she feels that she herself is always 'the spectator of the public, never part of it' but she and Mansfield make 'a public of two'[11] in that they see together when they consider writing and art. Eventually she states quite categorically that she 'gave me something no-one else can',[12] 'we had something in common which I shall never find in anyone else.'[13]

This elusive 'something' was based on their obsession with writing linked with their experience as 'edgewomen'; the personal writings of the two authors up until about the time of Mansfield's death will be used to explore 'something in common'. The argument in this and the following chapter traces similarity within obvious difference; it is concerned with highlighting what Woolf calls 'a queer sense of being "like"'.[14] Though they were literally foreigners to each other, with Mansfield prizing her colonial childhood increasingly as she grew older, they had border crossings in common: those traced in this chapter concern their abjection in illness, their bisexuality, their responses to childlessness, and their complex gender relationships with their editor husbands and with their fathers, as they move from late-Victorian childhood to young womanhood at the beginning of the new century. As the comparison develops, the tensions within

[7] Hermione Lee, *Virginia Woolf* (London: Chatto & Windus, 1996), 386.
[8] Ibid. 392.   [9] Gordon, *Virginia Woolf: A Writer's Life*, 186.
[10] VWL ii. 241, 15 May 1918.   [11] VWD i. 222, 30 Nov. 1918.
[12] VWL iii. 18, 2 Mar. 1923.   [13] VWD ii. 227, 16 Jan. 1923.
[14] Ibid. 45, 31 May 1920.

the friendship become clear. This can be interpreted through Kristeva's analysis of the effect on the self of the foreigner, who is also familiar, both homely and unhomely. Mansfield and Woolf recognized in each other a shared and total commitment to writing, and yet the differences were disturbing. Kristeva writes:

[T]he face that is so *other* bears the mark of a crossed threshold that irremediably imprints itself as peacefulness or anxiety. Whether perturbed or joyful, the foreigner's appearance signals that he is 'in addition.' The presence of such a border, internal to all that is displayed, awakens our most archaic senses through a burning sensation. Vivid concern or delight, set there in these other features, without forgetfulness, without ostentation, like a standing invitation to some inaccessible, irritating journey, whose code the foreigner does not have but whose mute, physical, visible memory he keeps.[15]

The journey that Woolf and Mansfield implicitly offered the other was challenging, frustrating, and enriching, and each provoked anxiety and searing jealousy in the other, always in relation to writing women's experience. Mansfield's independence and sexual freedom enabled her to write the body as Woolf was unable to do; Woolf's domestic security and her intellectual circle of friends seemed to Mansfield to enable fictional experiments which she herself could not encompass as she had to live by her writing. Both recognized in the 'foreigner' something that was inside themselves, that they wanted but also despised.

A sketch of both lives provides a framework for detailed comparisons. Woolf was born in 1882, the daughter of Julia and Leslie Stephen, sister of Vanessa, Thoby, and Adrian, and half-sister of Laura Stephen, and George, Gerald, and Stella Duckworth; both her parents had been married before and had been widowed suddenly. The extended family lived a comfortable middle-class life, with a holiday home, Talland House in St Ives, and a town house, 22 Hyde Park Gate; Leslie Stephen was a man of letters whose *magnum opus* was the *Dictionary of National Biography*, and Julia Stephen was actively engaged in running her household and caring for people round about her. Laura Stephen suffered from some kind of mental disability; she lived with the rest of the family until her early twenties when she

[15] Julia Kristeva, *Strangers to Ourselves* (London: Harvester Wheatsheaf, 1991), 4.

was sent to an asylum.[16] In 1895 Julia Stephen died, and Woolf suffered her first mental breakdown. She and her sister were educated at home; Stella Duckworth acted in a quasi-maternal role for Woolf until Stella died, shortly after her marriage, in 1897. Woolf attempted suicide soon after her father's death in 1904; she moved from the family home in Hyde Park Gate to share a house with her brothers and sister in the same year. In 1906 her brother Thoby died and the following year her sister married Clive Bell; Woolf began writing *The Voyage Out*. She married Leonard Woolf in 1912, finished the novel but attempted suicide again in 1913, and was mentally ill for over two years. When she recovered, she and her husband established the Hogarth Press, for which Woolf wrote. They lived in London and Rodmell, Sussex, until her suicide in 1941. Woolf's closest personal bonds were with her husband, her sister, and to a lesser extent with Vita Sackville-West.

Katherine Mansfield was born in New Zealand in 1888, to Australian parents whose families had moved to Wellington. Her father, Harold Beauchamp, was an ambitious man who became a director of the Bank of New Zealand; he demonstrated his upward mobility by constantly moving house. Katherine Mansfield (Kathleen Beauchamp) had three sisters and a brother, who was the youngest in the family; they were cared for by their maternal grandmother, who lived with them. Mansfield travelled to England with her family in 1903 and became a pupil at Queen's College, Harley Street, where she met Ida Baker who was to act as her companion throughout her life. She returned to live in Wellington in 1906 but yearned for Europe and persuaded her father to allow her to go back to London in 1908. She had already had a series of love affairs with women and men; in London she married G. C. Bowden after knowing him for only two or three weeks, but left him the same day. Her mother arrived and carried her off to a German spa, where Mansfield had a miscarriage; she also had an affair with Floryan Sobieniowski,

---

[16] Louise DeSalvo, *Virginia Woolf: The Impact of Childhood Sexual Abuse on Her Life and Work* (London: Women's Press, 1989), gives a different version of Laura's life, characterizing Leslie Stephen as sadistic and relating Laura to Woolf's development and writing; Hermione Lee's reading of Leslie Stephen's relationship with Laura 'suggests not a sadistic patriarchal conspiracy, but an unimaginative and disciplinarian response to the dilemma of caring for a child who was suffering from a mental disability, possibly a form of autism' (*Virginia Woolf*, 103).

by whom she may have been infected with the gonorrhoea she contracted at about this time. Moving constantly, and beginning to publish, she began a relationship with John Middleton Murry in 1911. They were engaged in precarious publishing ventures and were constantly worried about money; Mansfield left Murry for an affair with Francis Carco but returned to him in 1915, and both of them were involved in a stormy friendship with D. H. and Frieda Lawrence. Her only brother was killed in the First World War, and she was devastated by his death. She and Murry sometimes visited Lady Ottoline Morrell at Garsington, and moved within the same intellectual circle as the Woolfs, though there were class and other tensions between them. In 1917 Mansfield was diagnosed as definitely tubercular and advised to leave Britain in the winter; she and Murry married in 1918 but spent a great deal of time apart as his commitments kept him in Britain and she had to winter in warm climates. From 1918 she felt ill most of the time, writing a will in 1919, at the age of 31, and moving constantly in search of better health, though also writing and reviewing. Ironically, both she and her brother were victims of the imperial centre; lung disease reached almost epidemic proportions in London during the First World War:

It was not only the stress of war work which made young women susceptible; it was lack of air and sun, poor nutrition, crowding in urban housing, and general anxiety. Thus while young men died on the front, young women at home lived within the shadow of lung disease . . . In the London area, phthisis (as the last stage of tuberculosis was then called) was the leading single cause of death for women in their late teens and twenties, accounting for more than 45 percent of the fatalities in 1916.[17]

In October 1922 Mansfield moved, alone, to Gurdjieff's Institute for the Harmonious Development of Man at Fontainebleau; she wrote to Murry asking him to visit her early in 1923, and she died on the day he arrived.

Though Woolf was six years older than Mansfield she was clearly intimidated by a 'queer effect she produces of someone apart, entirely self-centred; altogether concentrated upon her "art" '.[18] She pursued the friendship after they first met, though

---

[17] Mary Burgan, *Illness, Gender, and Writing* (London: Johns Hopkins University Press, 1994), 124.   [18] VWD ii. 44, 31 May 1920.

she was hurt by apparent rebuffs and by Mansfield's review of her second novel *Night and Day*, in the *Athenaeum*. She invited Mansfield to her house in Sussex, sent her small presents, and for a while visited her weekly in London. They first met in 1916; by June 1917 Mansfield was expressing her delight at the relationship in a letter to Woolf: 'consider how rare is it to find some one with the same passion for writing that you have, who desires to be scrupulously truthful with you'.[19] After dining with 'the wolves' as she called them, she wrote to Ottoline Morrell saying how much she liked Woolf and 'the strange, trembling, glinting quality of her mind'.[20] Her story 'Prelude' was the second publication produced by the Woolfs' Hogarth Press; Virginia Woolf typeset parts of it. Mansfield spent a weekend at Asheham, the Woolfs' house in Sussex, in August 1917 and wrote to Woolf of the visit:

It was good to have time to talk to you. We have got the same job, Virginia & it is really very curious & thrilling that we should both, quite apart from each other, be after so very nearly the same thing. We are you know; there's no denying it.

But dont let THEM ever persuade you that I spend any of my precious time swapping hats or committing adultery—I'm far too arrogant & proud.[21]

This seems to be a reference to two of the major obstacles to their friendship: Woolf's timidity (snobbery?) about women of a different background from her own, and Bloomsbury gossip. The notorious description by Woolf of Mansfield as a 'civet cat that had taken to street-walking' but also 'so intelligent & inscrutable that she repays friendship'[22] may well have been conveyed through someone such as the gossipy Clive Bell to the Murrys. This would account for the 'steady discomposing formality & coldness'[23] that Woolf often comments on in Mansfield's manner. There was clearly rivalry, malice, and some hostility between 'the underworld', as Woolf describes Mansfield's friends, and Bloomsbury; 'To Hell with the Blooms Berries'[24] is a concluding anathema in the letter Mansfield wrote to Ottoline Morrell just before she left for her visit to Asheham.

[19] KMCL i. 313, 24? June 1917.   [20] Ibid. 315, 3 July 1917.
[21] Ibid. 327, 23 Aug. 1917.   [22] VWD i. 58, 11 Oct. 1917.
[23] Ibid. ii. 43-4, 31 May 1920.   [24] KMCL i. 326, 15 Aug. 1917.

Each writer sees the other as a foreigner, an alien. This is indicated by the fact that both refer critically to the smell of the other: Woolf comments that 'she stinks'[25] and Mansfield writes to Murry that 'the Woolves . . . are *smelly.*'[26] Patricia Moran remarks on Woolf's 'strange preoccupation with Mansfield's personal smell.'[27] Woolf often links Mansfield's smell with her fiction. In a letter written long after Mansfield's death she tells Vita Sackville-West that Mansfield's stories enabled her to 'permeate one with her quality; and if one felt this cheap scent in it, it reeked in ones nostrils.'[28] In the same letter she comments that Mansfield had 'knocked about with prostitutes', and dismisses her own respectability. She seems both to fear and envy the sexual experience that gives a dimension to Mansfield's prose that is lacking in Woolf's fiction; nowhere in Woolf's writing is there anything like the physical desirability of Pearl Fulton in 'Bliss', or the erotic tension in 'Psychology'. When Mansfield remarks on Woolf's smell she refers to a different kind of lack, though it too relates to the body. After commiserating with Murry in a letter because he has to visit the Woolfs, she comments on her own body emaciated by illness: 'I shall always be able to play on my bones.'[29] This may be an oblique reference to a Maori bone flute, and certainly implies that the source of her writing is physical hardship, in comparison with the settled comfort of the Woolfs' domestic life.

The edgy hostility between Mansfield and Woolf stemmed from professional jealousy and from class-consciousness; the Murrys struggled constantly with severe financial worries, and the rootlessness caused by Mansfield's illness. When she was told in December 1917 that she must avoid British winters she compared herself yearningly, in a letter to Murry, with her friend's settled domesticity, responding with what Kristeva calls a 'burning sensation' to the apparent peacefulness of the foreigner:

It isn't a married life at all—not what I mean by a married life. How I envy Virginia; no wonder she can write. There is always in her writing a calm freedom of expression as though she were at peace—her roof

---

[25] VWD i. 58, 11 Oct. 1917.   [26] KMCL ii. 77, 16 and 17 Feb. 1918.
[27] Patricia Moran, *Word of Mouth* (London: University Press of Virginia, 1996), 77.   [28] VWL iv. 366, 8 Aug. 1931.
[29] KMCL ii. 77, 16 and 17 Feb. 1918.

over her—her own possessions round her—and her man somewhere within call. Boge what have I done that I should have *all* the handicaps —plus a disease.[30]

Woolf was intensely envious of Mansfield, for different reasons; she thought that Vanessa Bell, her sister whose approval she always sought, would feel Mansfield to be a 'companion' because she 'seems to have gone every sort of hog since she was 17, which is interesting'.[31] Such wild experiments with experience were impossible for Woolf, who was felt to be in danger of a relapse into madness if she stayed up late or went to many parties, though she had family, friends, and a consistently entertaining social life whereas Mansfield's life became increasingly solitary and isolated. Woolf admitted, in letters and in her diaries, that the central focus of her envy was not Mansfield's uninhibited early love affairs but the writing that stemmed from them: 'I was jealous of her writing—the only writing I have ever been jealous of. This made it harder to write to her; & I saw in it, perhaps from jealousy, all the qualities I disliked in her.'[32] She may be thinking of her vindictive pleasure at what she sees as Mansfield's failure, expressed in her diary when she first reads Mansfield's story, 'Bliss': 'I threw down Bliss with the exclamation, "She's done for!" Indeed I dont see how much faith in her as a woman or writer can survive that sort of story.'[33] The lack of faith in Mansfield 'as a woman' is intriguing, as Woolf seems anxious to distance herself from the ambivalent sexuality of the story, with its combination of heterosexual desire and homoerotic yearning, possibly a fear of the foreigner within.[34]

There is throughout the record of the relationship in the letters and diaries of the two writers a sense of Woolf's intensity of feeling for Mansfield: admiration, love, and the hatred that stems from jealousy. Mansfield does not mention Woolf in her journal, and seems not to have kept many of Woolf's letters, whereas Woolf's diaries from 1917 until after Mansfield's death refer to her constantly, and she typed out Mansfield's letters to her for Murry after Mansfield was dead. The friendship continued from 1917, with frequent meetings when Mansfield was in

[30] Ibid. iii. 127–8, 30 Nov. 1919.   [31] VWL ii. 159, 27 June 1917.
[32] VWD ii. 227, 16 Jan. 1923.   [33] Ibid. i. 179, 7 Aug. 1918.
[34] This is analysed in detail in Moran, *Word of Mouth*, ch. 3.

London, surviving Mansfield's review of *Night and Day*. She described it in a letter to Murry as 'a lie in the soul',[35] and was very reluctant to review it as it seemed to her a regression from *The Voyage Out*, which she admired. She could not know that Woolf hoped she would not review it, recognizing that she had not taken risks in writing it; she said of it, 'no part of it taxed me as The Voyage Out did'.[36] She had consciously attempted to avoid the mental disturbance and phase of insanity that the earlier novel had caused her, so that what seemed to Mansfield a callous indifference ('The war has never been, that is what its message is'[37]) was a kind of therapy. There must have been a peculiar irony for Woolf in the way in which Mansfield, in her review of *Night and Day* for the *Athenaeum*, takes up the metaphor suggested by Woolf's first novel, *The Voyage Out*, to imply the limitations of *Night and Day*, referring specifically to the absence of scars. The implication is that, for the writing to succeed, the writer must expose her body to pain: 'To us who love to linger down at the harbour, as it were . . . comes the strange sight of *Night and Day* sailing into port serene and resolute on a deliberate wind. The strangeness lies in her aloofness, her air of quiet perfection, her lack of any sign that she has made a perilous voyage—the absence of any scars.'[38]

Similarly when Woolf speculates in her letters and diaries about Mansfield's apparent indifference to her, the reader of Mansfield's personal writings can explain her silence: late in 1918 she discovered that she was to some extent responsible for her own physical suffering. It was in early February of that year that she felt 'a great black bird flying over me'[39] but did not know what kind of bird it was; its identity became clear when she had her first pulmonary haemorrhage on 19 February. Dr Sorapure explained to her at the end of the year that many of her symptoms were caused by the gonorrhoea she had contracted years before when she was taking Oscar Wilde's advice, quoted in her journal: 'The only way to get rid of temptation is to yield to it.'[40] Her self-disgust and physical weakness were

---

[35] KMCL iii. 82, 10 Nov. 1919.   [36] VWD i. 259, 27 Mar. 1919.
[37] KMCL iii. 82, 10 Nov. 1919.
[38] Clare Hanson (ed.), *The Critical Writings of Katherine Mansfield* (London: Macmillan, 1987), 56–7.   [39] KMCL ii. 55, 3 and 4 Feb. 1918.
[40] KMJ 4, 1906.

compounded in the next two years by horror at what seemed to her Murry's brutal flirtations with other women, and his insensitivity to her needs. In March 1921 she wrote to Ottoline Morrell, 'even now I cant explain. Something happened—a kind of earthquake that shook everything and I lost faith and touch with everybody. I cannot write what it was . . . Let me say I was almost out of my mind with misery last year.'[41]

Kristeva defines abjection as being 'what disturbs identity, system, order. What does not respect borders, positions, rules.'[42] Mansfield was engulfed at this time by a sense of disintegration of the self, and by what Kristeva calls 'death infecting life. Abject.'[43] In spite of this, during the same time, she met the friend who had actually been out of *her* mind in the past as a result of grief and stress; they were observant about each other:

I lunched with K. M. & had 2 hours priceless talk—priceless in the sense that to no one else can I talk in the same disembodied way about writing; without altering my thought more than I alter it in writing here. (I except L. from this) . . . Then I said 'You've changed. Got through something;' indeed theres a sort of self command about her as if having mastered something subterfuges were no longer so necessary. She told me of her terrific experiences last winter—experience of loneliness chiefly.[44]

What Woolf responds to is Mansfield's experience of physical extremity and of the liminal moment when she wrote in her journal: 'I am (December 15, 1919) a dead woman, and I *don't care*.'[45] She felt herself to be outside the worlds of both the living and the dead though Ida Baker, who was her companion during this time at Ospedaletti in Italy, and Murry who was writing to her, both harried her with what she saw as trivial demands. She tried to conceal the severity of her physical condition from Murry. His apparent callousness and sense of self-sacrifice in letters precipitated her into writing three bitter poems, 'The New Husband', 'He wrote', and 'Et Apres', in which she imagines herself 'married' to death while her husband sends her a frisky and frivolous letter before she dies and

[41] KMCL iv. 192, 14 Mar. 1921.
[42] Julia Kristeva, *Powers of Horror* (New York: Columbia University Press, 1982), 4.   [43] Ibid.
[44] VWD ii. 45, 5 June 1920.   [45] KMJ 185, 15 Dec. 1919.

makes literary capital out of it afterwards. With astute self-scrutiny, she analysed the two definitive changes in herself in her notebook in December 1919, beginning with her response to his recent letters:

As I grew depressed, *he* grew depressed, but not *for* me. He began to write (1) about the suffering I caused him: *his* suffering, *his* nerves, *he* wasn't made of whipcord or steel, the fruit was bitter for *him*. (2) a constant cry about money . . . even in October I *clung* to him still—still the child—seeing as our salvation a house in the country, in England, *not later than next May* and then never to be apart again. The letters —ended all of it. *Was* it the letters? I must not forget something else.

All these two years I have been obsessed by the fear of death. This grew and grew and grew *gigantic*, and this it was that made me cling so, I think. Ten days ago it went, I care no more. It leaves me perfectly cold. Well it was that *and* the letters perhaps.[46]

The phrase 'It leaves me perfectly cold' is ambivalent; it suggests what she goes on to say, that she has experienced her own death in imagination, abjection. How much of all this she told Woolf we cannot know, but Woolf's admiration for Mansfield's self-control is evident, as is the wish for their intimacy to continue; she persistently asks her diary whether Mansfield will write. She herself wrote to Mansfield in 1921 because Murry had told her of Mansfield's acute loneliness. She was hurt by Mansfield's failure to reply, but acknowledged after her death that 'I never gave her credit for all her physical suffering & the effect it must have had in embittering her.'[47]

When Mansfield died Woolf expected to be haunted by the memory of her and it seems she was. Her first response to Mansfield's death early in 1923 combined her ambivalent feelings, jealousy and love, which are confronted in her diary:

[G]radually, blankness & disappointment; then a depression which I could not rouse myself from all that day. When I began to write, it seemed to me there was no point in writing. Katherine wont read it. Katherine's my rival no longer. More generously I felt, But though I can do this better than she could, where is she, who could do what I can't![48]

---

[46] KMCL iii. 158–9, 15 Dec. 1919 (entry in notebook).
[47] VWD ii. 227, 16 Jan. 1923.   [48] Ibid. 226, 16 Jan. 1923.

Throughout her life she suggests that she regrets not having persisted with even more determination, telling their mutual friend,
the painter Dorothy Brett, that 'it is terrible to me to think that
I sacrificed anything to this odious gossip'[49] and Ottoline Morrell
that she feels desolated by reading Mansfield's letters in 1928:
'What a waste!—and how wretched it is—her poverty, her illness
—I didn't realise how gifted she was either. And now never to—
but you will know all I mean.'[50]

The unique relationship Woolf and Mansfield enjoyed can be
explained partly in terms of the hints they give about their shared
attitudes to reading and writing; this will be explored more fully
later. But both imply that their intuitive understanding of each
other enabled their intellectual sympathy; Woolf expresses it like
this in 1920: 'I feel a common certain understanding between
us—a queer sense of being "like"—not only about literature—
& I think it's independent of gratified vanity. I can talk straight
out to her.'[51] What is intriguing about this is why they had the
'queer sense of being like', when the similarity was not connected
with literature. Ostensibly, they were in many respects different.
Woolf was part of the Bloomsbury establishment, homesick for
London when she was away from it for long; Mansfield felt that
geraniums in London gardens called her ' "a stranger—an alien" '
because she was a 'little Colonial walking in the London garden
patch—allowed to look, perhaps, but not to linger.'[52] Mansfield
as a girl boasts to her sister that she is more 'popular than
almost any girl here at dances'[53] in Wellington, whereas Woolf
describes how she lurks in frozen horror behind pillars at society
balls, and asserts rather poignantly that she 'would give all my
profound Greek to dance really well, and so would Adrian
[her brother] give anything he had.'[54] The obvious differences
between them persisted into adulthood. Woolf's married life was
secure, and rooted in Sussex and London, whereas Mansfield's
marriage was strained by separation and her necessarily restless search for a climate that would prolong her life. Woolf was
fascinated by intense passion but retreated from it herself; her
involvement with women lovers lacks the sexual bravado of
Mansfield's episode with Francis Carco. Mansfield's desperate

---

[49] VWL iii. 17–18, 2 Mar. 1923. [50] Ibid. 546, 15 Oct. 1928.
[51] VWD ii. 45, 31 May 1920. [52] KMJ 157, May 1919.
[53] KMCL i. 48, 12 June 1908. [54] VWL i. 63, 27? Dec. 1902.

retreat into a mystical cure at the Gurdjieff Institute was not an experiment that Woolf would have permitted herself.

However, for both of them what mattered was their art, and detailed exploration of their 'likeness' in human experience eventually spirals back to the preoccupations in their writing, to their determination to write even in extremity: 'the watermark that remains in the darkness and horror of night, allowing such a night, nevertheless, to be written' as Kristeva says of Céline.[55] On a superficial level one can compare their situations: both were busy reviewers, both of their husbands were editors, both couples had friends such as Ottoline Morrell, S. S. Koteliansky, Dorothy Brett, and T. S. Eliot in common. More significantly, both lived with chronic illness; readers of the letters and journals of both writers can rarely forget the presence of what Woolf, in a recurrent metaphor, calls 'that fin in the waste of waters which appeared to me over the marshes',[56] 'the old devil has once more got his spine through the waves.'[57] As Clare Hanson points out, the French *fin* gives this another dimension, and anticipates Woolf's death.[58] A similar satirical, observant and often self-mocking gaiety flickers through their most despondent personal writing, usually eschewing self-pity; Kristeva's comment applies: 'For, facing abjection, meaning has only a scored, rejected, ab-jected meaning—a comical one.'[59] As Mansfield is dying she notes in her journal 'the sense of humour I have found true of every single occasion of my life.'[60] In a wonderfully comic earlier letter to Murry, written when she was confronting the fact that she had '*acted* my sins . . . There IS waste—destruction, too',[61] she makes an implicit link between this and her youthful belief in resisting everything but temptation, by describing a dream in which she took Oscar Wilde home to her parents' house: 'He said would 12:30 tonight do? When I arrived home it seemed madness to have asked him. Father & Mother were in bed. What if Father came down & found that chap Wilde in one of the chintz armchairs? Too late now.'[62] Similarly Woolf, re-creating 22 Hyde Park Gate for the Bloomsbury Memoir Club

[55] Kristeva, *Powers of Horror*, 135–6. [56] VWD iv. 10, 7 Feb. 1931.
[57] Ibid. ii. 270, 15 Oct. 1923.
[58] Clare Hanson, *Virginia Woolf* (London: Macmillan, 1994), 135.
[59] Kristeva, *Powers of Horror*, 209. [60] KMJ 336, 17 Oct. 1922.
[61] KMCL iv. 92, 31 Oct. 1920. [62] Ibid. 95, 1 Nov. 1920.

and revealing the incestuous harassment she and her sister suffered from her stepbrother, George, writes with consistent and
pitiless humour of the painful memories:

He was fond of sending telegrams which began 'My darling mother'
and went on to say that he would be dining out. (I copied this style of
his, I regret to say, with disastrous results on one celebrated occasion.
'She is an angel' I wired, on hearing that Flora Russell had accepted
him, and signed my nickname 'Goat'. 'She is an aged Goat' was the
version that arrived, at Islay, and had something to do, George said,
with Flora's reluctance to ally herself with the Stephen family.)[63]

Though neither writer seems to have known the full menace
of the disease with which the other was grappling, the reader
of the personal writings recognizes comparable liminal psychological states arising from different physical circumstances. The
significance of some of the oblique comments in letters and diaries
only becomes evident in the light of subsequent biographies. In
the early diaries and letters of each writer, before Mansfield's
illness but after Woolf's first mental breakdown, there is evidence that each is intensely involved in a lesbian relationship,
crossing borders that their parents would have expected them
to respect. Bisexual experience is of course a liminal gender position, as Catharine Stimpson suggests: 'In cultural criticism, in
psychosexual practice, Woolf stands simultaneously outside, beside, and inside the borders of heterosexuality and of her sex.
These borders are as fluid, as subject to redrawing, as those of
counties and countries.'[64]
      Mansfield too is aware of crossing boundaries when she says
in 1907: 'I feel more powerfully all those so-termed sexual
impulses with her than I have with any man,'[65] while Woolf writes
to Violet Dickinson in 1906: 'When you wake in the night, I
suppose you feel my arms round you.'[66] The nature of the relationships appears, however, to be quite different: Mansfield is
stimulated physically by other women, and takes the initiative
in pursuing them: 'Do other people of my own age feel as I do

[63] Virginia Woolf, *Moments of Being* (St Albans: Triad/Panther, 1978), 169.
[64] Catharine R. Stimpson, 'Woolf's Room, Our Project: The Building of Feminist
Criticism', in Rachel Bowlby (ed.), *Virginia Woolf* (Harlow: Longman, 1992), 175.
[65] KMJ 12, 1 June 1907.   [66] VWL i. 244, 14 Nov. 1906.

I wonder—so absolutely powerful *licentious*, so almost physically ill . . . I want Maata—I want her as I have had her—
terribly. This is unclean I know but true. What an extraordinary
thing—I feel savagely crude—and almost powerfully enamoured
of the child.'[67] Woolf always appears to be dependent in her
sexual relationships, with Leonard Woolf and Vita Sackville-
West as in her early involvement with Violet Dickinson. She consistently describes herself as a vulnerable animal in her early
letters, after the mental breakdown caused by her mother's
death and at the time of her father's fatal illness; later in life
she sustains the animal nicknames and the fantasy that she is
both her sister Vanessa's child and her unrequited lover. This
mother/child relationship, lost once when her mother died and
again with the death of her half-sister Stella, is part of the
texture of her relationship with Violet Dickinson: 'I feel myself
curled up snugly in old mother wallabies pouch. My little claws
nestle round my furry cheeks. Is mother wallaby soft and tender
to her little one?'[68]

It is not immediately obvious that these diverse responses can
be used as part of an argument for 'a queer sense of being like':
in 1906 the 18-year-old Mansfield seems uninhibited in her sexual
experiments by the mores of her society whereas the 24-year-
old Woolf sounds cloyingly childish. By disparate routes however
both were damaged by their sexual experience, and arrived at a
sense of desolation at their resultant childlessness. Mansfield was
betrayed not simply by her own sexuality but by a late nineteenth-
century conception of artistic credentials: Wilde's maxim that ' "we
castrate our minds to the extent by which we deny our bodies" '
is noted in Mansfield's 1907 journal.[69] In pursuit of Wilde's injunction to be unafraid and experiment she contracted gonorrhoea,
probably infected by Floryan Sobieniowski. After her return to
London she became violently ill with peritonitis; Claire Tomalin's
account of this stage of her life states that her left fallopian
tube was removed because it was infected with gonococci. The
infection was spread by surgery as the gonococci entered the
bloodstream; systemic gonorrhoea causes infertility, arthritis, heart
trouble, and pleurisy, all symptoms that Mansfield developed

---

[67] KMCL i. 22, 1907, quoted from an unpublished notebook.
[68] VWL i. 244, 14 Nov. 1906.   [69] KMJ 11, Feb. 1907.

long before she was diagnosed as tubercular. Dr Sorapure identified the original disease late in 1918 and explained its nature to her, though Claire Tomalin speculates that she must have suspected for some time that her ill-health was traceable to her early sexual adventures. Mansfield's mature view is implied in an allusive comment on a quotation from Shakespeare, in a letter to Murry:

That is terrible, and it contains such a terribly deep psychological truth. 'That *rots* itself' . . . and the idea of it returning and returning, never swept out to sea finally. You may think you have done with it for ever, but comes a change of tide and there is that dark streak reappeared, more sickeningly rotten still. I understand that better than I care to. I mean—alas!—I have proof of it in my own being.[70]

A disgusted guilt rather than physical suffering resonates through this observation, combined with a weary sense of the ghosts of the past coming back to haunt her. The foreign body is psychologically and physically within her; in writing her journal and her stories she uses fear as, in Kristeva's interpretation, a writer with liminal experience does: 'discourse will seem tenable only if it ceaselessly confront that otherness, a burden both repellent and repelled, a deep well of memory that is unapproachable and intimate: the abject.'[71] Fear must be constantly inscribed if the writer is to avoid being frightened to death.

Possibly because she understood from her own experience the danger to a vulnerable body from a sensitive and ardent consciousness, Mansfield wrote, with uncanny perception, to Ottoline Morrell soon after she met Woolf that 'she seemed to me to be one of those Dostoievsky women whose "innocence" has been hurt'.[72] Her innocence was indeed hurt soon after her mother's death. Woolf's contributions to the Memoir Club, '22 Hyde Park Gate' and 'Old Bloomsbury', describe how her half-brother George preyed on her, creeping into her bedroom at night and flinging himself on her 'cuddling and kissing and otherwise embracing me in order, as he told Dr Savage later, to comfort me for the fatal illness of my father'.[73] In her 'A Sketch of the Past' she shows that she was molested by her other halfbrother when she was very small; he lifted her on to a shelf and she repeats

[70] KML ii. 183, 7 Feb. 1922. [71] Kristeva, *Powers of Horror*, 6.
[72] KMCL i. 315, 3 July 1917. [73] Woolf, *Moments of Being*, 184.

the phrase 'his hand' obsessively as she describes how he explored her 'private parts', and comments: 'I remember resenting, disliking it—what is the word for so dumb and mixed a feeling?'[74] Louise DeSalvo points out that, in a letter to Ethel Smyth, Woolf says how difficult it is for women to write openly about sexuality and compares it to breaking the hymen which is 'connected with all sorts of subterranean instincts.'[75] She then immediately associates this with the memory of Gerald's hand exploring her private parts, as if, in DeSalvo's reading, he either broke her hymen or she feared he had. The irony of Woolf's name, celebrating the virtue of which the Angel in the House was such a proponent, intensifies the sense of damaged innocence.

These half-brothers, who appeared to take a paternal and protective interest in Vanessa and Virginia Stephen and were admired by the old ladies of Kensington for it, created what Woolf calls 'our particular Hell'.[76] It is not surprising that the 'dumb and mixed' feeling seems to have recurred when Leonard Woolf, who was deeply in love with her, kissed her: '[I]s it the sexual side of it that comes between us? As I told you brutally the other day, I feel no physical attraction in you. There are moments—when you kissed me the other day was one—when I feel no more than a rock. And yet your caring for me as you do almost overwhelms me.'[77] She reports her loss of virginity, after her marriage, to Katherine Cox; she finds 'the climax immensely exaggerated'.[78] In the year after her marriage she went mad again, and attempted suicide. One can only guess at the effect of the furtive invasion of a sensitive mind and body by an apparent model of late-Victorian respectability, but Mansfield's remark that 'her innocence has been hurt' seems apt. Leonard and Virginia Woolf shared a bed for two or three years after their marriage, and a bedroom for a few years after that, but a sexual bond does not seem to have been a central aspect of what was in other ways a fulfilled and happy marriage. Woolf told her doctor, Octavia Wilberforce, that she could never remember any enjoyment of her own body;[79] when she was young, Mansfield

---

[74] Woolf, *Moments of Being*, 80.   [75] VWL vi. 460, 12 Jan. 1941.
[76] Ibid. ii. 393, 27 Oct. 1919.   [77] Ibid. i. 496, 1 May 1912.
[78] Ibid. ii. 6, 4 Sept. 1912.
[79] DeSalvo, *Virginia Woolf: The Impact of Childhood Sexual Abuse on her Life and Work*, 125.

celebrated the joys of the body, but that returned to punish her with unremitting physical suffering.

It is poignantly clear, particularly from the diaries, that both writers felt themselves to be abnormal and unfulfilled as women in their childlessness, and yet both are ambivalent about maternity; for each of them the norm was the large family into which they were themselves born, and both had sisters whose fertility sometimes aroused envy. Mansfield continued almost until her death to hope that she might have a child. One of the effects on women of gonorrhoea is to make the menstrual cycle irregular and her diaries indicate that she sometimes thinks she might be pregnant. As early as 1915 she writes yearningly to Murry: 'Why haven't I got a real "home", a real life—Why haven't I got a chinese nurse with green trousers and two babies who rush at me and clasp my knees—Im not a girl—Im a woman. I *want* things.'[80] Mansfield was then 26; Woolf wrote to her sister in 1911 that her 'hairy black' devils beset her during a storm: 'To be 29 and unmarried—to be a failure—childless—insane too, no writer.'[81] Some of the devils would subsequently be exorcized but the wistful longing for children permeates her diaries; she describes being 'in one of my moods' after Christmas in Sussex:

And what is it & why? A desire for children, I suppose; for Nessa's life; for the sense of flowers breaking all round me involuntarily . . . never pretend that the things you haven't got are not worth having; good advice I think. At least it often comes back to me. Never pretend that children, for instance, can be replaced by other things.[82]

In both cases it is possible to wonder whether the unfulfilled desire to experience motherhood led to the creation of fictional children: Kezia, the Sheridan children, the young Ramsays. Literature, as Kristeva says, juxtaposing maternity and writing, 'reveals a certain knowledge and sometimes the truth itself about an otherwise repressed, nocturnal, secret and unconscious universe'[83] as childbirth does. Certainly both writers see their work as a refuge from sterility and despair. The language they use to describe it suggests that it has a spiritually regenerative force for them;

---

[80] KMCL i. 177, 7? May 1915.   [81] VWL i. 466, 8? June 1911.
[82] VWD ii. 221, 2 Jan. 1923.
[83] Julia Kristeva, *The Kristeva Reader* (Oxford: Basil Blackwell, 1986), 207.

Mansfield describes work as her salvation: 'The longer I live the more I realise that in work only lies ones strength and ones salvation. And such *supreme joy* that one gives thanks for life with every breath.'[84] This is a central clue to her affinity with Woolf, who writes that she finds 'with Katherine what I don't find with the other clever women a sense of ease & interest, which is, I suppose, due to her caring so genuinely if so differently from the way I care, about our precious art.'[85] Using the language of mystical and quasi-sexual revelation to describe her own writing, Woolf explains 'my tunnelling process': 'One feels about in a state of misery—indeed I made up my mind one night to abandon the book—& then one touches the hidden spring.'[86]

For a woman to find her deepest realization of herself in her work was of course abnormal within the social codes of the first part of this century; Mansfield and Woolf, in their attitude to their childlessness, are probably reacting to the way in which femininity was constructed by their societies when they were growing up at the end of the nineteenth century. Part of their experience of liminality, shared with their contemporaries, was in being between centuries; both felt themselves to be in tune with a modernity that could not fulfil itself in colonial Wellington, or in Hyde Park Gate. Looking back in 1938 on the last years of the nineteenth century and the first years of the twentieth, including the First World War and the extension of suffrage to women in Britain, Woolf uses a threshold image to express it: 'in imagination perhaps we can see the educated man's daughter, as she issues from the shadow of the private house, and stands on the bridge which lies between the old world and the new'.[87] Both were part of large families with, at least in terms of gender relations, Victorian values. Mansfield's adolescent outbursts in her journal ('Damn my family! O Heavens, what bores they are! I detest them all heartily'[88]) have no counterpart in Woolf's early, much more reticent, writing, but Woolf makes clear later that she, like Mansfield, saw her father as a monstrous creature, preying on female energies. This is not by any means the whole story, but it is part of it.

---

[84] KMCL iv. 296, 15 Oct. 1921.   [85] VWD i. 258, 22 Mar. 1919.
[86] Ibid. ii. 272, 15 Oct. 1923.
[87] Virginia Woolf, *Three Guineas* (London: Hogarth, 1943), 30.
[88] KMJ 21, 21 Oct. 1907.

Mansfield describes Harold Beauchamp on the long sea voyage from Britain to New Zealand in 1906:

My Father spoke of my returning as damned rot, said look here, he wouldn't have me fooling around in dark corners with fellows. His hands, covered with long sandy hair, are absolutely cruel hands. A physically revolted feeling seizes me. He wants me to sit near. He watches me at meals, eats in the most abjectly, blatantly vulgar manner that is describable. He is like a constant offence, but I cannot escape from it, and it wraps me in its atmosphere.[89]

There is a certain Queen's College snobbery about colonial table manners expressed in the passage, but it also encapsulates some of the complexity of Mansfield's relationship with her father and, by extension, with other men. She resents his powerful physicality, presenting him almost as a werewolf or as Robert Louis Stevenson's Mr Hyde, and is exasperated by his curbing of her sexual freedom. But she is chained ('I cannot escape') and later in her life she writes nostalgically to her father of these voyages.

Virginia Woolf was similarly enmeshed; the ambivalence of the relationships is not unusual but it is crucial to an understanding of how gender issues are embodied in their writing. Julia Stephen's dying words to her daughter implied that feminine deportment mattered more than love: 'And there is my last sight of her; she was dying; I came to kiss her and as I crept out of the room she said: "Hold yourself straight, my little Goat." '[90] Leslie Stephen denied Woolf and her sister schooling; they were left at home after their mother's death with their father, while their brothers received education at Westminster School and Cambridge. Vanessa and Virginia Stephen formed 'a very close conspiracy', 'our private nucleus' in that 'world of many men'.[91] Their worst endurance test was the moment when the weekly accounts had to be presented by Vanessa to Leslie Stephen:

Down came his fist on the account book. There was a roar. His vein filled. His face flushed. Then he shouted 'I am ruined.' Then he beat his breast ... Never have I felt such rage and such frustration. For not a word of my feeling could be expressed ... Even now I can find nothing to say of his behaviour save that it was brutal. If, instead of words, he had used a whip the brutality would have been no greater.[92]

[89] Ibid., 6–7, Nov. 1906. [90] Woolf, *Moments of Being*, 98.
[91] Ibid. 144. [92] Ibid. 145.

Like Mansfield's, the father here is a monster, roaring, brutal, chest-beating like an ape, and suggestive of phallic potency as he swells with blood. The young woman looks on in greater subjection than Mansfield, apparently passive, and silenced by male authority. The sisters are in a master-and-slave relationship with their father; he has no knowledge of domestic life but expects them to make it run smoothly for his comfort and that of his sons and his stepsons. They are cast in the traditional female role of feather-brained spendthrifts, conspiring to subvert male responsibility and economy. These scenes never took place before male members of the family but Leslie Stephen had 'no shame in front of women', and his rages were 'sinister, blind, animal, savage'[93] to his daughters. Yet Woolf does not mention them in her letters, even to women; there her father 'says I am a very good daughter! He is the most delightful of people'.[94]

The double bind of resentment of and dependence on their fathers, both emotional and financial, finds constant expression in the letters and journals of both Mansfield and Woolf. Because Mansfield's father outlived her, he remains the patriarchal presence in her personal writings: 'I feel towards my Pa man like a little girl. I want to jump and stamp on his chest and cry "youve *got* to love me". When he says he does, I feel quite confident that God is on my side.'[95] She seeks all her life 'like a little girl' for the approval that she knows her conventional father can never bestow on her life or her fiction. His failure to understand the quality of her prose, capturing as it does the glinting evanescent moment, is suggested by the fact that he chose to have a tram shelter erected in memory of her in Wellington after her death with 'Katherine Mansfield Memorial' inscribed above it. Though she defies the Father's Law in her contempt for bourgeois values she simultaneously wants its permission to behave as she does. With worsening health, she increasingly indicates that God the Father, who is identified with her own father in the passage above, haunts her mental cosmos, as she quotes the General Confession[96] or prays, as though she were a transparent medium for the divine message, 'May I be found worthy to do it! Lord, make me crystal clear for thy light to shine through!'[97]

[93] Woolf, *Moments of Being*, 146, 147.   [94] VWL i. 123, 25 Jan. 1904.
[95] KMCL i. 120, May 1913.   [96] KMJ 279, 1 Jan. 1922.
[97] Ibid. 271, 21 Nov. 1921.

Mansfield and Woolf may wish to reject 'the metaphysical essentialism underlying patriarchal ideology, which hails God, the Father or the phallus as its transcendental signified'[98] in their creative writing, as Toril Moi suggests of Woolf, but both are in a liminal situation arising from the subject positions of their time. Both of them often identify the writing voice as masculine, as Patricia Moran makes clear in *Word of Mouth*. Mansfield's literary models are canonical male writers; she refers in her letters to her dependence for nourishment on Shakespeare, Dickens, and Chekhov. In spite of her critique of him, Woolf identifies herself with her literary father as she looks back in 'A Sketch of the Past', saying that she has 'a streak of the puritan' like him, who was 'spartan, ascetic, puritanical'.[99] She admires her mother's and sisters' famous beauty but has a horror of looking-glasses herself, and a phobia about buying new clothes; she says, with an abject's negation of her own body, that her ecstasies and raptures were never physical sensations. Though Woolf's upbringing was not orthodox, in that her parents were agnostics, she too quotes biblical law/lore; it is possible to give different inflections to such passages as this, quoting from Psalm 100, and referring to her intrusion, as a formally uneducated woman, into what had been her father's domain, that of the literary critic: 'My criticism seems to me pretty flimsy sometimes. But there is no principle, except to follow this whimsical brain implicitly, pare away the ill fitting, till I have the shape exact, & if thats no good, it is the fault of God, after all. It is He that has made us, not we ourselves. I like that text.'[100] The disparaging reference to her 'whimsical brain' is reminiscent of her father's essentialist view of gender, that women are by definition incapable of sustained thought, with the blame ultimately apportioned to God, very specifically here the Father.

Mansfield's and Woolf's personal writings reveal tensions in their marriages that are comparable with those in their relationships with their fathers. Theoretically both are clear and outspoken about men and marriage. The young Mansfield, whose country had extended the franchise to women as early as 1893, declares in 1908:

---

[98] Su Reid, *New Casebooks: Mrs Dalloway and To the Lighthouse* (London: Macmillan, 1993), 87. [99] Woolf, *Moments of Being*, 79.
[100] VWD ii. 299–300, 5 Apr. 1924.

I feel that I do now realise, dimly, what women in the future will be capable of. They truly as yet have never had their chance. Talk of our enlightened days and our emancipated country—pure nonsense! We are firmly held with the self-fashioned chains of slavery. Yes, now I see that they *are* self-fashioned, and must be self-removed.[101]

It is ironic that she sees the doctrine of love as one of those chains made by women for themselves, affirming 'we must get rid of that bogey'. When one remembers that her nickname for Murry was 'Bogey' and thinks of the struggles in the late journals to evolve an adequate doctrine of love, the complexity of bringing rational arguments and human experience into alignment becomes manifest. Nearly ten years later, Woolf finds 'something maniacal in masculine vanity',[102] and sometimes sees men almost as another species, as here, during the First World War in 1916: 'I become steadily more feminist . . . and wonder how this preposterous masculine fiction keeps going a day longer—without some vigorous young woman pulling us together and marching through it—Do you see any sense in it? I feel as if I were reading about some curious tribe in Central Africa—And now they'll give us votes'.[103]

The lucidity of these views blurs inevitably when they are complicated by private emotion. Both Mansfield and Woolf married editors, and submitted their work to their husbands, sometimes for publication and always for advice. As editors have the ultimate responsibility for the mediation of the text to the public, it was a familiar position for them to find themselves in: the female author could be rewritten by the male authority. In practice Leonard Woolf discussed his wife's work with her and she depended on his judgement, becoming nervous before he read each completed book, but he did not tamper editorially with the fiction; Murry, having had his fingers burned before, received instructions such as these from the mature Mansfield: 'You know how I *choose* my words; they can't be changed. And if you don't like it or think its wrong *just as it is* Id rather you didn't print it.'[104] Professional dependence was reinforced by the periodic helplessness of Mansfield and Woolf when they were ill; this was double-edged as was the professional relationship.

[101] KMJ 36–7, May 1908. [102] VWD ii. 186, 28 July 1922.
[103] VWL ii. 76, 23 Jan. 1916. [104] KMCL iv. 66, 11 Oct. 1920.

Leonard Woolf and Middleton Murry both recognized and respected their wives' creativity: Woolf was an asset to the Hogarth Press and Mansfield published many of her stories in Murry's various journals. But both writers at different times bitterly resented the patriarchal power their husbands exercised:

It is remarkable how much there is of the ordinary man in J. For instance, finding no towels in his room tonight, his indignation, sense of injury, desire so to shut his door that it would bring the house down— his fury in fact at having to look for the blasted things—all was just precisely what one would have expected of his Father.[105]

Woolf constantly records her gratitude for her husband's care of her, but at the same time resents it. He did not wish to attend Bloomsbury parties when they lived in Richmond; she found them personally and creatively stimulating. If she went to parties he insisted that she should leave by 11 p.m., so she had less leeway than Cinderella. His fear was that tiredness would cause another phase of insanity; what she resents about him is the puritanical quality she admired in her father:

[I]sn't he too much of a Puritan, of a disciplinarian, doesn't he through birth & training accept a drastic discipline too tamely, or rather, with too Spartan a self control? There is, I suppose, a very different element in us; my social side, his intellectual side. This social side is very genuine in me. Nor do I think it reprehensible. It is a piece of jewellery I inherit from my mother—a joy in laughter, something that is stimulated, not selfishly wholly or vainly, by contact with my friends. And then ideas leap in me.[106]

This passage from Woolf's diary sounds almost like the kind of self-justifying internal monologues that adolescents need for articulating their resentment of their parents, particularly in her assertion that her social side is not reprehensible: this is immediately undercut by the implication that it is a decoration (a piece of jewellery) and therefore not as essential as she claims, almost acquiescing in Leonard Woolf's masculinist view of social life. 'Ideas leap in me' is oddly reminiscent of the biblical phrase 'the babe leaped in her womb',[107] suggesting the creative significance that Woolf attaches to social interaction.

---

[105] KMJ 147–8, Oct. 1918.   [106] VWD ii. 250–1, 28 June 1923.
[107] Luke 1: 41.

Mansfield shared this feeling, writing enviously to Murry from her isolation at Ospedaletti of her mother, and of him and his access to lively conversation, though he was notoriously silent on social occasions and resented their intrusion on his time. Mansfield's tone is critical of her husband, even sneering. She describes her mother as protected from her own ill-health and awareness of death by her family:

She had her husband her children, her home, her friends—physical presences—darling treasures to be cherished—and Ive not one of these things. I have only my work. That might be enough for you in like case—for the fine intelligence capable of detachment—but God! God! Im *rooted* in Life. Even if I hate Life I cant deny it. I spring from it and feed on it.[108]

Murry's existence is almost negated in 'Ive not one of these things', as are his efforts to create a home by house-hunting and collecting furniture; the fecund metaphor she uses to describe herself implies his sterility.

Mansfield's deployment of the rather banal opposition between thinking and being reveals a central similarity between herself and Woolf; both see intellectuality as in some ways antithetical to life though both are envious of the confidence their husbands derive from their Oxbridge education. They are again between borders, generally seen as intellectuals because they review, but aware of their own academic inadequacy. Mansfield articulates these conflicting attitudes in her journal, comparing Murry's ability to concentrate on his writing with her vivid memories of the girls, teachers, and buildings that composed her experience of Queen's College, but her total failure to absorb any scholarly information. Woolf's *A Room of One's Own* and *Three Guineas* provide an oblique gloss on Mansfield's experience of education, articulating the different attitudes that informed the provision of education for women and for men. While Leonard Woolf at St Paul's School and Murry at Christ's Hospital were given a sense of direction and prepared for Oxbridge, Mansfield's education was unfocused, part of the ethos that locks women out, as Woolf is excluded from the Cambridge library by a man who resembles the cherubims who bar the way to the Garden of Eden which contains the tree of knowledge:

[108] KMCL iii. 107, 21 Nov. 1919.

I was actually at the door which leads into the library itself. I must have opened it, for instantly there issued, like a guardian angel barring the way with a flutter of black gown instead of white wings, a deprecating, silvery, kindly gentleman, who regretted in a low voice as he waved me back that ladies are only admitted to the library if accompanied by a Fellow of the College.[109]

Woolf's tone is as bitter as Mansfield's hostility to Murry's aloof intellectuality when she explores the implications for women of their menfolk's education; women such as the Brontës had to scrimp and save in order to provide their brothers with a superior education. Echoing Thackeray's *Pendennis*, Woolf refers accusingly to this process as Arthur's Education Fund, in which sisters sacrifice comfort and prospects while their brothers disport themselves at Eton and Cambridge. Woolf's use of the following epigraph from Johnson's *Life of Gray* for *The Common Reader*, and the title itself, together with her assertion that the second volume was 'an unprofessional book of criticism' make the point that she dissociates herself from the self-conscious intellectualism of many of her male friends and contemporaries: 'I rejoice to concur with the common reader; for by the common sense of readers, uncorrupted by literary prejudices, after all the refinements of subtility and the dogmatism of learning, must be generally decided all claim to poetical honours.' Mansfield anticipated this view when she participated in a debate as a pupil at Queen's College, proposing the motion that 'pastors and masters, parents and guardians, commentators and cranks have done their best to spoil the taste of Shakespeare for us by making a duty of it instead of a pleasure.'[110] It may reflect the conformity of her fellow pupils that she lost the motion by 1 vote to 21.

Throughout both writers' preoccupation with male and female roles there is an abiding sense that women cannot choose their parts. While Leslie Stephen can be full of melodramatic self-pity one moment, and ordinarily conversational the next, women have the part written for them in advance by men. Mansfield writes to Murry that she 'can only play the servant with very bad grace indeed':

---

[109] Virginia Woolf, *A Room of One's Own* (London: Hogarth, 1929), 12.
[110] *Queen's College Magazine*, Apr. 1905, 273.

As though I were a dilatory housemaid! I loathe myself, today. I detest this woman who 'superintends' you and rushes about, slamming doors & slopping water—all untidy with her blouse out & her nails grimed. I am disgusted & repelled by the creature who shouts at you 'you might at least empty the pail & wash out the tea leaves!'[111]

The alienation from the self is profound; she both is 'this woman', 'the creature' and at the same time observes herself conforming to the time-honoured role of the harassed, overworked house-wife. Virginia Woolf writes of her role as drawing-room orna-ment: 'Dress and hair-doing became far more important than pictures and Greek . . . Down I came: in my green evening dress; all the lights were up in the drawing room; and there was George, in his black tie and evening jacket . . . He looked me up and down as if [I] were a horse turned into the ring.'[112] The agony of the fractured self, the reluctant actress who is reduced to an animal by the gaze of her male master, is clear, as it is later when, released from Hyde Park Gate, she entertains her own and her brother's male friends in Bloomsbury. She writes to Vanessa: 'He began to tell stories about shooting policemen and challenging Hugh Lane which I had to answer, across the room, and every-one sat silent.'[113] The phrase 'I had to answer' reveals how fully she had absorbed her mother's belief that a woman's duty is to 'transact all those trifling businesses which, as women feel instinctively, are somehow derogatory to the dignity which they like to discover in clever men'.[114]

Perhaps in Woolf's case and certainly in Mansfield's, the response to being forced into pre-scripted and prescriptive roles was to write an alternative script. Like the huge cavern where the seaweed-gathering selves mumble together intimately in her suspended moment by the sea, Mansfield had a whole series of aliases and pseudonyms when she was a young woman in Europe: Kathleen Beauchamp became Julian Mark, Kathi Bowden, K. Bendall, Matilda Berry, Katherine Schonfeld, Kathe Beauchamp-Bowden, and the familiar KM, or Katherine Mans-field. Even at Queen's College she went to the junior fancy-dress party in the singularly inappropriate guise of Dolly Varden, who is 'the pink and pattern of good looks, in a smart little

[111] KMCL i. 126, ?May–June 1913.   [112] Woolf, *Moments of Being*, 151.
[113] VWL i. 415, 25 Dec. 1909.   [114] Woolf, *Moments of Being*, 43.

cherry-coloured mantle', 'a little straw hat trimmed with cherry-coloured ribbons, and worn the merest trifle on one side', 'a cruel little muff, and such a heart-rending pair of shoes.'[115] Mansfield disconcerted friends by altering her appearance radically; in 1910 she visited a Japanese exhibition and changed her clothes and hairstyle in imitation of what she saw. Woolf said she 'had her look of a Japanese doll'.[116] She showed a homely image to one friend, a bohemian one to another: the constant motif in all this is the necessity of the mask and an awareness of multiple subjectivities. Her first husband was bemused by the roles she played, as he told Alpers: 'This time she was dressed "more or less Maori fashion," with some sort of scarf or kerchief over her shoulders, and there was "something almost eerie about it, as though of a psychic transformation rather than a mere impersonation." '[117] She wrote to Murry in 1917, with evident experience, 'dont lower your mask until you have another mask prepared beneath— As terrible as you like—but a *mask*.'[118] She fantasized and acted parts, literally as an extra on a film set but also in her romantically self-conscious expedition to join Francis Carco at the front during the First World War. Her description of the episode in her journal suggests that she is seeing herself as an actor in a drama, possibly *Tristan and Isolde*; she supplies the stage directions and set:

It was like an elopement.
    We went into a room on the ground floor, and the door was shut ... Laughing and trembling we pressed against each other—a long long kiss, interrupted by a clock on the wall striking five. He lit the fire ... The sword, the big ugly sword, but not between us, lying in a chair.[119]

Woolf herself was the recipient of one of Mansfield's scripts for her life; she writes to Violet Dickinson that Mansfield has 'had every sort of experience, wandering about with traveling circuses over the moors of Scotland'.[120] This could be either Mansfield's or Woolf's invention. Mansfield's clearest expression of life as a series of impersonations is in her journal in 1920:

[115] Charles Dickens, *Barnaby Rudge*, ch. 19.
[116] VWD ii. 226, 16 Jan. 1923.
[117] Antony Alpers, *The Life of Katherine Mansfield* (New York: Viking, 1980), 87.
[118] KMCL i. 318, late July 1917.   [119] KMJ 77–8, 20 Feb. 1915.
[120] VWL ii. 248, 10 June 1918.

True to oneself! which self? Which of my many—well really, that's what it looks like coming to—hundreds of selves? For what with complexes and repressions and reactions and vibrations and reflections, there are moments when I feel I am nothing but the small clerk of some hotel without a proprietor, who has all his work cut out to enter the names and hand the keys to the wilful guests.[121]

The fact that she likens herself to a male clerk heightens the impression that there may be no 'true self', no proprietor, at the core of the role-playing. Her letters confirm the image; the whimsical affectation of her letters to Ottoline Morrell seems to stem from a different personality than does the dutiful affection for her family and for New Zealand expressed in her letters to her father. Anne Estelle Rice 'has also left a record of a self-conscious and self-dramatizing Katherine who appeared at the Closerie des Lilas on different nights in clothes so different they seemed almost disguises, now a hat covered in cherries, another time a cloak and a white fez, or a turban, with bright, red-lipsticked mouth'.[122] Her language indicates her awareness of Freudian thought, 'complexes and repressions'; the pressure of modernity can be felt in her account of a subject position, rather than a unified identity.

Virginia Woolf similarly wrote her own script, sometimes for her own entertainment, sometimes for the protection or enjoyment of others. Like Mansfield, she had a series of aliases and nicknames: Apes, *Singes*, Billy Goat, Billy, the Goat, Capra, Ginia, Goatus, *il Giotto*, Sparroy, Sp, Wallaby, Mandril. These were affectionate family names, not used in public. On one occasion, in February 1910, she participated in the Dreadnought hoax, when she and five male friends disguised themselves as the Emperor of Abyssinia and his suite and paid a 'state' visit to HMS *Dreadnought* which was anchored at Weymouth. More painfully, she sustained an extraordinary fiction about her brother Thoby for her friend Violet Dickinson. Thoby Stephen and Violet Dickinson both contracted typhoid fever when they, Woolf, and Vanessa Stephen were on holiday in Greece. They returned to

[121] KMJ 205, Apr. 1920.
[122] Claire Tomalin, *Katherine Mansfield: A Secret Life* (London: Viking, 1987), 114.

Britain, where Thoby Stephen died on 20 November 1906. For almost a month Woolf wrote to Violet Dickinson, who was desperately ill, protecting her from possibly fatal mental anguish by pretending that Thoby was getting better; five days after the death of her much-loved brother she writes: 'Thoby is going on splendidly. He is very cross with his nurses, because they wont give him mutton chops and beer; and he asks why he cant go for a ride with Bell, and look for wild geese.'[123] She sustained the illusion until Dickinson, by then out of danger, came across an obituary notice of Thoby Stephen.

Her family and friends, in *Recollections of Virginia Woolf*, all comment on her power to transform reality, pushing back the borders of mundanity; her niece describes how Woolf took her to the theatre and persuaded her that 'the King and Queen would be here, they would be wearing their crowns sparkling with diamonds and rubies, their embroidered silk robes and ermine cloaks'.[124] Young writers comment on the way she would 'build up the most extraordinary sort of inverted pyramid of what she imagined your life was',[125] bringing Matisse, Picasso, and Gide together with princesses wearing tiaras into the imagined existence of a young man who happened to be living in Paris. Leonard Woolf told of a journey to London from Sussex at the beginning of the Second World War 'during which Virginia insisted, in a stage whisper, that a perfectly innocent nun who got into their carriage was a Nazi spy in disguise.'[126] Her pleasure in her transformations of the drab and everyday is evident from her letters, though what were creative fictions or exaggerations to her seemed malicious lies to some of those implicated, as was the case with some of Mansfield's victims. Mansfield and Woolf can be seen as part of a tradition of female storytellers for whom transformation of the mundane into the magical, crossing a border, is of the essence, from Scheherezade to their contemporary, Karen Blixen. Both describe that particular gift of dramatizing life as an attribute of their mothers. Woolf remembered her mother's transformations:

[123] VWL i. 250, 25 Nov. 1906.
[124] Joan Russell Noble (ed.), *Recollections of Virginia Woolf* (London: Sphere, 1989), 22.   [125] Ibid. 204.
[126] Ibid. 53.

She stamped people with characters at once; and at St Ives, or on Sunday afternoons at Hyde Park Gate, the scene was often fit for the stage; boldly acting on her conception she drew out from old General Beadle, or C. B. Clarke, or Jack Hills, or Sidney Lee, such sparks of character as they have never shown to anyone since. All lives directly she crossed them seemed to form themselves into a pattern and while she stayed each move was of the utmost importance.[127]

In a letter written after her mother's death, Mansfield recounts an anecdote her father told her about an incident that happened just after the family's move to the Grange which shows her mother's indifference to business conventions:

He was at a board meeting & was called away 'in the thick of it' to the telephone. A voice said 'its Mrs Beauchamp of The Grange speaking'. He couldn't make out what was happening & thought she wanted to ring up the *office* to give a 'wholesale order'. But when she heard his voice Father said 'all she said was "Hal dear, Im at home. I love this house. I simply love it. Thats all." and rang off.'[128]

When one reads Leonard Woolf's account of Mansfield, one can see why she appealed to Virginia Woolf in her ability to embroider reality, and how much the two women had in common with each other and with their mothers:

I don't think anyone has ever made me laugh more than she did in those days. She would sit very upright on the edge of a chair or sofa and tell at immense length a kind of saga, of her experiences as an actress ... There was not the shadow of a gleam of a smile on her mask of a face, and the extraordinary funniness of the story was increased by the flashes of her astringent wit.[129]

The significant 'mask' recurs, and 'the queer sense of being "like"—not only about literature' is confirmed. The ability to inhabit multiple positions is clearly related to the kind of fiction that each wanted to write; echoing Keats's distinction between 'negative capability' and Wordsworth's 'egotistical sublime', Woolf writes in her diary that 'the danger is the damned egotistical self; which ruins Joyce & [Dorothy] Richardson to my mind'.[130] A few months later she records a conversation with Mansfield that

---

[127] Woolf, *Moments of Being*, 40–1.   [128] KMCL iii. 116, 24 Nov. 1919.
[129] Leonard Woolf, *Autobiography*, iii. 204, quoted in Tomalin, *Katherine Mansfield: A Secret Life*, 180.   [130] VWD ii. 14, 26 Jan. 1920.

seems to refer both to social life and to fiction: 'I said how my own character seemed to cut out a shape like a shadow in front of me. This she understood (I give it as an example of her understanding) & proved it by telling me that she thought this bad: one ought to merge into things. Her senses are amazingly acute'.[131]

In some respects Julia Stephen's training prepared her daughter for her role as a novelist as both she and Mansfield saw it; constant attention to her father's emotional and spiritual state must have heightened her awareness of otherness, just as in tricky social situations with her brother's friends she had consistently tried to imagine what response they needed. Merging into other things and people, shifting perspectives, and registering difference are all implied both in Mansfield's and Woolf's social behaviour and in their beliefs about the nature of fiction, expressed in a letter by Mansfield: 'I find my great difficulty in writing is to learn to submit. Not that one ought to be without resistance—of course I dont mean that. But—when I am writing of "another" I want so to lose myself in the soul of the other that I am not'.[132] This might imply that both writers had an essentialist view of gender, and that they defined themselves as not-male. Underlying the fascination with the multifariousness of human personality, however, is a belief in both of them in a face behind the masks, in a subject that is not prescribed by negatives and that dismantles the binary oppositions that define traditional notions of identity. Mansfield writes to Murry of her admiration for Emily Brontë's poetry because 'it is not Emily disguised—who writes—it is Emily . . . It *is* so tiring, isnt it, never to leave the Masked Ball'.[133] What each writer values in her relationship with the other is the fact that disguises can be discarded: 'I can talk straight out to her'[134] writes Woolf, and Mansfield, in a letter to Woolf, invites her to 'consider how rare is it to find some one with the same passion for writing that you have, who desires to be scrupulously truthful with you'.[135] It is characteristic of their personal writing that the distinction between living and writing blurs, and a comment on one can refer equally to the other. Constant fissure and slippage in the sense of self are intimately connected with artistic exploration, and both writers are wary of the 'personal', monolithic

---

[131] Ibid. 61–2, 25 Aug. 1920.
[133] Ibid. ii. 334, 27 June 1919.
[135] KMCL i. 313, 24? June 1917.

[132] KMCL iv. 180, 12 Feb. 1921.
[134] VWD ii. 45, 31 May 1920.

identity. Kristeva claims that, in crossing the border, the foreigner disseminates 'the actor's paradox: multiplying masks and "false selves" he is never completely true nor completely false'.[136] As a result she asserts that the foreigner, the edgeman, has no self: 'I do what *they* want *me* to, but it is not "me"—"me" is elsewhere, "me" belongs to no one, "me" does not belong to "me," ... does "me" exist?'[137] '*Is there a Me?*'[138] Mansfield asks, a fortnight before her death. The liminal place, the landing or the crossover between life and death, sanity and madness, is one where the demands of the personal drop away, and there is no place for masks and play-acting, only for an awareness of the stranger within, which produces a momentarily heightened consciousness. Woolf, at the time of Mansfield's death, believes that she must 'like things for themselves: or rather, rid them of their bearing upon one's personal life. One must throw that aside; & venture on to the things that exist independently of oneself.'[139] Similarly Mansfield distinguishes between the self and the personal, describing in her journal what Woolf might have called a 'moment of being' in which memory, the unconscious, and the present fuse, not in a permanent unified self or identity but in a transient transformation:

Is it not possible that the rage for confession, autobiography, especially for memories of earliest childhood, is explained by our persistent yet mysterious belief in a self which is continuous and permanent; which, untouched by all we acquire and all we shed, pushes a green spear through the dead leaves and through the mould, thrusts a scaled bud through years of darkness until, one day, the light discovers it and shakes the flower free and—we are alive—we are flowering for our moment upon the earth? This is the moment which, after all, we live for,—the moment of direct feeling when we are most ourselves and least personal.[140]

The ideas embodied here, the metonymic mode of expression, and, centrally, the distinction between the self and the personal all manifest Mansfield's affinity with Woolf. The 'rage for confession' associated with 'earliest childhood' leads into another area of mutual preoccupation, which requires to be considered in relation to the writers' conception of time and memory.

[136] Kristeva, *Strangers to Ourselves*, 8.   [137] Ibid.
[138] KML ii. 266, 26 Dec. 1922.   [139] VWD ii. 221, 2 Jan. 1923.
[140] KMJ 205, Apr. 1920.

3
Sense of Echo

A woman caring as I care for writing is rare enough I suppose to give me the queerest sense of echo coming back to
me from her mind the second after I've spoken.[1]

VIRGINIA WOOLF's phrase 'the queerest sense of echo' used
of her relationship with Katherine Mansfield indicates her own
awareness of recognizing Mansfield as the foreigner within, other
but familiar, both frightening in her alien similarity and reassuring in her capacity to understand a shared obsession with writing.
What Ann L. McLaughlin describes as an 'uneasy sisterhood'[2]
is acknowledged in June 1920 when Woolf remarks of her friendship with Mansfield that 'this fragmentary intermittent intercourse
of mine seems more fundamental than many better established
ones.'[3] It predates Woolf's relationship with another writer,
Vita Sackville-West, and was intellectually and artistically more
significant for Woolf: its centrality becomes evident to the reader
of the personal writings of both women. The two writers are preoccupied by exploring the liminal territory they inhabit, between
life and death or sanity and madness, between tradition and experiment, suspended between past and present, between 'feminine'
dependence and artistic adventurousness which both gender
at different times as masculine. A discussion of the danger to
Mansfield's and Woolf's vulnerable sensibilities in the process of
exploration, and of their dependence on literary husbands and
canonical fathers, leads into the major subject of this chapter:
their preoccupation with childhood, time, and memory. As Louise
Bernikow says: 'This constellation of female illness, masculine
nurture, and the price of being taken care of, the abandonment

[1] VWD ii. 61, 25 Aug. 1920.
[2] Ann L. MacLaughlin, 'An Uneasy Sisterhood: Virginia Woolf and Katherine
Mansfield' in Jane Marcus (ed.), *Virginia Woolf: A Feminist Slant* (Lincoln, Nebr.:
University of Nebraska Press, 1983), 152–61.   [3] VWD ii. 46, 5 June 1920.

of not being taken care of, is an uncanny mirror in the lives of Mansfield and Woolf.'[4]

There is a directness in Mansfield's letters to Woolf that is lacking, for instance, in the more frequent and fulsome ones to 'My dearest ever dearest Ottoline'.[5] Often this involves a discovery, an experience that excites both writers; in the following message from Mansfield to Woolf the subject is a letter by Chekhov: '[W]hat the writer does is not so much to *solve* the question but to *put* the question. There must be the question put. That seems to me a very nice dividing line between the true & the false writer—Come & talk it over with me.'[6] The sense of recognition and the assumption that Woolf will understand is evident, as is the unaffected playfulness of the language, perhaps imitating the way in which their mutual friend Koteliansky spoke about Chekhov. On one of the rare occasions when Murry and Mansfield have a fairly settled home in London, Mansfield writes to Woolf in a different mood, showing her awareness that they share the same pleasures when her peripatetic existence permits: 'A husband, a home, a great many books & a passion for writing—are very nice things to possess all at once—It is pleasant to think of you & Leonard together—I often do.'[7] Their pleasure in books, and in discussing others' writing as well as their own, is evident from the references to their religious meetings in praise of Shakespeare, and in their correspondence. They were part of an intellectual and artistic milieu which was gossipy and argumentative but also deeply engaged with issues of modernity. Both of them read voraciously in their girlhood, though the impression gained from their responses to the reading is that Mansfield was looking for role models, as there were no writers in her family and immediate social circle, whereas Woolf was responding to stylistic influences. Mansfield's enthusiasm for symbolist writing[8] led her to enact what she read there; in her journal in 1906 she quotes Wilde's injunction to ' "[p]ush everything as far as it will go" ',[9] a notion that was deeply at odds with the mores of colonial Wellington. In a curiously prophetic

---

[4] Louise Bernikow, *Among Women* (New York: Harmony Books, 1980), 132.
[5] KMCL ii. 333, 27 June 1919.   [6] Ibid. 320, 27 May 1919.
[7] Ibid. 314, Apr. 1919.
[8] Clare Hanson and Andrew Gurr, *Katherine Mansfield* (London; Macmillan, 1981), 21–3, discusses this.   [9] KMJ 3, 1906.

few sentences in the journal she comments that 'I should like to write a life much in the style of Walter Pater's *Child in the House*'[10] and then outlines a story that is almost an account of her own life and death, as if her art writes her life. Pater was also influential for Woolf,[11] but she had the freedom of her father's library, and became a reviewer early in her writing life; the scope of her reading was ambitious, and she was from the beginning exactingly professional in the tasks she set herself. Though she felt herself to be ill-educated, to Mansfield she seemed to have a secure and established place among the intelligentsia. The barriers between Mansfield and Woolf seem to have dissolved, temporarily at least, when they met because of their mutual interest in Chekhov's apparently inconsequential stories and plays, in Dostoevsky, or in modern writing in general. Woolf's diaries show the intellectual stimulus she gained from their encounters: 'The inscrutable woman remains inscrutable I'm glad to say; no apologies, or sense of apologies due. At once she flung down her pen & plunged, as if we'd been parted for 10 minutes, into the question of Dorothy Richardson; & so on with the greatest freedom and animation on both sides until I had to catch my train.'[12] Both were part of the busy, pressured world of publishing, editing, reviewing, and writing, but both were precipitated out of it at frequent intervals into silence and solitude, Mansfield because she had to leave London in the winter, and Woolf because she had to rest if she was becoming too anxious and excited.

It could be argued that the tracing of the affinity between Woolf and Mansfield, developed in the previous chapter and continued in this one, is based too exclusively on what the writers reveal about themselves in letters and journals; that any kind of autobiographical writing is notoriously unreliable and only a version of what the writer may have wished to present as the truth about herself. This in itself however circles back to patriarchal power, and the intervention of male editing processes in the posthumous production of the two writers' investigation of their own female selves. Though the initial versions of Mansfield's letters (1928), her journal (1927), and Woolf's *A Writer's Diary* (1953)

[10] Ibid. 37, May 1908.
[11] Perry Meisel, *The Absent Father: Virginia Woolf and Walter Pater* (New Haven: Yale University Press, 1980), explores this.   [12] VWD i. 257, 22 Mar. 1919.

seem constructed to confirm the tragedy of the death that the reader anticipates, the full versions of the diaries and letters reveal malice, snobbery, and jealousy, among other unendearing human traits; their venom is sometimes directed at each other. Woolf wrote to Janet Case in 1922 of 'Bliss' that 'it was so brilliant,— so hard, and so shallow, and so sentimental that I had to rush to the bookcase for something to drink';[13] Mansfield, in the previous year, wrote contemptuously of 'Virginia Woolf tittering over some little mechanical contrivance to "relieve virgins" —that I abhor & abominate & am ashamed of.'[14] The overreaction in each case may suggest the danger of recognizing the foreigner within; the alien aspect of the double evokes intensely personal responses in Mansfield. She feels humiliated by what she sees as Woolf's prurience, as if it were her own. Both women were, of course, part of a literary environment and may have been writing with a consciousness that anything they penned might eventually find its way into print. Writing themselves and their friends as the Bloomsbury Group did, they must always have known that their letters probably would be published, but their rage, venom, and jealousy seem freely expressed, whereas there is slightly sinister evidence in his letters that Murry had an eye to his future as a widower. After he received a letter from Mansfield in 1918 in which she confesses, echoing Keats, to spitting 'bright arterial blood',[15] Murry writes to her with elephantine casualness, using a revealing metaphor of the mortality of his letters: 'Another thing, if any of my letters are alive still, will you keep them? I have all yours—and I think they may be important to us one day'.[16]

In spite of this threat that the editor husband will make literary capital out of his wife's most intimate writing, both Woolf and Mansfield seem to assume that at least their diaries are essentially private. Mansfield's warning in her Home Diary for 1915 that it is private property is echoed in 1922: 'Queer, this habit of mine of being garrulous. And I don't mean that any eye but mine should read this. This is—*really private*. And I must say —nothing affords me the same relief.'[17] In the letter that was essentially her will, Mansfield writes to her husband, 'All my

---

[13] VWL ii. 514, 20 Mar. 1922.   [14] KMCL iv. 270, 29 Aug. 1921.
[15] KMCL ii. 79, 19 Feb. 1918.   [16] KMMML 130, 10 Mar. 1918.
[17] KMJ 255, 14 July 1921.

manuscripts I leave entirely to you to do what you like with. Go through them one day, dear love, and destroy all you do not use. Please destroy all letters you do not wish to keep & all papers. You know my love of tidiness. Have a clean sweep, Bogey, and leave all fair—will you?'[18] Although they were not acted upon, these instructions seem as unambiguous as Woolf's speculation about what will happen to her diaries: 'But what is to become of all these diaries, I asked myself yesterday. If I died, what would Leo make of them? He would be disinclined to burn them; he could not publish them. Well, he should make up a book from them, I think; & then burn the body.'[19] The reiteration of text as body underlines the identification both the Murrys and the Woolfs made between the life of the text and the life of the body. In each case the husband, as survivor, is entrusted with disposal of the physical corpse and the body of work. Leonard Woolf had his wife's body cremated and her ashes buried under a tree in the garden of their house in Sussex. Mansfield was buried in Fontainebleau, though Murry forgot to pay the bill for the funeral. As a result her body was moved to an unmarked pauper's grave until her father heard of it and had her grave moved again, and a tombstone carved. Neither body of remaining personal writings was burnt of course, though rather like Mansfield, Woolf's final request to her husband was: 'Will you destroy all my papers.'[20]

Whether the retention of the mummified body in each case should be regarded as an act of betrayal, of hagiography, of agonized bereavement, or of the triumph of editorial judgement over marital obligation, remains an unanswerable question. The possibilities are not totally incompatible though some of her friends regarded Mansfield's papers as a body which Murry had cannibalized: Sylvia Lynd, referring to Murry's practice of publishing scraps of Mansfield's personal writing and unfinished stories in his own magazine, 'spoke of Murry "boiling Katherine's bones to make soup" ',[21] an opinion shared by Leonard and Virginia Woolf. Ultimately power over their wives' surviving unpublished texts resided with Leonard Woolf and Murry; both

[18] KMMML 363, 7 Aug. 1922. [19] VWD iii. 67, 20 Mar. 1926.
[20] VWL vi. 487, 28 Mar. 1941.
[21] Claire Tomalin, *Katherine Mansfield: A Secret Life* (London: Viking, 1987), 241.

initially mediated and censored those texts, subjecting the body to posthumous cosmetic surgery. Murry published the first edition of Mansfield's journal in 1927 and of the letters in 1928, adding *The Scrapbook of Katherine Mansfield* in 1939, with a 'definitive' version of the journal in 1954. He justified the venture in 1928 by asserting that 'Katherine Mansfield's one concern was to leave behind her some small legacy of truth, and because I believe that not a little of her "truth" is contained in these letters, I have tried to make the record as complete as I could.'[22] Ian Gordon provides a detailed factual account of the stages of publication[23] of what others call Murry's manufacture of the Mansfield Myth; those who knew her felt that in 'Murry's editing of the *Journal*, KM the mimic, the cynic, the mystic, the flirt who had to try her charm on every man, was ignored; neglected also was the "masked" pretender.'[24] Tomalin also sees Murry's role as exploitative of his dead wife, manipulating the tragedy of her early death, 'puffing and promoting Katherine's work through his own magazine, and running with Constable a well-organized and enormously successful publishing campaign in which segments of her work, fragments of stories, reissues, scraps of letters and pieces of journal (followed by the 'definitive' versions of the same) were issued to the public all through the 1920s, and indeed into the 1950s.'[25] Leonard Woolf began to plan how to use his wife's unpublished material even before her body had been found; Lee's repeated term for his function is significant:

He planned to 'husband' it, to bring it out at carefully timed intervals 'over a long period of years'. Leonard would make the decisions which set the terms of her posthumous reception and reputation: that the diary should be produced in severely edited form, as *A Writer's Diary*, in 1953; that the essays should be published in selections without dates or annotations; that the first biography should be written by a member of the family. His 'husbanding' of her posthumous resources controlled our access to Virginia Woolf for many years.[26]

22 KML i. p. viii.
23 Ian Gordon, 'The Editing of Katherine Mansfield's Journal and Scrapbook', in Jan Pilditch (ed.), *The Critical Response to Katherine Mansfield* (Westport, Conn.: Greenwood, 1996), 77–81.
24 Ruth Elvish Mantz, 'Katherine Mansfield: Tormentor and Tormented', ibid. 128.   25 Tomalin, *Katherine Mansfield: A Secret Life*, 241.
26 Hermione Lee, *Virginia Woolf* (London: Chatto & Windus, 1996), 767.

Like Murry he edited his wife's character; in *A Writer's Diary* he 'cut most of the gossip and malice in which Virginia delighted, and the resulting book made nonsense of his claim, in the preface to that volume, to detest "a Royal Academy picture" which would elide "the wrinkles, warts, frowns and asperities".'[27] It is ironic that patriarchal control, which Mansfield and Woolf so much resented and resisted, should finally have been exercised so definitively by both husbands ignoring direct requests to destroy papers and 'leave all fair'.

Whatever their intentions about publication, the essence of the comparison between Woolf and Mansfield lies, not in their assertions of friendship or of similarity, but in the fact that the reader of the personal writings is repeatedly made aware of the 'queer sense of their being "like" ' in their casual use of the same metaphors and phrases, and in the unconscious echoes of one in the other's psychic and private experience. This is nowhere more evident than in their sense of imminent disintegration, through disease and death, and in their experience of the liminal as a place of habitation, rather than of transition, a place which they recognize as they re-enter it and which is made tolerable only through memory. Mansfield writes to Murry of her exposure to death:

I get overwhelmed at times that it *is* all over, that we've seen each other for the last time (imagine it!) ((no, don't imagine it)) and that these letters will one day be published and people will read something in them—in their queer finality—that 'ought to have told us' . . . Once the defenses are fallen between you and Death they are not built up again. It needs such a little push—hardly that—just a false step—just not looking—and you are over.[28]

Similarly Woolf writes to her husband with a controlled desperation about crossing her private threshold: 'I feel certain that I am going mad again: I feel we cant go through another of those terrible times. And I shant recover this time. I begin to hear voices, and cant concentrate.'[29] This, of course, is the source of power in their fiction: that they live with a heightened awareness of danger, and of the transient beauty of the mortal world, like

[27] Peter F. Alexander, *Leonard and Virginia Woolf. A Literary Partnership* (London: Harvester Wheatsheaf, 1992), 195.
[28] KMCL iii. 106–7, 21 Nov. 1919.   [29] VWL vi. 481, 18? Mar. 1941.

the liminar who sees the familiar world made strange at the end of a rite of passage. When Mansfield writes to Murry that 'We see death in life as we see death in a flower that is fresh unfolded'[30] she is describing Woolf's experience, though the observation arises from a negative response to *Night and Day*. Learning through liminality is summed up in Mansfield's terse and dismissive contrasting of herself with Murry, an implicit comparison with Woolf's experience: 'Not being an intellectual I always seem to have to learn things at the risk of my life—but I do learn.'[31]

So the reader of the personal writings becomes aware of something which the writers themselves may not have known, the extent to which their psychic experience, connected always with their fiction, is similar. The other side of the domestic happiness which both express simply in their journals is their sense of menace and terror; of course in both cases this is heightened by the constant awareness of disease and death. Woolf feels that life is 'like a little strip of pavement over an abyss'[32] and likes 'to question people about death. I have taken it into my head that I shan't live till 70'[33] while Mansfield describes how she 'fell into the dark hollow which waits for me always'[34] when Murry seemed indifferent to her after their marriage. She, like Woolf, feels suspended between a perilous refuge and an abyss: 'Hanging in our little cages on the awful wall over the gulf of eternity we must sing—sing—'[35] The funereal image of the dark hollow persists when she writes to Ottoline Morrell of her horror at the victory celebrations after the First World War, 'all these toothless old jaws guzzling for the day—and then all of that beautiful youth feeding the fields of France' while 'I see nothing but black men, black boxes, black holes'.[36]

Not surprisingly, Mansfield's personal writings become increasingly obsessed with mortality, sometimes in throwaway remarks like the description of a little boat at Ospedaletti as 'a little black spot like the spot on a lung'[37] or the reference to 'that policeman with his scythe'.[38] There are more extended

[30] KMCL iii. 97, 16 Nov. 1919.
[31] Ibid. 216, 11 Feb. 1920.
[32] VWD ii. 72, 25 Oct. 1920.
[33] Ibid. 167, 17 Feb. 1922.
[34] KMCL ii. 197, 27 May 1918.
[35] Ibid. iii. 37, 20 Oct. 1919.
[36] Ibid. ii. 339, 13 July 1919.
[37] Ibid. iii. 36, 20 Oct. 1919.
[38] Ibid. 51, 27 Oct. 1919.

glimpses of the horror she lived in her isolation, such as this journal entry about a dream in 1919 where she experiences death in life:

And suddenly I felt my whole body *breaking up*. It broke up with a violent shock—an earthquake—and it broke like glass. A long terrible shiver, you understand—and the spinal cord and the bones and every bit and particle quaking. It sounded in my ears—a low, confused din, and there was a sense of flashing greenish brilliance, like broken glass ... It slowly dawned upon me—the conviction that in that dream I died ... The *spirit* that is the enemy of death and quakes so and is so tenacious was shaken out of me. I am (December 15, 1919) a dead woman.[39]

Murry's 'reassuring' letter, written after she had this dream of spiritual and physical disintegration, suggests that he sees himself as her benign undertaker; his promise never to shut the lid appropriates to himself an unthinking patriarchal power: 'I shall never forget: never do forget, even for a minute, that I nearly lost you once. Now I intend to put you in a box and keep you there. Don't be frightened. I'll never shut the lid.'[40] Woolf's early experience of death within her family and her own fragile state of health provide an affinity with Mansfield's '*feeling of finality*'.[41] She writes that 'death & tragedy had once more put down his paw, after letting us run a few paces. People never get over their early impressions of death I think. I always feel pursued.'[42] Both use the image of grasping the nettle; Woolf writes, 'Still I dont pluck the nettle out of me'[43] while Mansfield quotes in her journal the lines from Shakespeare's *1 Henry IV* which were to become her epitaph: 'But I tell you my Lord fool, Out of this nettle, danger, we pluck this flower, safety.' Grasping the nettle requires courage in a world where, as Woolf says, 'Unhappiness is everywhere; just beyond the door'.[44]

Their sense of danger is central to their conception of what fiction should be, stylistically as well as thematically. Woolf writes in her diary of the public response to a novel by Romer Wilson: 'another proof that what people dread is being made to feel

[39] KMJ 184–5, 15 Dec. 1919.
[40] Alexander Turnbull Library archive, letter of 12 Oct. 1919.
[41] KMCL iii. 77, 8 Nov. 1919.   [42] VWD ii. 299, 5 Apr. 1924.
[43] Ibid. 73, 25 Oct. 1920.   [44] Ibid.

anything: a certain kind of rhapsody makes them feel wild & adventurous; & they then make out that this is passion & poetry—so thankful to be let off the genuine thing.'[45] Two years earlier Mansfield comes to a similar opinion as she struggles with a review for the *Athenaeum*: 'But one always seems to arrive at the same conclusion—nothing goes deep enough—the *risk* has not been taken'.[46] Writing to Koteliansky about *Aaron's Rod*, Mansfield compares Lawrence's vitality with the work of writers who refuse to grasp the nettle:

And it is written by a living man, with *conviction*. Oh, Koteliansky, what a relief it is to turn away from these little pre-digested books written by authors who have nothing to say! . . . But these seekers in the looking glass, these half-female, frightened writers-of-today—You know, they remind me of the greenfly in roses—they are a kind of blight.[47]

The reader is reminded of Beryl gazing at herself in the mirror at the end of 'Prelude', and Kezia's parodic version of the scene as she holds the dirty calico cat up to the mirror with the top of a cream jar over its ear: ' "Now look at yourself," said she sternly.'[48] Just as this scene mocks Beryl's perception of herself through an imagined male gaze as a sexual object, so Mansfield attacks her contemporaries' narcissistic preoccupation with identity rather than the kind of selving that recognizes the foreigner within. 'Half-female' seems to suggest, rather than androgyny, that for Mansfield there is an identification between masculinity and the writing self like that in the suspended moment beside the sea.

Both Mansfield and Woolf had taken risks in living as well as in writing when they were young, ignoring the disapproval they incurred, Mansfield for her sexual experiments and Woolf for her determination to live with her friends and contemporaries after her father's death. Exploration and discovery remain key concepts for both of them; the journeys are inner rather than outer, and recognize that mapping is fragmented and tentative. Woolf writes that '[b]y nature, both Vanessa and I were explorers, revolutionists, reformers'[49] and, self-mockingly but with

---

[45] VWD ii. 117, 9 May 1921.   [46] KMCL ii. 326, 10 June 1919.
[47] KML ii. 229, 17 July 1922.   [48] CS 60.
[49] Virginia Woolf, *Moments of Being* (St Albans: Triad/Panther, 1978), 147.

insight into her own motivation, that 'my inveterate romanticism suggests an image of forging ahead, alone, through the night: of suffering inwardly, stoically; of blazing my way through to the end'.[50] The word 'discovery' recurs in Mansfield's writing; as she plans 'The Garden Party' she remarks that 'there seems to be a moment when all is to be discovered',[51] and writing to the painter, Brett, she asks what urges them as artists to 'feel that you *must* make *your* discovery and that I *must* make *mine*?'[52] The tentative and often frustrating process of exploration must culminate in some way, though it will not be definitive. Mansfield admires Lawrence, in comparison with his contemporaries, for his 'living book': 'I am so sick of all this modern seeking which ends in seeking. *Seek* by all means, but the text goes on "and ye shall find." And although, of course, there can be no ultimate finding, there is a kind of finding by the way which is enough, is sufficient.'[53]

Finding through risk is achieved for both writers through memory. Superficially this could seem a form of escapism rather than confrontation but again a significant trope recurs in the personal writings of both. What they explore and remember is not just the idyllic lost world of childhood, even though Mansfield imagines a photograph of herself at the age of 3 months 'firmly gripping a spade, showing even then a longing to dig for treasure with her own hands'.[54] It is a remembered fear of death: of being shut in, in the dark, the uncanny sense of being buried alive. As a woman, Mansfield's heart 'begins to cry as if it were a child in an empty room'[55] and she feels like 'a tiny girl whom someone has locked up in the dark cupboard—even though its daytime'[56] while Woolf remembers 'being afraid of being shut in, as a child'[57] and finds that when her husband is ill her 'mind turned by anxiety, or other cause, from its scrutiny of blank paper, is like a lost child—wandering the house, sitting on the bottom step to cry.'[58] The reader is reminded of Kezia's horror of the empty house in 'Prelude', and Cam's fear at bedtime in *To the Lighthouse*; the small children in 'At the Bay' have to confront

[50] VWD ii. 221, 2 Jan. 1923.
[51] KMJ 314, 3 May 1922.
[52] KMCL iii. 262, 26 Mar. 1920.
[53] KML ii. 229, 17 July 1922.
[54] KMCL iii. 59, 30 Oct. 1919.
[55] Ibid. i. 158, 19–20 Mar. 1915.
[56] Ibid. ii. 81, 20 Feb. 1918.
[57] VWD i. 224, 3 Dec. 1918.
[58] Ibid. 315, 5 Dec. 1919.

terrors in their attempt to map their world: 'The pink and the blue sunbonnet followed Isabel's bright red sunbonnet up that sliding, slipping hill. At the top they paused to decide where to go and to have a good stare at who was there already. Seen from behind, standing against the sky-line, gesticulating largely with their spades, they looked like minute puzzled explorers.'[59] The personal significance of the distant view, in time as well as space, of these small figures is articulated in Mansfield's letter to Brett about the writing of 'At the Bay' in which she says how strange it is to bring the dead back to life again.[60]

These depictions of childhood danger, exclusion, and terror are echoed overtly in their memories of their own infancy. Virginia Woolf uses specific memories to define what she calls a moment of being, an instant that remains in the consciousness as a point of clarity 'embedded in a kind of nondescript cotton wool'[61] which is how we spend most of our waking lives; as George Eliot describes it in a similar phrase, 'the quickest of us walk about well wadded with stupidity.'[62] Two of the three instances Woolf gives end in despair; this existential experience is one of them:

somehow I overheard my father or my mother say that Mr Valpy had killed himself. The next thing I remember is being in the garden at night and walking on the path by the apple tree. It seemed to me that the apple tree was connected with the horror of Mr Valpy's suicide. I could not pass it. I stood there looking at the grey-green creases of the bark—it was a moonlit night—in a trance of horror. I seemed to be dragged down, hopelessly, into some pit of absolute despair from which I could not escape.[63]

This momentary experience of passing into a liminal space anticipates what will become a more familiar mental territory in her later life. In a letter to one of her sisters thanking her for a birthday present, Mansfield recalls what was evidently a traumatic moment, a birthday in her infancy, showing her resentment of being cast in the conventional female role even then, and evidently feeling bitterly that her family conspired against her in the matter of gifts. Though this is deeply felt, however, it is not a

[59] CS 214.   [60] KMCL iv. 278, 12 Sept. 1921.
[61] Woolf, *Moments of Being*, 81.   [62] George Eliot, *Middlemarch*, ch. 20.
[63] Woolf, *Moments of Being*, 82–3.

liminal experience; it is social and emotional rather than existential: 'I remember the birthday when you bit me! It was the
same one when I got a dolls pram & in a rage let it go hurling
by itself down the grassy slope outside the conservatory. Father
was *awfully* angry & said no one was to speak to me.'[64] This
passage is oddly contextualized, as the letter begins 'My little
sister' and continues, after the events recorded: 'anyone who says
to me "do you remember" simply has my heart.' Yet the memory
is full of bitterness against her father in his manifestation as patriarch punishing his daughter for her unfeminine behaviour, and
against the rest of the family for victimizing and isolating the
small Katherine, with her aggressive sense of who she is and
what she wants. The reader remembers what a hasty retreat Kezia
beats in 'Prelude' when she is threatened with accompanying
Isabel and her 'neat pramload of prim dolls'.[65]

These passages suggest the central role that memory plays
in the thought and fiction of both writers. In recounting the
episodes they remember, they are also recording a process of discovery of the self and of the nature of moments of being; there
is an integral connection for them between discovery and the
nettle, danger, with its menacing abyss, as well as the possibility
of the flower, safety. In one of the fragments in Mansfield's notebooks written in 1915, where the distinction between fiction
and autobiography is blurred as she remembers and mourns the
death of her brother, she records how she and her brother were
involved in their own version of the creation story in Genesis.
In an idyllic orchard that 'stretched right over to the edge of the
paddocks—to the clump of wattles bobbing yellow in the bright
sun and the blue gums with their streaming sickle-shaped
leaves'[66] a rare apple tree was accidentally discovered which their
father forbade them to touch. All through the story the father
swells and struts with self-importance, for 'father was a self-made
man and the price he had to pay for everything was so huge
and so painful that nothing rang so sweet to him as to hear his
purchase praised.'[67] Yet when the children are eventually permitted
to taste an apple, '[o]ur mouths were full of a floury stuff, a hard,

[64] KMCL iv. 294, 14 Oct. 1921.   [65] CS 26.
[66] Ian A. Gordon (ed.), *Undiscovered Country: The New Zealand Stories of
Katherine Mansfield* (London: Longman, 1974), 96.   [67] Ibid. 97.

faintly bitter skin—a horrible taste of something dry . . .'[68] Though the children take a conspiratorial pleasure in their father's fallibility, they also learn through a significant and in some ways disappointing experience; father can declare a tree forbidden but he is not God, and the spectacular apples which look as if they have been dipped in wine are the bitter fruit of the tree of knowledge. Yet their experience is shared, and remains in the recognizable world, not the borderland that Woolf evidently knew from childhood. In a recollection of her brother and the resonant events of childhood Woolf writes of another liminal moment:

I was fighting with Thoby on the lawn. We were pommelling each other with our fists. Just as I raised my fist to hit him, I felt: why hurt another person? I dropped my hand instantly, and stood there, and let him beat me. I remember the feeling. It was a feeling of hopeless sadness. It was as if I became aware of something terrible; and of my own powerlessness. I slunk off alone, feeling horribly depressed.[69]

The awareness of something terrible, which disempowers her and leaves her isolated in her own space, is familiar to her before the onset of her illness.

Childless and ill themselves in their adult lives, both Mansfield and Woolf take an intense delight in the children they meet in the present. Woolf writes of her nephews and nieces:

And of course children are wonderful & charming creatures . . . There's a quality in their minds to me very adorable: to be alone with them, & see them day to day would be an extraordinary experience. They have what no grown up has—that directness . . . the walls of her mind all hung round with such bright vivid things, & she doesn't see what we see.[70]

When Mansfield was caught in Paris during the bombardment in April 1918, for which she uses a biblical archetype, she was temporarily distracted from her suffering and misery by a 2-year-old boy to whom she offered a piece of chocolate: 'How fine and lovely little children can be. When he sat on my lap I felt a moment of almost *peace* as though the Sodom & Gomorrah world had stopped just for an instant.'[71]

[68] Ian A. Gordon (ed.), *Undiscovered Country: The New Zealand Stories of Katherine Mansfield* (London: Longman, 1974), 98.
[69] Woolf, *Moments of Being*, 82.   [70] VWD ii. 315–16, 29 Sept. 1924.
[71] KMCL ii. 149, 1 Apr. 1918.

Both use images of harvest to express the way in which they contemplate childhood and use their own childhood in their adult work. Woolf writes when she is about to go to Cornwall on holiday:

Why am I so incredibly & incurably romantic about Cornwall? One's past, I suppose: I see children running in the garden. A spring day. Life so new. People so enchanting. The sound of the sea at night. And now I go back 'bringing my sheaves'—well, Leonard, & almost 40 years of life, all built on that, permeated by that: how much so I could never explain.[72]

Mansfield also sees children running in a garden and hears the sound of the sea at night when she remembers her childhood; she says that there is 'no harvest to be reaped' out of London whereas a 'young country is a real heritage, though it takes one time to recognise it.'[73] After her brother's death she records that she wants 'to write recollections of my own country. Yes, I want to write about my own country till I simply exhaust my store.'[74] The metaphors of discovery and of harvest, storing, come together as she wonders, 'Is there another grown person as ignorant as I?'[75] and concludes that she was too busy absorbing all the detail of school life to pay any attention to lessons: 'My mind was just like a squirrel. I gathered and gathered and hid away, for that long "winter" when I should rediscover all this treasure—and if anybody came close I scuttled up the tallest, darkest tree and hid in the branches.'[76]

In many ways Woolf's and Mansfield's specific childhood experiences were similar, though they took place on opposite sides of the globe. Sibling rivalry is clearly a part of the texture of their adult lives. The tone of a letter that Mansfield wrote to her mother in 1918, when she was nearly 30, is difficult to interpret; it sounds so childish that it may be intended as a parody of a childhood whine: 'By the way, my dear, re, again, your letter to Belle and Chaddie this talk of woolen jackets really does begin to make my mouth water. If you can toss them off <their> your knitting pegs like positive pancakes—why cant your poor little K have one? It is mean; Im older than Jeanne.'[77]

[72] VWD ii. 103, 22 Mar. 1921. [73] KML ii. 199, 18 Mar. 1922.
[74] KMJ 93–4, 22 Jan. 1916. [75] Ibid. 105, Feb. 1916.
[76] Ibid. 103–4. [77] KMCL ii. 18–19, 18 Jan. 1918.

Whatever the exact tone, the insistence that she should not be excluded, and that she is at once her mother's daughter and has her place in the family hierarchy is manifest. Woolf is not aggressive in her envy of her sister; she repeatedly measures her life against Vanessa's and usually finds her own wanting. At the beginning of 1923 she wonders why she is depressed:

A desire for children, I suppose; . . . Here's Angelica—here's Quentin & Julian. Now children dont make yourself ill on plum pudding tonight. We have people dining. There's no hot water. The gas is escaping in Quentin's bedroom—I pluck what I call flowers at random. They make my life seem a little bare sometimes.[78]

What might be interpreted here as wearing domestic trials rather than flowers are obviously attractive to Woolf because they remind her of her conception of normality, created before she was aware of the impressions she was absorbing, when her busy mother ran her household as Vanessa Bell runs hers; they are the flowers of at least apparent safety and belonging. Her mother had little time for her individually, and she felt displaced by her younger brother, Adrian, 'mother called him her Benjamin',[79] the beloved youngest child: 'she had not time, nor strength, to concentrate, except for a moment if one were ill or in some child's crisis, upon me, or upon anyone—unless it were Adrian. Him she cherished separately; she called him "My Joy"'.[80] Mansfield describes a similar experience in the section of her journal entitled 'A Recollection of Childhood'; she was very young because 'I remember standing on tiptoe and using both hands to turn the big white china door-handle'.[81] She finds her mother lying in bed and her grandmother holding a new baby; 'My mother paid no attention to me at all.' Her grandmother tells her to kiss her mother but 'mother did not want to kiss me. Very languid, leaning against the pillows, she was eating some sago.'[82] Mansfield's sense that both the baby and her mother exclude her is strong; the reader is reminded of Linda Burnell who is, in 'Prelude' and 'At the Bay', also 'very languid' and indifferent to whether Kezia has or has not been tossed by a bull. Though these experiences for each writer of displacement within the family are ordinarily traumatic, their liminal

---

[78] VWD ii. 221, 2 Jan. 1923.   [79] Woolf, *Moments of Being*, 125.
[80] Ibid. 96.   [81] KMJ 101, Feb. 1916.   [82] Ibid.

significance is recognized and reworked in what happens in the fiction to Kezia, Jacob, and James.[83]

A central link in the chain of connection between childhood memories, discovery of lost treasure or unrealized significance, the black hole or abyss, and writing, is the fact that both women had beloved brothers who died in their early twenties. Mansfield's anguish is articulated at the time of Leslie Beauchamp's death in her journal and in letters. In a letter to Koteliansky she records that her brother's friend told her that, just before he died as a result of a hand-grenade accident, he said, ' "Lift my head, Katy I can't breathe" ',[84] an uncanny foreshadowing of her own death from tuberculosis. Woolf's reaction to Thoby's death is recorded many years after the event. In 1929 she feels that 'no-one knows how I suffer, walking up this street, engaged with my anguish, as I was after Thoby died—alone; fighting something alone. But then I had the devil to fight'.[85] Thoby died in 1906; in 1931 she wrote in her diary that *The Waves* was completed: 'I have been sitting these 15 minutes in a state of glory, & calm, & some tears, thinking of Thoby & if I could write Julian Thoby Stephen 1881—1906 on the first page. I suppose not.'[86] She had finally paid what Mansfield calls a 'debt of love'[87] to her brother, though neither she nor Mansfield used the dedications they planned. After Mansfield's brother Leslie was killed in France in October 1915 she felt herself to be as dead as he was:

I feel I have a duty to perform to the lovely time when we were both alive. I want to write about it, and he wanted me to. We talked it over in my little top room in London. I said: I will just put on the front page: To my brother, Leslie Heron Beauchamp. Very well: it shall be done.[88]

The impetus in both writers is to retrieve the 'undiscovered country' of childhood 'in a kind of *special prose*' which will recreate the past 'because in my thoughts I range with him over all the remembered places. I am never far away from them. I long to renew them in writing.'[89] Woolf's preoccupation with childhood is not as evident in her fiction as Mansfield's is, but

---

[83] Patricia Moran, in *Word of Mouth* (London: University Press of Virginia, 1996), makes a persuasive case for seeing these rejections as part of a source of matrophobia in the two writers.

[84] KMCL i. 200, 19 Nov. 1915.   [85] VWD iii. 259–60, 11 Oct. 1929.
[86] Ibid. iv. 10, 7 Feb. 1931.   [87] KMJ 94, 22 Jan. 1916.
[88] Ibid. 90, Nov. 1915.   [89] Ibid. 94, 22 Jan. 1916.

it permeates her personal writing with a sense of yearning for the lost self whose world was securely inhabited by parents and brother: 'Do you like yourself as a child? I like myself, before the age of 10, that is—before consciousness sets in.'[90]

Woolf of course could and did revisit her childhood places. After their father's death, and eleven years after their last family holiday there, the four Stephen children, by this time young adults, had a holiday in Cornwall and saw Talland House, which had for many years been their holiday home:

It is a strange dream to come back here again. The first night we groped our way up to Talland House in the dark, and just peeped at it from behind the Escalonia hedge. It was a ghostly thing to do: it all looked quite unchanged. Old people meet us and stop and talk to us, and remember us playing on the beach.[91]

It was ghostly partly because their mother, father, and stepsister had died in the intervening years, and also because they saw their former selves wherever they went. As she says in a letter a month later, 'We all walk and wander like so many disembodied ghosts.'[92] The family decision to give up the lease of Talland House coincided with the beginning of the disintegration of the family life; much later Woolf speculates on whether there were any advantages in this, dwelling on her own need for discovery. The metaphor of the family as a moving vehicle or a secure shelter gives way to a violent trope ('gashes') suggesting the physical and mental wounds Woolf suffered in the loss of her imagination's home, and the liminal space on the edge of insanity she inhabited as one form of controlled exploration gave place to another ineluctable kind:

Would it not have been better (if there is any sense in using good and better when there is no possible judge) to go on feeling at St Ives the rush and tumble of things? to go on exploring and adventuring privately, while all the while the family as a whole continued its solid rumbling progress, from year to year? . . . But at fifteen to have that protection removed, to be tumbled out of the family shelter, to see cracks and gashes in that fabric, to be cut by them, to see beyond them —was that good?[93]

---

[90] VWL ii. 462, 28 Mar. 1921.   [91] Ibid. i. 203–4, 13? Aug. 1905.
[92] Ibid. 207, 17 Sept. 1905.   [93] Woolf, *Moments of Being*, 137.

The metaphor is powerful; Woolf was damaged by the fragmenta-
tion of the family that she depended on for her security, so that
the lost world 'before consciousness sets in' bringing madness
with it is almost as elusive as Mansfield's was to her. Mansfield
could only return to her childhood place in her mind; as it becomes
increasingly clear that she cannot survive the long voyage home
she records in her journal 'A long typical boat dream. I was,
as usual, going to N.Z.'[94] Perhaps because the irrecoverable past
is in another country, a colonial society in which the process of
exploration, mapping, and naming was still part of ordinary life,
she persistently uses images of territory, exploration, and discovery in her personal writing to express her sense of the danger
and excitement of human relationships. After her brother's death
she and Murry created 'the world of two' which she places on
an Edenic island: 'I think we ought to develop together . . . and
make ourselves, on our island, a palace and gardens and arbours
and boats for you and flowery bushes for me—and we ought not
to court other people at all yet awhile.'[95] As her disease develops
she reiterates the theme that they have a territory of their own
which they create and in which they can make the rules, just
as they are among the few writers who realize that prose is a
hidden country whose possibilities are only just beginning to be
explored, though the use of 'undiscovered country' belies the
unexpressed awareness of death, referring as it does to Hamlet's
'undiscover'd country, from whose bourn | No traveller returns':[96]
'my whole soul waits for the time when you and I shall be
withdrawn from everybody—when we shall go into our own
undiscovered darling country and dwell therein.'[97] In a letter to
Ida Baker written when she is living in London with Murry and
planning to move to what she hoped would be a permanent
home in Hampstead, Mansfield tries to explain her possessive-
ness: 'You see out of all my external world only the house remains
just now. Its all my little world & I want to make it *mine beyond
words*'.[98]

The idea of creating her own world, accomplished most
securely not beyond words but in words, pervades Mansfield's
personal writing. She writes of her mother, after her death, when

[94] KMJ 281, 5 Jan. 1922.   [95] KMCL i. 220, 19–20 Dec. 1915.
[96] *Hamlet*, iii. i.   [97] KMCL ii. 227, 8 June 1918.
[98] Ibid. 262, 1 Aug. 1918.

she herself is in the liminal world of incapacitating illness and coughing blood: 'My little Mother, my star, my courage, my *own*. I seem to dwell in her now. We live in *the same world*. Not quite this world, not quite another.'[99] The appropriation of her mother may reflect the fact that she now only lives in Mansfield's fiction, and has come under her control as she never did in life; the mother who tried to mould her daughter to conform with bourgeois Wellington now inhabits liminal territory in Mansfield's imagination. But Mansfield's living friend and rival is also admitted to the private world: 'I wonder why I feel an intense joy that you are a writer—that you live for writing—I do. You are immensely important in my world, Virginia.'[100] The need to inhabit a world of writing and of personal memory becomes stronger as the dream of the world of two disintegrates and Murry's Englishness becomes oppressive to her when he is in his native environment and she is not. In an extraordinarily obtuse letter to her in 1918, Murry writes: 'My darling, you and I are English, and because we are truly English we are set apart from our generation . . . You are a perfect flower of England.'[101] When his brother visits them the following year, 'They were of one nation, I of another, as we sat talking,'[102] and she hates Murry's Englishness though she loves him in spite of it, denying the banal identification he makes of her as an English flower: 'I would not care if I never saw the English country again. Even in its flowering I feel deeply antagonistic to it'.[103] The feeling drives her back to the world of childhood, which is inaccessible but where she was at home, and makes her feel that the present is unreal. London flowers, geraniums, provoke this response, evoking the Tinakori hills where she lived as a small child:

But why should they make me feel a stranger? Why should they ask me every time I go near: 'And what are *you* doing in a London garden?' They burn with arrogance and pride. And I am the little Colonial walking in the London garden patch—allowed to look, perhaps, but not to linger. If I lie on the grass they positively shout at me: 'Look at her, lying on *our* grass, pretending she lives here, pretending this is her garden, and that tall back of the house, with the windows open and

---

[99] KMJ 154, 19 May 1919.   [100] KMCL ii. 288, 7 Nov. 1918.
[101] Turnbull Archive, letter of 30 Mar. 1918.   [102] KMJ 159, May 1919.
[103] Ibid.

the coloured curtains lifting, is her house. She is a stranger—an alien. She is nothing but a little girl sitting on the Tinakori hills and dreaming: "I went to London and married an Englishman, and we lived in a tall grave house with red geraniums and white daisies in the garden at the back." *Im*-pudence!'[104]

This hostile house is the one around which her dreams of creating a perfect private world centre in earlier letters; she consistently turns in her disappointments with Murry and in her inability to control her illness to the remembered world and her recreation of it in her writing. She constantly sees fiction as territory to be mapped; in a letter to the painter J. D. Fergusson she marvels at how content writers have been 'with the chance encounter or a matrimonial stodge. All that lies between is almost undiscovered and unexplored'.[105] In a letter to Koteliansky about their translation of one of Chekhov's letters she says that it 'seems to me one of the most valuable things I have ever read. It opens—it discovers rather, a new world.'[106] In responding to Joyce's *Ulysses* and disliking its 'peculiar *male* arrogance' she expresses her belief in English prose: 'People have never explored the lovely medium of prose. It is a hidden country still—I feel that so profoundly.'[107]

When the two hidden countries, New Zealand and prose, intersect in her recreation of the lost world of childhood there is a fleeting glimpse, through inhabiting the threshold space of discovery, of 'the moment which, after all, we live for,—the moment of direct feeling when we are most ourselves and least personal',[108] for the reader as well as the writer. At the end of her life she is still struggling with the difficulty of attaining the unified moment, a positive moment of being, as she explains in the letter quoted earlier (p. 19): '[A]ll we have said of "individuality" and of being strong and single, and of growing—I believe it. I try to act up to it. But the reality is far far different. Circumstances still hypnotise me. I am a divided being . . . I am always conscious of this secret disruption in me'.[109] Testimony to the different forms taken by the attempt to be reconciled to the fragmented self permeate the letters and journals; the 'world

[104] Ibid. 157, May 1919.
[105] KMCL ii. 275, Sept. 1918.
[106] Ibid. 324, 6 June 1919.
[107] Ibid. 343, 19 or 26 July 1919.
[108] KMJ 205, May? 1920.
[109] KML ii. 260, 19 Oct. 1922.

of two' is one attempt at cohesion, but the most lasting effort to heal the wound, the 'secret disruption', is through re-entering the world of childhood where the initial ruptures happened before she was conscious of them. She writes to Brett about what she tries to achieve in 'At the Bay':

It is so strange to bring the dead to life again. Theres my grandmother, back in her chair with her pink knitting, there stalks my uncle over the grass. I feel as I write 'you are not dead, my darlings. All is remembered. I bow down to you. I efface myself so that you may live again through me in your richness and beauty.' And one feels *possessed*. And then the peace where it all happens. I have tried to make it as familiar to 'you' as it is to me. You know the marigolds? You know those pools in the rocks? You know the mousetrap on the wash house window sill? And, too, one tries to go deep—to speak to the secret self we all have—to acknowledge that.[110]

This passage is about discovery in the widest sense: the discovery of reader by writer, of the writer's unconscious and relationship with her physically irretrievable people and places, and of the resources of prose. The sense of possession by her writing is expressed most strongly when she writes about the Burnell family in New Zealand; as she writes to Koteliansky, she feels 'an infinite delight and value in *detail*—not for the sake of detail but for the life *in* the life of it.'[111] In an earlier letter to Brett about 'Prelude' she describes what happens to her at such moments, suspended liminal moments when she is between the remembered past and the encoding of it. She is referring apparently to the scene in 'Prelude' where Pat takes the children to catch a duck and kill it:

When I write about ducks I swear that I am a white duck with a round eye, floating in a pond fringed with yellow blobs and taking an occasional dart at the other duck with the round eye, which floats upside down beneath me. In fact this whole process of becoming the duck ... is so thrilling that I can hardly breathe, only to think about it. For although that is as far as most people get, it is really only the 'prelude'. There follows the moment when you are *more* duck, *more* apple or *more* Natasha than any of these objects could ever possibly be, and so you *create* them anew.[112]

---

[110] KMCL iv. 278, 12 Sept. 1921. [111] Ibid. i. 192, 17 May 1915.
[112] Ibid. 330, 11 Oct. 1917.

This passage suggests that the title of the story indicates the mode of fiction that she is beginning to develop, under the pressure of grief for her brother and distance from the home where they grew up together. In an entry in her journal written at the time when she is rewriting 'The Aloe' and turning it into 'Prelude', she says that the 'plots of my stories leave me perfectly cold' and that 'I feel no longer concerned with the same appearance of things.'[113] She remembers details of domestic life, but is concerned with how her prose can transform them, fusing two undiscovered countries:

Ah, the people—the people we loved there—of them, too, I want to write. Another 'debt of love'. Oh, I want for one moment to make our undiscovered country leap into the eyes of the Old World. It must be mysterious, as though floating. It must take the breath. It must be 'one of those islands . . .' I shall tell everything, even of how the laundry-basket squeaked at 75. But all must be told with a sense of mystery, a radiance, an afterglow, because you, my little sun of it, are set.[114]

In the letter to Brett about 'Prelude' she makes clear that the form of the story, its twelve-cell structure,[115] arises out of the nature of childhood memories, not viewed nostalgically but re-created through a child's consciousness of how things felt and looked and tasted, with 'that directness' that Woolf admired in children's minds:

What form is it? you ask. Ah, Brett, its so difficult to say. As far as I know its more or less my own invention. And how have I shaped it? This is about as much as I can say about it. You know, if the truth were known I have a perfect passion for the island where I was born . . . Well, in the early morning there I always remember feeling that this little island has dipped back into the dark blue sea during the night only to rise again at beam of day, all hung with bright spangles and glittering drops—(When you ran over the dewy grass you positively felt that your feet tasted salt.) I tried to catch that moment—with something of its sparkle and its flowers. And just as on those mornings white milky mists rise and uncover some beauty, then smother it again and then again disclose it, I tried to lift that mist from my people and let them be seen and then to hide them again.[116]

[113] KMJ 93, 22 Jan. 1916.   [114] Ibid. 94.
[115] The phrase, taken from Ian Gordon, is explained in subsequent chapters.
[116] KMCL i. 331, 11 Oct. 1917.

The essence of this passage is exploration and revelation of the flexibility of prose, of the nature of childhood memories where feet taste the saltiness of the grass, of the otherness of the island sea and landscape, and of family connectedness as a subject for fiction. The adolescent girl who wrote in her journal: 'Damn my family! O Heavens, what bores they are! I detest them all heartily'[117] has become the woman who finds her subject and her own fictional form in trying to 'lift that mist from my people' but also in hiding them again, so that they remain ephemeral and elusive, fragmented, ghostly.

There is a direct parallel with Mansfield's obsession with her childhood place in Woolf's experience; as a mature woman she comments on it: 'The strength of these pictures—but sight was always then so much mixed with sound that picture is not the right word—the strength anyhow of these impressions makes me again digress. Those moments—in the nursery, on the road to the beach—can still be more real than the present moment.'[118] She is referring to St Ives; Talland House was her equivalent of the seaside cottage at Muritai that Harold Beauchamp rented as a summer home for his family, and she felt that when 'they took Talland House, my father and mother gave me, at any rate, something I think invaluable.'[119] She records her memories of the house in a manner reminiscent of Mansfield's memory of the squeak of the laundry-basket: 'You entered Talland House by a large wooden gate, the sound of whose latch clicking comes back: you went up the carriage drive, with its steep wall scattered with mesembryanthemums; and then came to the Lookout place on the right.'[120] Reading this, it is easy to interpret Virginia Woolf's response to 'Prelude', which surprised Mansfield: 'I threw my darling ['Prelude'] to the wolves and they ate it and served me up so much praise in such a golden bowl that I couldn't help feeling gratified.'[121] The sharply detailed account of the drive and the flowers Kezia notices must have been recognizable to Woolf; in her memories of the sea in St Ives her observations compare with Mansfield's memories of the beach in New Zealand, and focus on the pleasure of being suspended between waking and sleeping, between sea and land:

---

[117] KMJ 21, 21 Oct. 1907.   [118] Woolf, *Moments of Being*, 77.
[119] Ibid. 128.   [120] Ibid. 130.   [121] KMCL i. 330–1, 11 Oct. 1917.

The quality of the air above Talland House seemed to suspend sound, to let it sink down slowly, as if it were caught in a blue gummy veil. The rooks cawing is part of the waves breaking—one, two, one, two— and the splash as the wave drew back and then it gathered again, and I lay there half awake, half asleep, drawing in such ecstasy as I cannot describe.[122]

Inextricably linked with this are impressions of her mother; she herself says that she exorcized the memory of her mother to some extent by writing *To the Lighthouse*: 'Until I was in the forties—I could settle the date by seeing when I wrote *To the Lighthouse*, but am too casual here to bother to do it—the presence of my mother obsessed me.'[123] Her diaries attest to the truth of this remark; on the anniversary of her mother's death, she relives the experience and records it, and references to her are as frequent as Mansfield's references to her beloved grandmother Dyer, and to her mother: 'Cant I hear her "child you mustnt be left here ONE INSTANT" and then shed make miracles happen'.[124] Woolf shows in her diary her own awareness that she is confronting an obsession in *To the Lighthouse*: 'This is going to be fairly short: to have father's character done complete in it; & mothers; & St Ives; & childhood; & all the usual things I try to put in—life, death & c.'[125]

The link between the past, the fictional embodiment of it, and personal discovery is as clear here as it is in Mansfield's personal writing; Woolf comments on the way in which she laid her mother's ghost for herself in *To the Lighthouse*, saying, 'I suppose that I did for myself what psycho-analysts do for their patients. I expressed some very long felt and deeply felt emotion.'[126] The repression she half acknowledges hints at matrophobia, at the fear of being so trapped within the mother that she becomes her, particularly because the mother was absent during her adolescence and so only an imaginary self-definition could take place. Underlying her reflections on her fiction is the metaphor of discovery, of exploration, of pushing back boundaries and frontiers in the darkness, as there is in Mansfield's journal; Woolf writes in 1920:

---

[122] Woolf, *Moments of Being*, 76–7.
[123] Ibid. 93.
[124] KMCL iii. 135, 4 Dec. 1919.
[125] VWD iii. 18, 14 May 1925.
[126] Woolf, *Moments of Being*, 94.

What the unity shall be I have yet to discover: the theme is a blank to me; but I see immense possibilities in the form I hit upon more or less by chance 2 weeks ago . . . I must still grope & experiment but this afternoon I had a gleam of light. Indeed, I think from the ease with which I'm developing the unwritten novel there must be a path for me there.[127]

This is integrally related to her sense, like Mansfield's, that life has secrets to reveal, and that she is constantly on the edge of discovering them, through living and through writing, though the reiterated revelation is of multiple rather than unified selves, as she indicates three years after Mansfield's death, in 1926:

Yet I have some restless searcher in me. Why is there not a discovery in life? Something one can lay hands on & say 'This is it'? My depression is a harassed feeling—I'm looking; but that's not it—thats not it. What is it? And shall I die before I find it? . . . Who am I, what am I, & so on: these questions are always floating about in me.[128]

The reader can see how much this questioning of the past, of place and of fiction attuned Woolf to the priorities of her friend who writes a few days before her death with the same terrier-like worrying of the problem of the secret self as ever: 'You see, the question is always: *Who am I?* and until that is discovered I don't see how one can really direct anything in one's self. *Is there a Me?*'[129] The secret selves, the foreigners within, the border country that they both inhabit, including that between the mother and the self, drive them back into the past in search of the wholeness and unity with the mother, and they encode in fiction the fear both of the severance from the mother and of being engulfed by her.

This chapter and the preceding one have focused on the biographical links between Mansfield and Woolf which moulded their fiction. Both write of being haunted, partly by each other: after Mansfield's death Woolf refers to her as 'that strange ghost'[130] and in her first letter to Woolf Mansfield tells her that she has been 'a bit "haunted" ' by her.[131] The dominant phantoms for both of them, I have suggested, are the Angel in the House, a maternal figure of great apparent sweetness and self-sacrifice which

[127] VWD ii. 14, 26 Jan. 1920.
[129] KML ii. 266, 26 Dec. 1922.
[131] KMCL i. 313, 24? June 1917.

[128] Ibid. iii. 62, 27 Feb. 1926.
[130] VWD ii. 317, 17 Oct. 1924.

mediates the Father's Law for her daughters, and the vampire, the undead creature that preys on the energies of the living, corrupting and destroying them, which is how at their worst they saw themselves, though Woolf does not use the vampire image of herself. The Angel, as Woolf's and Mansfield's intimate private writing suggests, fluttered round both of them with the persistence of an irrational obsession; Mansfield wrote to Woolf in 1919, as to one who would understand her dilemma: 'I could get on without a baby—but Murry? I should like to give him one'.[132] The Angel would approve of the concept that a baby is a present which a wife gives her husband; a woman who can express herself like this is in danger of admitting the Angel as guardian. The Angel and the vampire collude, engendering guilt and envy in women who try to define themselves primarily as writers; both Mansfield and Woolf partly wanted what Vanessa Bell appeared to have, a central role as matriarch, though Bell's daughter's autobiography reveals that her house, full of life, painting, hospitality, conversation, and children, was not quite as paradisal as it seemed.[133] The definition of the self as vampire interacts with the preoccupation with the Angel; Woolf's final letter to her husband, moving though it is, shows that in refusing to sustain the role of what she saw as predator, vampire, she like Mansfield had never succeeded in exorcizing the Angel. The letter assumes that Leonard's work must have priority over everything else, and that the public perception of their marriage must be that he has been preyed upon by a life-sapping woman: 'I know that I am spoiling your life, that without me you could work. And you will I know . . . You have been entirely patient with me and incredibly good. I want to say that—everybody knows it. If anybody could have saved me it would have been you . . . I cant go on spoiling your life any longer.'[134] The language used, for instance 'patient with me', defines Woolf herself as a trying child, peripheral to her husband's central concerns, casting him in the role of God the Father, with the capacity to save, and implicitly asking forgiveness for what she is about to do which breaks the Father's Law, his canon 'gainst self-slaughter, as Hamlet calls it.

---

[132] Ibid. ii. 311, 10 Apr. 1919.
[133] Angelica Garnett, *Deceived with Kindness: A Bloomsbury Childhood* (London: Chatto & Windus, 1984), clarifies this. [134] VWL vi. 481, 18? Mar. 1941.

Woolf and Mansfield characteristically took their final fare-wells of their husbands in writing, Mansfield because she was choked by a haemorrhage as she died and Woolf because she had to conceal her intention to commit suicide. As in so much else, there is a remarkable and surprising similarity in their final preoccupations, acknowledging and affirming as both do, not a sense of disintegration but of the joy that love has brought them. The last line of Woolf's letter reads: 'I dont think two people could have been happier than we have been,'[135] while Mansfield, nearly twenty years earlier, writes to Murry: 'In spite of everything—how happy we have been. I feel no other lovers have walked the earth together more joyfully—in spite of all.'[136] The sense of echo which is so evident to readers of the two writers' personal writings, the uncanny doubling within differ-ence, can be traced in two works in which the form is controlled by memory, 'Prelude' and *To the Lighthouse*.

[135] VWL vi. 481, 18? Mar. 1941.   [136] KMMML 363, 7 Aug. 1922.

4

Shifts in 'Prelude' and
To the Lighthouse

I couldn't tell anybody *bang out* about those deserts. They
are my secret. I might write about a boy eating strawberries
or a woman combing her hair on a windy morning & that
is the only way I can ever mention them. But they *must*
be there.[1]

IN an essay written in 1933, the Italian critic Salvatore Rosati
celebrates what he calls Woolf's 'psychological impressionism'
in *To the Lighthouse*: 'In the last section, in particular, the inter-
penetration of the present with past memories creates, in a dream-
like atmosphere, a continuity of psychological texture and an
evocative power which shows a close relationship between the
art of Virginia Woolf and that of Katherine Mansfield'.[2] The
encoding of psychological rather than chronological or linear
time, offering the reader a prose that is textured differently,
is comparable with what Kristeva defines as revolutionary in
modernist French poetry, which 'with its abrupt shifts, ellipses,
breaks and apparent lack of logical construction is a kind of
writing in which the rhythms of the body and the unconscious
have managed to break through the strict rational defences of
conventional social meaning.'[3] Toril Moi links Kristeva's theory
with Woolf's practice: she says that for Kristeva 'there is a *specific
practice of writing* that is itself "revolutionary", analogous to
sexual and political transformation, and that by its very existence testifies to the possibility of transforming the symbolic order
of orthodox society from the inside.'[4] This chapter focuses on

[1] KMCL iii. 97–8, 16 Nov. 1919.
[2] Robin Majumdar and Allen McLaurin (eds.), *Virginia Woolf: The Critical
Heritage* (London: Routledge & Kegan Paul, 1975), 317.
[3] Su Reid (ed.), *New Casebooks: Mrs Dalloway and To the Lighthouse* (London: Macmillan, 1993), 89.   [4] Ibid.

two works by Mansfield and Woolf, which have been linked by other critics, both of which use shifts and ellipses to transform the symbolic order from the inside, using the characters' thresholds and experience of being between borders to do it.

Lyndall Gordon hints at the disruption of narrative expectations in the writers' representation of psychological time in the two works when she writes:

Virginia admired the most memory-ridden of Katherine Mansfield's stories, *Prelude*, a frieze of scenes from her New Zealand childhood, written after her beloved brother, Chummie (Leslie Heron Beauchamp), was killed in 1915. There was the same elegiac motive when Katherine Mansfield said of her brother: 'I hear his voice in the trees and flowers, in scents and light and shadow. Have people, apart from these far-away people, ever existed for me?' She wanted to seal their shared past 'because in my thoughts I range with him over all the remembered places'. Virginia Woolf's elegiac novel of childhood, *To the Lighthouse*, may have been inspired, in part, by *Prelude*. Mrs Ramsay, like *Prelude*'s mother, Linda Burnell, soothes family crises, charms and placates her husband, yet is inwardly remote, craving solitude.[5]

Similarly, Clare Hanson suggests that 'Prelude' 'might have offered one of the models for *To the Lighthouse*, with its domestic setting, use of the house as a psychic structure, and the presence of an ambivalent (phallic?) title image ("Prelude" was originally called "The Aloe").'[6] The writers' mothers and families dominate the works; Mansfield recognizes in her journal about New Zealand as she is writing 'Prelude'[7] that she must pay her debts of love. Woolf writes in response to a letter from Vanessa Bell about *To the Lighthouse*:

I'm in a terrible state of pleasure that you should think Mrs Ramsay so like mother. At the same time, it is a psychological mystery why she should be: how a child could know about her; except that she has always haunted me, partly, I suppose, her beauty; and then dying at that moment, I suppose she cut a great figure on one's mind when it was just awake, and had not any experience of life.[8]

---

[5] Lyndall Gordon, *Virginia Woolf: A Writer's Life* (Oxford: Oxford University Press, 1986), 185–6.

[6] Clare Hanson, *Virginia Woolf* (London: Macmillan, 1994), 147.

[7] 'Prelude' was first published by the Hogarth Press as a self-contained volume and so is sometimes presented as *Prelude*; I consider it as one of Mansfield's *Collected Stories* and present it accordingly.   [8] VWL iii. 383, 25 May 1927.

Vanessa Bell had written that it was 'almost painful to have her so raised from the dead' as 'It was like meeting her again with oneself grown up and on equal terms'.[9] Thresholds pervade these comments: that between the remembered dead and the living, an uncanny crossing from death back to life, lost places that live in the memory, and women's rites of passage. It is not surprising that the woman who was to write *To the Lighthouse* should have chosen 'Prelude' as one of the first publications for her press, nor that, when Woolf could not attend one of her parties, Mansfield should have regretted it because 'I wanted the small private satisfaction of looking at the party *with* you.'[10] Their ways of seeing, as they are expressed in their prose, are remarkably similar, as 'Prelude' and *To the Lighthouse* testify.

In a poem that was written in 1910 and published in *Rhythm* Mansfield encodes a mother's control over her daughter in a liminal territory, between sea and land. The poem could be read autobiographically, as Mansfield had incurred her mother's wrath by marrying impetuously not long before the poem was written. Her mother arrived in England, took her daughter to a German spa where she had a miscarriage, then Mrs Beauchamp sailed for New Zealand and cut Mansfield out of her will. Mansfield returned to England, had an operation, and was recuperating when she wrote the poem. She may have felt in a limbo between London, the town, and New Zealand, the place of the 'sifting sand', but the poem is more significant for its suggestion of the ambivalence of the mother/daughter relationship; the poem is permeated by those anxieties that Kristeva defines as experience of abjection, when the female child is rendered uncertain about the boundaries between the self and the mother. The mother 'fashions', creates the child, then drives her away from home, and rejects her a second time when the broken girl returns:

The Sea Child

Into the world you sent her, mother,
Fashioned her body of coral and foam,
Combed a wave in her hair's warm smother,
And drove her away from home.

---

[9] Ibid. 572, 11 May 1927.   [10] KMCL ii. 320, 27 May 1919.

> In the dark of the night she crept to the town
>   And under a doorway she laid her down,
> The little blue child in the foam-fringed gown . . .
>
> She sold her corals; she sold her foam;
>   Her rainbow heart like a singing shell
> Broke in her body: she crept back home.
>
> Peace, go back to the world, my daughter,
>   Daughter, go back to the darkling land;
> There is nothing here but sad sea water,
>   And a handful of sifting sand.[11]

The mother's power to create a daughter in her own image and then to leave her in limbo is unambiguously expressed, and is echoed in both Linda Burnell, Kezia's mother in 'Prelude', and in Mrs Ramsay's attitude to her daughters in *To the Lighthouse*. The two works pivot on a series of thresholds and rites of passage. The small children, Kezia, Cam,[12] and James, are testing their own apprehension of the world against adult versions of it; the older girls, Beryl and Prue, are aware of their own sexuality but unsure what to do with it; the adult women, Linda and Mrs Fairfield, and Lily Briscoe and Mrs Ramsay, are caught either in the embrace of, or in a struggle with the Angel in the House. Apart from Mrs Ramsay's errand of mercy to the town, all four adult women are seen exclusively in the house or garden; they do not, like the children, stray to the paddocks or take a boat to the lighthouse.

The texts' preoccupation with liminality, being on the edge, is reflected in the idiosyncrasy of the form of the two works. As Mansfield began to write 'Prelude' she wrote in her notebook: 'Only the form that I would choose has changed utterly. . . . Now—now I want to write recollections of my own country.'[13] Using threshold language, Woolf writes, at the time she is finishing *To the Lighthouse*, in a similar way about her experience of trying to write about life as she perceives it:

---

[11] Vincent O'Sullivan (ed.), *The Poems of Katherine Mansfield* (Oxford: Oxford University Press, 1988), 32.

[12] Jane Marcus (ed.), *Virginia Woolf and Bloomsbury: A Centenary Celebration* (London: Macmillan, 1987), 170–88, contains an essay on Cam's role in the novel.

[13] KMJ 93, 22 Jan. 1916.

[I]t is not oneself but something in the universe that one's left with. It is this that is frightening & exciting in the midst of my profound gloom, depression, boredom, whatever it is: One sees a fin passing far out . . . Life is, soberly & accurately, the oddest affair; has in it the essence of reality. I used to feel this as a child—couldn't step across a puddle once I remember, for thinking, how strange—what am I?[14] . . . The method of writing smooth narrative cant be right: things dont happen in one's mind like that.[15]

The significance of this lies in the impetus to capture the disintegrating sense of self in writing, to record what it feels like, in comparison with Vita Sackville-West's prose which Woolf finds too fluent; as Kristeva has it, the self that 'shows itself to be a strange land of borders and othernesses ceaselessly constructed and deconstructed'.[16]

To the Lighthouse is full of echoes of 'Prelude', some at a surface level. Kezia recovers from the trauma of the duck's death by discovering that Pat, the handyman, 'wore little round gold ear-rings. She never knew that men wore ear-rings. She was very much surprised.'[17] Cam, sitting in the boat with her father on the way to the lighthouse thinks that 'now this was real; the boat and the sail with its patch; Macalister with his earrings'.[18] Pat and Macalister have a similar function: Pat kills the duck and encourages the children to watch its headless corpse running about, while Macalister's boy cuts a square out of the side of a fish for bait, then the 'mutilated body (it was still alive) was thrown back into the sea' (p. 243). There is an obvious suggestion about how gender roles are transmitted to children; in both instances a sensitive boy is present and the death of the duck disturbs Rags as much as Kezia, but it is Cam and Kezia who notice contradictions in what seems a definitively gendered identity.

Susan Gubar suggests that Lily Briscoe's final line in her painting is a flowering family tree of life, resembling Mansfield's aloe.

---

[14] VWD iii. 113, 30 Sept. 1926.   [15] Ibid. 126–7, 12 Feb. 1927.
[16] Julia Kristeva, *Strangers to Ourselves* (London: Harvester Wheatsheaf, 1991), 191.
[17] Katherine Mansfield, *Collected Short Stories* (Harmondsworth: Penguin, 1981), 47. All future references to the text are to this edn.; page refs. will hereafter be given in the text.
[18] Virginia Woolf, *To the Lighthouse* (Oxford: Oxford University Press, 1992), 225. All future refs. are to this edn.; page refs. will hereafter be given in the text.

She continues: 'The flower that names the painter, the lily so dear to Mansfield, implies that Lily's Chinese eyes, as well as her sardonic self-protectiveness, constitute if not a fictional portrait of Mansfield then a tribute on Woolf's part to Mansfield's achievement.'[19] Certainly the description of Lily is reminiscent of Woolf's pen portrait of Mansfield, 'She had her look of a Japanese doll.'[20] Gubar's comparison between the aloe and Lily's tree is a provocative one, but I want to focus on the link between the aloe and the lighthouse in the structure of the two works.[21] When he first read *To the Lighthouse*, Roger Fry wrote to Woolf saying how much he liked it but that 'there's lots I haven't understood . . . for instance, that arriving at the Lighthouse has a symbolic meaning which escapes me'.[22] In her rather tart reply, Woolf rejects a response which, she implies, smacks of the male intellectualism that she and Mansfield resisted. The intensity of her language suggests that she wants to identify with the common reader rather than the super-subtle critic:

I meant *nothing* by The Lighthouse. One has to have a central line down the middle of the book to hold the design together. I saw that all sorts of feelings would accrue to this, but I refused to think them out, and trusted that people would make it the deposit for their own emotions—which they have done, one thinking it means one thing another another. I can't manage Symbolism except in this vague, generalised way. Whether its right or wrong I don't know, but directly I'm told what a thing means, it becomes hateful to me.[23]

'Hateful to me' is a phrase that Mansfield might have used, and the whole description of the function of symbolism in the novel

---

[19] Carolyn G. Heilbrun and Margaret R. Higonnet (eds.), *The Representation of Women in Fiction* (Baltimore: Johns Hopkins University Press, 1983), 48.

[20] VWD ii. 226, 16 Jan. 1923.

[21] There are several illuminating analyses of the significance of the lighthouse in *To the Lighthouse*, e.g. Makiko Minow-Pinkney, *Virginia Woolf and the Problem of the Subject* (Brighton: Harvester, 1987), 84–116; Mary Jacobus, ' "The Third Stroke": Reading Woolf with Freud', in Rachel Bowlby (ed.), *Virginia Woolf* (Harlow: Longman, 1992), 102–20; Hanson, *Virginia Woolf*, 72–93; Rachel Bowlby, *Feminist Destinations and Further Essays on Virginia Woolf* (Edinburgh: Edinburgh University Press, 1997), 54–68; Sue Roe, *Writing and Gender* (Hemel Hempstead: Harvester Wheatsheaf, 1990), 63–80; Gillian Beer, *Virginia Woolf: The Common Ground* (Edinburgh: Edinburgh University Press, 1996), 41, says that *To the Lighthouse* is a post-symbolist novel. [22] VWL iii. 385, 27 May 1927.

[23] Ibid. 27 May 1927.

could apply equally to 'Prelude'. The central line in each work is a trope around which associations cluster, but those accrued meanings are different for each character in the work, and for each reader. The aloe and the lighthouse bear a physical resemblance to each other, one which, from the pens of writers familiar with the work of D. H. Lawrence, might seem inevitably to suggest a phallic significance. But Mansfield specifically resisted what she regarded as Lawrence's obsession with the phallus, writing to her friend Beatrice Campbell when she was living in Cornwall as Lawrence's neighbour: 'I shall *never* see sex in trees, sex in the running brooks, sex in stones & sex in everything. The number of things that are really phallic from fountain pen fillers onwards!'[24]

It is almost as if Mansfield had this in mind when she wrote 'Prelude'. Kezia is the first person to see the aloe, as the culmination of her characteristically solitary exploration of the garden; she sees it and its plants in terms of the human body: 'pink smooth beauties opening curl on curl', 'a bed of pelargoniums with velvet eyes', 'dividing the drive into two arms that met in front of the house' (pp. 33–4). But she is a child of about 5 so the aloe has not the significance for her that it has for her mother. She is engaged in sibling battles, and particularly in resisting the domination of her older sister Isabel who wants Kezia to conform to her gender role, and to her junior place in the family: ' "Well, let's play ladies," said Isabel. "Pip can be the father and you can be all our dear little children." "I hate playing ladies," said Kezia. "You always make us go to church hand in hand and come home and go to bed" ' (p. 43). Though she notices the aloe's stem, she is preoccupied by its age; her anxiety about her grandmother's age is articulated clearly in 'At the Bay'. What she sees when she looks at the aloe is 'one huge plant with thick, grey-green thorny leaves, and out of the middle there sprang up a tall stout stem. Some of the leaves of the plant were so old that they curled up in the air no longer; they turned back, they were split and broken; some of them lay flat and withered on the ground' (p. 34). She focuses on the decaying parts of the aloe, whereas Linda, who joins her and can name the plant, sees in it what she fears. The text implies that she is pregnant with her

[24] KMCL i. 261, 4 May 1916.

fourth child, and terrified of her husband's sexuality as it results in ' "great lumps of children" ' (p. 54). When she looks at the aloe she sees:

the fat swelling plant with its cruel leaves and fleshy stem. High above them, as though becalmed in the air, and yet holding so fast to the earth it grew from, it might have had claws instead of roots. The curving leaves seemed to be hiding something; the blind stem cut into the air as if no wind could ever shake it. (p. 34)

When Linda is most frightened she imagines that small things are swelling and coming alive, like the 'sticky, silky petals, the stem, hairy like a gooseberry skin' (p. 27) of poppies on her bedroom wallpaper; both the phallus and the growing foetus are suggested, implying that Linda is on the verge of panic and abjection. Boundaries are being overstepped and are failing; she is being engulfed. The aloe seems to confront her with a phallocentric world, invincible, the power of the phallus cruel, animal, and indomitable; her private image for her husband, Stanley, is ' "my Newfoundland dog . . . that I'm so fond of in the daytime" ' (p. 53). Yet at the end of the section in which the reader, Kezia, and Linda meet and identify the aloe, Kezia asks if the aloe ever flowers and her mother replies: ' "Once every hundred years" ' (p. 34). This shifts the reader's perception of the aloe, as throughout the story flowers are identified with women: Mrs Fairfield wears a dress patterned with purple pansies, Linda picks and rubs a piece of verbena, Beryl wears a bunch of pansies in her dress or syringa in her hair, Kezia makes flower surprises in a matchbox for her grandmother. No such associations exist with the male characters. It is as if Linda envies the aloe, suddenly gendered as female, its infertility; it only gives birth every hundred years, whereas she will ' "go on having children and Stanley will go on making money and the children and the gardens will grow bigger and bigger" ' (p. 54). The grammatical imprecision suggests that Stanley will make the children but she will have to give birth to them, implying both resignation and abjected resentment.

It is evidently impossible to say, in Woolf's terms, what the aloe means, or that it means any one thing; it has different suggestions for different characters at different times of day. When Linda speaks directly to her daughter her response is different from her first impression of the aloe. When she looks at it again she is with her mother, not with the small girl who so resolutely resists taking dolls for a walk in a pram or playing mothers and fathers. Linda's mother is content with her domestic role, and is pictured in the kitchen as part of it: Linda 'thought her mother looked wonderfully beautiful with her back to the leafy window' (p. 31). When they go into the garden together at night they have entered a liminal space and they see differently; they are bathed with the moonlight in which Linda has felt earlier 'that she was being strangely discovered' (pp. 38–9). They use 'the special voice that women use at night to each other as though they spoke in their sleep or from some hollow cave' (p. 53) like the ancient seaweed gatherers in Mansfield's cave of the selves. The implication is that this gendered space elicits different responses from that in the male-dominated daytime world, and what Mrs Fairfield sees in this light, accompanied by her pregnant daughter, is that the aloe is about to flower, anticipating the change in Linda in 'At the Bay' when she feels a spasm of love for her baby boy. Linda does not disagree with her mother; she too sees the buds on the aloe, but now sees the aloe as a ship with oars lifted. Her attraction to the hollow cave, or the crossing-place from one world to another, is suggested by the way in which she now visualizes the plant:

[T]he high grassy bank on which the aloe rested rose up like a wave, and the aloe seemed to ride upon it like a ship with the oars lifted. Bright moonlight hung upon the lifted oars like water, and on the green wave glittered the dew . . . She dreamed that she was caught up out of the cold water into the ship with the lifted oars and the budding mast. Now the oars fell striking quickly, quickly. They rowed far away over the top of the garden trees, the paddocks and the dark bush beyond. Ah, she heard herself cry: 'Faster! Faster!' to those who were rowing.

How much more real this dream was than that they should go back to the house where the sleeping children lay and where Stanley and Beryl played cribbage. (pp. 52–3)

What Linda imagines for herself is a traditionally male role, taking command of a ship and escaping into exploration of an unknown world, the dark bush; the dream is an alternative to the journey she has reluctantly embarked on towards childbirth. In 'At the Bay' she thinks that 'it was as though a cold breath had chilled her through and through on each of those awful journeys; she had no warmth left to give' her children (p. 223). Holding her mother's arm she approaches the aloe, saying that she likes it better than anything else in the garden. Looking at the long sharp thorns on the leaves she reaches a moment of epiphany when she recognizes her hatred of her husband at night, when he makes love to her and then is humble and submissive. As she realizes this she snatches her hand from her mother's arm and hugs her folded arms, thinking:

It had never been so plain to her as it was at this moment. There were all her feelings for him, sharp and defined, one as true as the other. And there was this other, this hatred, just as real as the rest. She could have done her feelings up in little packets and given them to Stanley. She longed to hand him that last one, for a surprise. She could see his eyes as he opened that . . .   (p. 54)

The reader is reminded of Kezia's little packets for her grandma and the pleasure that the child, who resists her gender role but is not yet sexually active, wants to give the old woman. Linda, however, snatches her hand from her mother's arm and hugs herself because it was this old woman, loving and domestic as she is, who prepared what Linda experiences as the trap of marriage for her. As Moran observes,[25] when Linda enters the kitchen of the new house she says that it expresses her mother because everything is in pairs, hinting at Mrs Fairfield's ideological commitment to marriage and motherhood. This is confirmed when Linda asks her mother what she has been thinking while Linda confronted her feelings about Stanley, and Mrs Fairfield replies that she has been wondering whether the fruit trees and currant bushes will supply fruit for jam.

The aloe does not recur but it does not need to; it acts as a central line to hold the design together. The prelude of the title can be interpreted as Kezia's first encounter with intimations of sexual love and of death, in the form of the duck; the younger adults in the story, Beryl, Stanley, and Linda, are also engaged in wrestling with their gender identities, while Mrs Fairfield accepts these as 'natural'. Kezia approaches a threshold and Linda crosses it by appropriating the aloe, which at first represented masculine dominance, and making it her ship; she casts herself

---

[25] Patricia Moran, *Word of Mouth* (London: University Press of Virginia, 1996), 107.

as a kind of Flying Dutchman who is seeking to avoid rather than find a mate.

The use of the lighthouse trope in *To the Lighthouse* also pivots on gender roles, and also resists monolithic significance. It is first imaged in Mrs Ramsay's mind as a place of heroic masculine endeavour, and she sympathizes with her 6-year-old son's desperate wish to go there. There is no question of her going, but she is playing the Angel's role and knitting socks for the lighthouse-keeper's little boy. As she thinks about it, the reader becomes aware of Mrs Ramsay's desire to fashion her daughters' consciousness, inviting them to imagine the lighthouse-keeper's life, but also, more obliquely, the imperatives of male sexuality:

For how would you like to be shut up for a whole month at a time, and possibly more in stormy weather, upon a rock ... to see the same dreary waves breaking week after week, and then a dreadful storm coming, and the windows covered with spray, and birds dashed against the lamp, and the whole place rocking ... How would you like that? she asked, addressing herself particularly to her daughters.
(pp. 9–10)

This initiates the parental definition of male heroism which is sustained throughout the novel. For Mr and Mrs Ramsay heroes are solitary men at war with their environment, either physical or intellectual, though Mr Ramsay's part in the heroic endeavour is undermined by comedy from the moment when Mrs Ramsay sees her distinguished philosopher as 'the great sea lion at the Zoo tumbling backwards after swallowing his fish and walloping off' (p. 46). He wallops off, reassured by domesticity, to the garden where he tries to push his splendid mind a little further; the imagery evokes traditional gendering, and links him with the lighthouse-keeper:

Feelings that would not have disgraced a leader who, now that the snow has begun to fall and the mountain-top is covered in mist, knows that he must lay himself down and die before morning comes, stole upon him, paling the colour of his eyes, giving him, even in the two minutes of his turn on the terrace, the bleached look of withered old age. Yet he would not die lying down; he would find some crag of rock, and there, his eyes fixed on the storm, trying to the end to pierce the darkness, he would die standing. (p. 49)

Pointing the way like the lighthouse in a passage that reflects his phallocentricity the patriarch resolves to endure, standing to the last, with a comic nod in the direction of his fathering of eight children; the poems he quotes as he rampages round the garden are overtly also about male heroism and female submission, like the fragments of Tennyson's 'The Charge of the Light Brigade' and Cowper's 'The Castaway'. His heroes are doomed but resolute. The insistent comedy suggests that his identification with the lighthouse is part of his self-pity, and self-deception, and that men need to see themselves mirrored in admiring female eyes to achieve lighthouse status. The savagely reductive comment in *A Room of One's Own* seems to underlie the depiction of Mr Ramsay: 'Women have served all these centuries as looking-glasses possessing the magic and delicious power of reflecting the figure of man at twice its natural size.'[26] Mrs Ramsay supplies that reflection, with a sense that there is something demeaning to both of them about it, but after Mrs Ramsay's death Lily Briscoe refuses to do so. The language that she uses of herself suggests that she is measuring herself by Mrs Ramsay's yardstick, privileging sexual potency and fertility over her own kind of creativity although she is, in her picture, forming a version rather than a reflection of the Ramsays' life:

The Lighthouse! What's that got to do with it? he thought impatiently. Instantly, with the force of some primeval gust (for he really could not restrain himself any longer), there issued from him such a groan that any other woman in the whole world would have done something, said something—all except myself, thought Lily, girding at herself bitterly, who am not a woman, but a peevish, ill-tempered, dried-up old maid presumably. (p. 205)

The final image of Mr Ramsay surprisingly restores to him his identity as solitary hero, with another contradictory sequence of associations. As the party finally reach the lighthouse, ten years after the initial hopes of going, Mr Ramsay is identified in his son's mind with the lighthouse:

He rose and stood in the bow of the boat, very straight and tall, for all the world, James thought, as if he were saying, 'There is no God,' and Cam thought, as if he were leaping into space, and they both rose

---

[26] Virginia Woolf, *A Room of One's Own* (London: Hogarth, 1929), 53.

to follow him as he sprang, lightly like a young man, holding his parcel, on to the rock. (pp. 279–80)

Lily senses that he has arrived: ' "He has landed," she said aloud. "It is finished" ' (p. 280). As his tall pointing figure suggests his bold assertion of atheism to his son, Lily seems to associate his journey with Christ's crucifixion and his final words on the cross, identifying Mr Ramsay with the archetypal solitary hero. Nothing is simply one thing, as James thinks on the journey to the lighthouse:

James looked at the Lighthouse. He could see the white-washed rocks; the tower, stark and straight; he could see that it was barred with black and white; he could see windows in it; he could even see washing spread on the rocks to dry. So that was the Lighthouse, was it?

No, the other was also the Lighthouse. For nothing was simply one thing. The other was the Lighthouse too. It was sometimes hardly to be seen across the bay. (p. 251)

The other, also the lighthouse, which is sometimes imaged as the male body, is also imaged as the female body and is linked with Mrs Ramsay's fecundity. She is perceived as a column by her son, James; as he stands between her knees James visualizes her potency in ways reminiscent of the bursting buds in 'Prelude'. Even her knitting-needles flash, like weapons or the light from the lighthouse, 'and James, as he stood stiff between her knees, felt her rise in a rosy-flowered fruit tree laid with leaves and dancing boughs' (p. 53). His father is 'an arid scimitar' but his mother is a living column, seeming to combine male and female sexual characteristics, while his father is seen as destructive and violent. James hates his father with an Oedipal intensity at this moment, 'if there had been an axe handy, a knife, or anything with a sharp point he would have seized it and struck his father through the heart' (p. 252), and his preoccupation with the lighthouse perhaps underlies this ambivalent passage, with the phallic associations of 'erect' and 'column of spray':

Mrs Ramsay . . . seemed to raise herself with an effort, and at once to pour erect into the air a rain of energy, a column of spray, looking at the same time animated and alive as if all her energies were being fused into force, burning and illuminating . . . and into this delicious fecundity, this fountain and spray of life, the fatal sterility of the male plunged itself, like a beak of brass, barren and bare. (p. 52)

James's view of her is confirmed later in the first part, interlaced with images of the lighthouse as the embodiment of solitary male suffering, when she is alone knitting and waiting for the third stroke of the light 'for she was stern, she was searching, she was beautiful like that light' (p. 87). She seems again to combine within herself male and female sexual characteristics as the stroke of the light, with its sensual connotations, is both herself and outside her:

[B]ut for all that she thought, watching it with fascination, hypnotized, as if it were stroking with its silver fingers some sealed vessel in her brain whose bursting would flood her with delight, she had known happiness, exquisite happiness, intense happiness, and it silvered the rough waves a little more brightly, as daylight faded, and the blue went out of the sea and it rolled in waves of pure lemon which curved and swelled and broke upon the beach and the ecstasy burst in her eyes and waves of pure delight raced over the floor of her mind and she felt, It is enough! It is enough!   (pp. 88–9)

This extended and orgasmic experience empowers Mrs Ramsay, ironically enough, to continue as the Angel in the House; regenerated, she moves out into the garden and organizes the evening's events, which culminate in the celebratory *bœuf en daube* dinner.

As with the aloe, the reader's attention is drawn to conflicting ways of seeing the lighthouse. Mrs Ramsay reads Grimm's 'The Fisherman and his Wife' to James in the first part of the novel, and it provides an oblique commentary on her own position. Ilsabil, in the story, is overtly domineering, sending her pusillanimous husband to the all-powerful flounder with demands that reflect her accelerating monomania. She becomes pope, but when she asks to become God the flounder makes the dark sea boil with fury and sends her husband home to find that it has reverted to being the original chamber-pot. That Mrs Ramsay should influence her children's imaginative life by telling them such stories is not surprising; the husband is punished for not standing up to his wife, and the wife gets her reward for wanting to assume masculine authority. Mrs Ramsay, however, has almost as much power as the omnipotent flounder through her manipulation of her own beauty and persona; the power comes from the Angel's role. She can create the world for her husband

and children: 'He must be assured that he too lived in the heart of life; was needed; not here only, but all over the world. Flashing her needles, confident, upright, she created drawing-room and kitchen, set them all aglow; bade him take his ease there, go in and out, enjoy himself' (pp. 52–3).

Though the lighthouse is associated with both Mr and Mrs Ramsay in shifting and contradictory ways, it also has a significance of its own which links it with 'Prelude'. It marks the passing of time in the central section of the novel, and seems to mock Mrs Ramsay's identification of herself with it as its regular illumination reveals the destruction of what she has made. She created the illusion of safety for Cam by wrapping the boar's skull in her shawl, veiling its aggressive masculinity but assuring James that it was still there. In the central passage her death is mentioned parenthetically, and the death of her daughter, Prue, who had accepted her mother's insistence that she must marry, and died in an illness connected with childbirth. The light still caresses the room, but it reveals Mrs Ramsay's powerlessness:

When darkness fell, the stroke of the Lighthouse, which had laid itself with such authority upon the carpet in the darkness, tracing its pattern, came now in the softer light of spring mixed with moonlight gliding gently as if it laid its caress and lingered stealthily and looked and came lovingly again. But in the very lull of this loving caress, as the long stroke leant upon the bed, the rock was rent asunder; another fold of the shawl loosened; there it hung, and swayed. (pp. 180–1)

This is the liminal moment of transition for the house itself, the crossover point for the fabric and, by implication, for the world that Mrs Ramsay built within it. The lighthouse is impassive observer rather than sexual symbol as the house teeters on the edge of extinction:

Only the Lighthouse beam entered the rooms for a moment, sent its sudden stare over bed and wall in the darkness of winter . . . For now had come that moment, that hesitation when dawn trembles and night pauses, when if a feather alight in the scale it will be weighed down. One feather, and the house, sinking, falling, would have turned and pitched downwards to the depths of darkness. (p. 188)

The liminal image is strong, and the Angel's way of being is threatened; Prue has died as a result of pregnancy and Andrew, the brilliant mathematician, has been killed serving as a soldier in the Great War, releasing the childless poet Carmichael into an unprecedented burst of elegiac creativity. The empty house is on the threshold of its own destruction, and is itself a threshold: if it is restored, will it be the same?

The empty house in 'Prelude' is rightly felt to be liminal territory by Kezia; in it, at the in-between time of twilight, she experiences a moment of terror, Woolf's fin under the water:

As she stood there, the day flickered out and dark came. With the dark, crept the wind snuffling and howling. The windows of the empty house shook, a creaking came from the walls and floors, a piece of loose iron on the roof banged forlornly. Kezia was suddenly quite, quite still, with wide open eyes and knees pressed together. She was frightened. She wanted to call Lottie and to go on calling all the while she ran downstairs and out of the house. But IT was just behind her, waiting at the door, at the head of the stairs, at the bottom of the stairs, hiding in the passage, ready to dart out at the back door.   (p. 15)

Kezia's position on the stairs accentuates the sense that she is on the edge, a feeling that is confirmed later in the story when the snuffling and lurking animal in Kezia's imagination recurs in Linda's horror of her husband's sexuality: 'If only he wouldn't jump at her so, and bark so loudly, and watch her with such eager, loving eyes. He was too strong for her; she had always hated things that rush at her, from a child. There were times when he was frightening—really frightening' (p. 54). Though Kezia's responses are identified with her mother's, Kezia's source of danger is Linda. Just as Mrs Ramsay's control drove Prue to her death and Minta and Paul Rayley into an unhappy marriage, so the text suggests that Linda's exclusion of Kezia places her in limbo, like the sea child in the poem. Kezia is first seen, 'all ready for the fray', being abandoned by her mother, who is taking with her to the new house only her ' "absolute necessities" '. These do not include two of her children. Her body language indicates her self-absorption and rejection of a maternal role when, the next day, the grandmother says she would like her to keep an eye on her children but knows she will not:

'Of course I will, but you know Isabel is much more grown up than any of us.'
'Yes, but Kezia is not,' said Mrs Fairfield.

'Oh, Kezia has been tossed by a bull hours ago,' said Linda, winding herself up in her shawl again.

But no, Kezia had seen a bull through a hole in a knot of wood in the paling that separated the tennis lawn from the paddock. But she had not liked the bull frightfully.   (p. 32)

Earlier, Kezia has told the storeman, ' "I hate rushing animals like dogs and parrots" ' (p. 17). Like her mother, she fears and avoids a rushing masculine beast, but her mother makes no effort to protect her from it, instead wrapping herself rather than a child in a shawl. That Kezia and possibly Lottie know their insecurity is evident from their game, in which a naked baby girl is left behind:

'Oh, good morning, Mrs Smith. I'm so glad to see you. Have you brought your children?'
'Yes, I've brought both my twins. I have had another baby since I saw you last, but she came so suddenly that I haven't had time to make her any clothes yet. So I left her . . . How is your husband?'   (p. 40)

The ellipsis signals a gulf, a terror of the mother's premature ejection of the child. Earlier in the story, the journey from the deserted house to the new one is a rite of passage for Kezia and her sister, like the journey in 'The Voyage' and 'The Little Governess': 'It was the first time that Lottie and Kezia had ever been out so late. Everything looked different' (p. 16). Lottie sleeps through most of the experience, but for Kezia it is a voyage of discovery as she leaves behind the familiar town and goes into territory that for her is unmapped: 'Now everything familiar was left behind. Now the big dray rattled into unknown country, along new roads' (p. 17). The question she puts to the storeman in the darkness is: ' "What is the difference between a ram and a sheep?" ' (p. 17). His rather evasive response, that a ram has horns and runs at you, and her dislike of the prospect, anticipate her mother's sexual terrors, and Kezia strokes the storeman's sleeve, 'it felt hairy' (p. 17), as Linda later strokes the wallpaper and feels the poppy on it 'hairy like a gooseberry skin' (p. 27). Kezia arrives at the new house and, lifted by the storeman, seems 'to come flying through the air'; Lottie arrives on the new threshold but staggers 'on the lowest veranda step like a bird fallen out of the nest' (p. 18). The sinister implication is sustained that these birds have been pushed out of the nest before they can fly, ejected from maternal protection too soon. They are not sure of a welcome; the veranda, a threshold, is an area of anxiety for them as it is for their father. Stanley panics as he drives home and Linda opens the glass door to meet him: 'At the sound of her his heart beat so hard that he could hardly stop himself dashing up the steps and catching her in his arms' (p. 37). If he did, he would be identifiable with the ram or the bull; his anxiety springs from insecurity about how to manage his masculine role, and he is disconcerted when Linda undermines it by hanging cherries on his ear, a small echo of Kezia's surprise that Pat wears an ear-ring.

The journey in *To the Lighthouse*, from the island to the lighthouse, is in a literal and metaphoric sense a crossing and, as Lily thinks about such moments, they have an intensity. This passage is like a description of the return to the familiar world after the liminar's rite of passage, when the familiar is made strange:

It was a way things had sometimes, she thought, lingering for a moment and looking at the long glittering windows and the plume of blue smoke: they became unreal. So coming back from a journey, or after an illness, before habits had spun themselves across the surface, one felt that same unreality, which was so startling; felt something emerge. Life was most vivid then. (pp. 258–9)

For Cam the journey clarifies her childhood fear, like Kezia's, of the boar's skull, which her mother concealed but did not remove. As she sits in the boat with her father, James, and the boatmen, she thinks of her pact against her father with James, but resents James because his Oedipal resistance of his father is easier to sustain than her 'pressure and division of feeling, this extraordinary temptation' (p. 229). The echo of Woolf's own nexus of emotion about her father expressed in her diaries and memoirs is evident here, as is Kristeva's revisioning of the disintegration of the symbolic order's binary opposites:

For no one attracted her more; his hands were beautiful to her and his feet, and his voice, and his words, and his haste, and his temper, and his oddity, and his passion, and his saying straight out before everyone, we perish, each alone, and his remoteness. (He had opened his book.) But what remained intolerable, she thought, sitting upright, and watching Macalister's boy tug the hook out of the gills of another fish, was that crass blindness and tyranny of his which had poisoned her childhood and raised bitter storms, so that even now she woke in the night trembling with rage and remembered some command of his; some insolence: 'Do this,' 'Do that,' his dominance: his 'Submit to me.'

(p. 229)

This is neither the Angel nor the vampire. Cam resists flattering her father and asks nothing of him, but, temporarily perhaps, she disintegrates the tensions that may have been created by her mother's mystification and deception: 'Now I can go on thinking whatever I like, and I shan't fall over a precipice or be drowned, for there he is, keeping his eye on me, she thought' (p. 276).

Lily makes the journey in imagination as Cam travels, and Lily is also making a journey of her own as she experiences the crossover between the real world and her painting. She feels as if she is among waves: '[B]efore she exchanged the fluidity of life for the concentration of painting she had a few moments of nakedness when she seemed like an unborn soul, a soul reft of body, hesitating on some windy pinnacle and exposed without protection to all the blasts of doubt' (pp. 214–15). The doubts are mostly engendered by men like Charles Tansley, who say that women can't write or paint, and women like Mrs Ramsay who think that Lily is not attractive enough to marry and 'one could not take her painting very seriously' (p. 25). Gradually, as she is possessed by her painting, Lily begins to appropriate the language that has so far been used only of masculine achievement. She thinks of herself as engaged on a dangerous mission: 'Out and out one went, further and further, until at last one seemed to be on a narrow plank, perfectly alone, over the sea' (p. 232). Mrs Ramsay has meditated on 'this admirable fabric of the masculine intelligence, which ran up and down, crossed this way and that, like iron girders spanning the swaying fabric, upholding the world' (p. 143) but now Lily sees her picture combining what Mrs Ramsay has thought of as definitively gendered differences: 'Beautiful and bright it should be on the surface, feathery and evanescent, one colour melting into another like the colours on a butterfly's wing; but beneath the fabric must be clamped together with bolts of iron' (p. 231).

The assertion at the end of the novel denies the power of the Angel in the House and the vampire. In the first section of the novel Lily remembers an encounter with Mrs Ramsay that fluctuates between the homoerotic and a desire for the protection of the maternal body; Lily sits with her arms round Mrs Ramsay's knees wondering 'What art was there, known to love or cunning, by which one pressed through into those secret chambers? What device for becoming, like waters poured into one jar, inextricably the same, one with the object one adored?' (p. 70). By the end of the novel she has given birth to Mrs Ramsay by resurrecting her and putting her and the house into the picture. It frees her to say: 'I have had my vision' (p. 281) and links her with Woolf herself, who, like Mansfield, has had no children but has created her parents in the image she chooses to give them. Both hint at the vision obliquely: at the awareness of the joys and terrors of sexuality and mortality that are part of the fluctuating experience of an ordinary mind on an ordinary day. When Mansfield was wrestling with her review of *Night and Day*, and wondering why it seemed to deny the tragic knowledge that the First World War had brought with it, she described her own use of symbolism, and the passage applies equally to Woolf's fictions other than *Night and Day*. Quoting Marvell's metaphor for death in 'To His Coy Mistress', 'yonder all before us lie | Deserts of vast eternity', Mansfield tries to explain in a letter to Murry how she writes death in life:

But of course you dont imagine I mean by this knowledge 'let us eat and drink-ism'. No, I mean 'deserts of vast eternity'. But the difference between you and me is (perhaps Im wrong) I couldn't tell anybody *bang out* about those deserts. They are my secret. I might write about a boy eating strawberries or a woman combing her hair on a windy morning & that is the only way I can ever mention them. But they *must* be there.[27]

Though the affinity between Woolf and Mansfield is clearly evident when memory is bringing the dead to life again, hinting at the deserts of vast eternity that separate the dead from the living, their rapport can also be traced in their early experimental fiction written before they met. This is the concern of the next chapter.

[27] KMCL iii. 97–8, 16 Nov. 1919.

5

Early Writings and Rites of Passage

The english language is damned difficult but its also damned rich and so clear and bright that you can search out search out [*sic*] the darkest places with it.[1]

IN an unfinished story by Mansfield called 'Weak Heart', an adolescent boy hurtles away from a funeral and runs back to the home of the girl who has just been buried. She was a promising pianist. He rushes into the house and up to the drawing-room, calling her name: 'But cold, solemn, as if frozen, heavily the piano stared back at Roddie. Then it answered, but on its own behalf, on behalf of the house and the violet patch, the garden, the velvet tree at the corner of May Street, and all that was delightful: "There is nobody here of that name, young man!" '[2] The piano appears to have a life of its own, and to speak for the comfortable bourgeois present, denying the ephemeral existence of Edie though, earlier in the story, 'Edie and the piano seem to plunge together into deep dark water, into waves that flow over both, relentless' (p. 503). The symbolic significance of the piano, here and in other texts of colonial life, is ambivalent, contradictory and tantalising. Edie speaks through the piano; in the anthropomorphic language of the story 'the piano sounds gay, tender, laughing' (p. 502) but after her death it stares and answers Roddie 'on its own behalf'. The piano denies Edie's being though it is implicated in her death as she plays it 'until her nose is white and her heart beats' (p. 503). The title implies that her passionate playing is too much for her, and that the piano has killed her.

What is central to 'Weak Heart', is a rite of passage for girls and women. This chapter will pivot on literal and metaphorical

---

[1] KMCL ii. 96, 27 Feb. 1918.

[2] Katherine Mansfield, *Collected Short Stories* (Harmondsworth: Penguin, 1981), 505. All page refs. are from this edn., unless another source is indicated.

voyages made by girls and young women in the fiction of Mansfield and Woolf, beginning with works that they wrote before they met and read each other's writing, *The Urewera Notebook*, 'The Woman at the Store', 'The Wind Blows', and *The Voyage Out*, and then looking at the thematically similar stories they produced at the time when their relationship with each other was at its most influential, 'The Garden Party' and 'Kew Gardens'. Various tropes are repeated within these voyages and journeys: pianos, the sea, and encounters with indigenous people, that raise the complex question of colonialism in Woolf's writing as well as in Mansfield's. *Night and Day* is omitted because both Woolf and Mansfield disliked it and saw it as a denial of the urgent need to experiment with both the content and form of fiction. Twenty years later, Woolf wrote about the way she modelled it on existing fictions:

I was so tremblingly afraid of my own insanity that I wrote Night and Day mainly to prove to my own satisfaction that I could keep entirely off that dangerous ground. I wrote it, lying in bed, allowed to write only for one half hour a day. And I made myself copy from plaster casts, partly to tranquillise, partly to learn anatomy. Bad as the book is, it composed my mind.[3]

Because she knew nothing of these circumstances, Mansfield was mystified and appalled by the novel which she felt to be 'a lie in the soul . . . the novel cant just leave the war out . . . I feel in the *profoundest* sense that nothing can ever be the same that as artists we are traitors if we feel otherwise'.[4] Her review entitled 'A Ship Comes into the Harbour' implies that this novel is the sedate antithesis of Woolf's first novel, *The Voyage Out*.

The piano as a cultural icon, with an apparent life of its own, often appears in writing by women in the colonies, for example in the memoirs of a Canadian writer and painter, Emily Carr, who was roughly contemporary with Mansfield. She was born in Victoria, British Columbia, in 1871, and as a small girl befriended a settler who told her of an intrepid pioneering piano:

Mrs Lewis told, too, of the coming of their piano from England. It sailed all round Cape Horn and was the first piano to come into the Colony of British Columbia. It landed at Esquimault Harbour and was carried

---

[3] VWL iv. 231, 16 Oct. 1930.   [4] KMCL iii. 82, 10 Nov. 1919.

on the backs of Indians in relays of twenty at a time through a rough bush trail from Esquimault to Langford. The tired Indians put the piano down in a field outside the house to rest a minute. The Langford girls rushed out with the key, unlocked and played the piano out there in the field. The Indians were very much astonished. They looked up into the sky and into the woods to see where the noise came from.[5]

The piano sounds like a confident imperial explorer, travelling half-way round the world, arriving and being carried by natives to its destination. The syntax of the third sentence is ambiguous and could mean that the piano rather than the tired Indians needed to rest. Again, it is girls who have the key in two senses, and who play the piano; its invasive sounds leave indigenous people bemused about what has happened to their environment.

The physical presence of the piano looms in other colonial writing. Robin Hyde was born in Capetown in 1906, and moved with her parents to New Zealand when she was a baby; in her novel, *The Godwits Fly*, a piano dominates Eliza's memory of removal in Wellington:

If she waited long enough in the memory-dream, she could see the furniture-van drawn by two old horses, straining slowly uphill. Suddenly one of the horses slipped and fell. It lay plunging about, and two men in blue overalls leapt down and ran to the back of the van, while a woman in a near-by garden shrieked: 'Mind that pianner!— you dratted, lazy stots, mind that pianner!'[6]

The neighbouring woman, whose business it is not, identifies with the piano rather than with the injured horse and the distressed men ('stots' are oafs); she assumes that they are idle and are ill-treating the piano, and intervenes to defend it.

The implications of the relationship between a woman or girl and a piano in a colonial context are explored retrospectively in Jane Campion's *The Piano* (1992). When Ada arrives in New Zealand with her daughter and her piano, her new husband arrives on the shore but refuses to move the piano, and it is left on the beach looking both imposing and absurd, with the tide coming in round its legs. A powerful liminal image is created as Ada sits on the beach playing the piano while her daughter

[5] Emily Carr, *The Book of Small* (Toronto: Irwin, 1986), 83–4.
[6] Robin Hyde, *The Godwits Fly* (Auckland: Auckland University Press, 1970), 2–3.

dances round her. Ada and her daughter claim the shore temporarily as their space in between the old world and the new, inscribing on it an outline image of a sea-horse, but they are at the mercy of the tides and dependent on male power; like Mansfield's multiple selves in a sea cave, they communicate through a private language of music and signs, sleeping together when they settle in their new home as if the boundaries between mother and child are still fluid. When the daughter is precipitated violently out of this pre-Oedipal state she causes a crisis and they leave in a Maori canoe. Ada insists on taking the piano, against the Maoris' advice; when it has to be jettisoned she is accidentally tied to it by the ankle and is dragged under the water with it, echoing the trope in 'Weak Heart' where 'Edie and the piano seem to plunge together into deep dark water, into waves that flow over both, relentless.' Ada, unlike Edie, surfaces, resurrected and reborn as if from amniotic fluid, while the piano plummets to the seabed. As a post-colonial reading of colonialism the film heightens awareness of the iconic significance of a piano as part of colonial experience, specifically as both a voice and an impediment for women. What they express through a piano may be something that their society does not want to hear, as it is when the headmaster at her Melbourne school disapproves of Laura's heartfelt rendering of 'There's no place like home' in Henry Handel Richardson's *The Getting of Wisdom*, but it may also be too indirect a method of offering a critique of patriarchy, avoiding the responsibility of coherent self-expression. The language Ada has such difficulty in articulating is structured by patriarchy and alien to her, as the piano itself is; as it sits incongruously on the beach it is clearly the product of an industrial society, unwieldy beside the image of the sea-horse. It has to be knocked into shape and tuned by a male expert, just as Ada's husband tries to retune her to a prescribed role within the society. The language Ada and her daughter share is private, inaccessible to patriarchy, expressed through the eloquent fingers that also play the piano. When her husband cuts off one of her fingers he is intervening in her two most intimate languages, and attempting to sever a relationship that seems still to retain qualities of the semiotic, the stage that precedes entry into the symbolic order, where the female child and the mother do not clearly differentiate themselves.

The liminal area in the fictions about rites of passage is one of transition, passing from one state to another, and is frequently represented by travelling, as it is in 'The Little Governess', 'The Voyage', '*Je ne parle pas français*', 'An Indiscreet Journey', and 'The Stranger'; in 'The Wind Blows' and 'The Garden Party' the journey is framed by piano-playing. Mansfield's characters are as restless as she was; Woolf's fiction does not involve her characters in constant journeys, but *The Voyage Out* is a significant exception, and shows a fascination with the colonial life of which Mansfield had direct experience. For both writers, what is challenging about the encounter with indigenous people is what Kristeva calls the recognition of our own strangeness: 'Strangely, the foreigner lives within us: he is the hidden face of our identity, the space that wrecks our abode, the time in which understanding and affinity founder.'[7] The outer limit of Rachel's voyage comes when she encounters the colonized natives of the South American country to which she has travelled, playing her piano on the ship. When Evelyn asks her what she does, ' "I play," she said with an affectation of stolid composure. "That's about it!" Evelyn laughed. "We none of us do anything but play." '[8] Rachel becomes engaged to Terence, who wants to write a novel about silence, about the things that are not said. The interaction between a man who is intensely interested in the position of women and a woman who is anxious about whether her practice is playing in a frivolous sense, and is inarticulate except when she expresses herself through a man's music (she plays Bach, Beethoven, Mozart, and Purcell), focuses on the nature of silence. When Rachel and Terence stroll round the colonized village, where the inhabitants have become the objects of the tourists' curiosity and entrepreneurial activity, the silence of the native women is beyond the things that are not said: 'their long narrow eyes slid round and fixed upon them with the motionless inexpressive gaze of those removed from each other far far beyond the plunge of speech' (pp. 331–2). These women make both Rachel and Terence feel like an invading army; they 'felt themselves treading cumbrously like tight-coated soldiers among these soft instinctive people' (p. 332). Though Rachel feels excluded

---

[7] Julia Kristeva, *Strangers to Ourselves* (London: Harvester Wheatsheaf, 1991), 1.
[8] Virginia Woolf, *The Voyage Out* (Oxford: Oxford University Press, 1992), 288. All future refs. included in the text are to this edn.

by what she sees as the male world of European intellectual discourse, and Terence perceives her to be silenced by it, both are
gendered as imperial male aggressors in relation to the Amerindian village women, whose music is not instrumental but song
which 'settled again upon the same low and melancholy note'
(ibid.). Rachel is defined here as part of the incomprehensible
invasion and yet Woolf writes elsewhere that a woman may resist
patriotism and national identity because she recognizes aspects
of the colonial experience within her own life: ' "What does
'our country' mean to me an outsider? . . . 'Our country' . . .
throughout the greater part of its history has treated me as a
slave; it has denied me education or any share in its possessions.
'Our' country still ceases to be mine if I marry a foreigner." '⁹
In such a case, a woman becomes a foreigner. Rachel's inability
to express herself in words implies a link between her and the
indigenous women; within patriarchal culture, she is a foreigner
who can only make music. The reader infers that it is in the
village, or at least on the river journey, that Rachel catches the
disease that kills her; her experience is both parallel and antithetical to Kurtz's in *Heart of Darkness*, in that she is aware that
looting is going on though she is powerless to control it, and
seems unaware of its implications. Mrs Flushing, who organizes
the expedition, is ruthlessly if aristocratically exploitative; she
shows Rachel mounds of fabrics and jewellery: ' "The women wore
them hundreds of years ago, they wear 'em still," Mrs Flushing
remarked. "My husband rides about and finds 'em; they don't
know what they're worth, so we get 'em cheap. And we shall
sell 'em to smart women in London" ' (p. 272). The placing of
different European women in relation to the colonial process is
one of many intriguing partial silences in *The Voyage Out*; the
situation is opened up but remains unexplored as the novel with-
draws into a partially predictable study of the behaviour of British
guests in a foreign hotel. Nevertheless the tropes of the piano
and the sea interact as they do in some of Mansfield's early
writing, suggesting a similarity of vision in the two writers before
they were aware of each other's work.

   The Urewera Notebook is concerned with neither pianos
nor the sea but it is a record of one of Mansfield's own rites

---

⁹ Virginia Woolf, *Three Guineas* (London: Hogarth, 1943), 195, 197.

of passage; it was transcribed from what Mansfield called 'A Rough Notebook' by the New Zealand scholar, Ian Gordon. He explains in the introduction that she began the notebook in Wellington in November 1907 and took it to England with her in 1908; characteristically, she continued to add to it and finished it in Belgium in 1909. The first half of the notebook forms a self-contained episode which becomes *The Urewera Notebook*; Mansfield was one of a camping party that made a month-long trip through the North Island of New Zealand in November and December 1907. Though she is exploring her own country, Mansfield is in some respects in the same position as Rachel in *The Voyage Out*; her journey is one of self-discovery, suggested by a preoccupation with playing in the sense that unnerves Rachel: 'How we play inside the house while Life sits on the front door step and Death mounts guard at the back.'[10] This rather self-conscious and melodramatic style drops away as she becomes involved in the life of the bush, enjoying the freedom of the journey ('we laugh with joy all day', p. 40) but also newly aware of the stories that colonial life suppresses. One of those is the isolated existence of settlers in the bush; the hotel keepers at Rangitaiki 'do not seem glad or surprised to see us—give us fresh bread—all surly and familiar—and they seem troubled' (p. 86). The middle-class life she and her family live in Wellington is ironically placed by the roadman's wife, who greets them when they arrive at her cottage to camp for the night: ' "Come in and doss for a bit. I haven't got my drorin' room boots on" ' (ibid.). The isolation of the lonely women in the bush is part of a wider fascination with the inadequacy of language in the context of the magnificent landscape and its suppressed history.

The idea of the secret, the hidden, the foreigner within, recurs on the journey as Mansfield hears of her country's history: 'visions of long dead Maoris—of forgotten battles and vanished feuds —stirred in me' (p. 37). In spite of the fact that she is only 19 and has had the kind of education that represses awareness of the violence of colonial history, she seems conscious that set-tler life in the present encourages amnesia; though her travelling

[10] Katherine Mansfield, *The Urewera Notebook* (Oxford: Oxford University Press, 1978), 35. All future page refs. included in the text are to this edn.

companions are 'ultra-Colonial' (p. 45) she finds that, in the bush, 'it is all so gigantic and tragic—and even in the bright sunlight it is so passionately secret' (p. 55). This response may be prompted by the whares, Maori houses, that they pass: 'we pass several little whares deserted—and grey—they look very old and desolate—almost haunted' (ibid.). The implication is that it is the writer herself who is haunted by the empty houses and by what she perceives as an alien race of people. She takes every opportunity to talk to the Maori people she meets, and to play with their children, but she portrays them as Woolf depicts the Amerindian people in *The Voyage Out*, as other and alien: 'There is one great fellow I see—who speaks English—black curls clustering round his broad brow—rest almost languor in his black eyes—a slouching walk and yet there slumbers in his face passion might and strength' (p. 59). It is the antipodean equivalent of an orientalist gaze in that she feels superior to the man and yet there is a powerful discourse of desire for the man's unfamiliar physicality in the passage, as there is in the 'Vignette' when she watches a young Maori girl beside a lake. What she calls vignettes are imagined pieces based on observed reality; here she creates for herself an ideal situation for a writer, observing someone who does not know that she is seen, and so reveals herself:

She is dressed in a blue skirt and white soft blouse—Round her neck is a piece of twisted flax and . . . a long piece of greenstone—is suspended from it—Her black hair is twisted softly at her neck—she wears long white and red bone earrings—She is very young — . . . She sits —silent—utterly motionless—her head thrust back—All the lines of her face are passionate violent—crudely savage—but in her lifted eyes slumbers a tragic illimitable peace. (pp. 84–5)

The passage is a curious mixture of desire and guilt, as one very young girl depicts another; the repetition of 'soft' resembles Woolf's description of the 'soft instinctive' village people but it seems at odds with 'violent—crudely savage'. The phrase 'tragic illimitable peace' implies that the girl accepts the dispossession and possible annihilation of her people, and yet there is an awareness that she has qualities that the watcher envies; like the 'great fellow' she is full of unaroused passion. Of both of them the word 'slumbers' is used, which is at once a stereotypical view of 'native' peoples' passivity and an indicator of a wish to be the agent of arousal. Of herself she says: 'I am alone—I am hidden' (p. 84), a phrase which suggests that the journey is a rite of passage for her. In solitary exploration, that key word in her writing, she is discovering not just new territory and the evidence of a history that European narratives want to rewrite or suppress; she is finding her subject, 'the secret self we all have',[11] and the beginning of an awareness of the foreigner within.

She expressed both discoveries in the first story that she sent to John Middleton Murry in 1912, which he published in *Rhythm*, 'The Woman at the Store'; the story derived from her experience of the camping trip. Though it has an element of narrative denouement which is unusual in Mansfield's work, it is also an exploration of a liminal state on the borders of madness for the protagonist and a transitional one for the country as its communications improve but some of its inhabitants become dangerously isolated. It is disorientating both to the reader and the characters from the beginning, inverting the conventions of European writing as, for instance, larks are no longer blithe spirits which pour out their full hearts 'in profuse strains of unpremeditated art'[12] but instead they screech: 'Hundreds of larks shrilled; the sky was slate colour, and the sound of the larks reminded me of slate pencils scraping over its surface.'[13] A sundowner is not a pink gin on the veranda at sunset but a menacing tramp who turns up at nightfall looking for somewhere to sleep; the sun does not sink but plummet: 'It was sunset. There is no twilight in our New Zealand days, but a curious half-hour when everything appears grotesque—it frightens—as though the savage spirit of the country walked abroad and sneered at what it saw' (p. 554). Nothing is what it seems, and the reader sometimes feels as if she is being sneered at; all three of the weary riders who appear at the beginning of the story are covered with pumice dust, their whiteness exaggerated and pantomimic, so that 'Jim rode beside me, white as a clown; his black eyes glittered and he kept shooting out his tongue and moistening his lips' (p. 551). The woman at the store greets them by saying that she ' "thought you was three 'awks" ' (p. 552); their appearance is

[11] KMCL iv. 278, 12 Sept. 1921.   [12] Percy Bysshe Shelley, 'To a Skylark'.
[13] CS 550.

macabre, and predatory as she suggests, with one of them wearing a noose-like white spotted handkerchief 'knotted round his throat' which 'looked as though his nose had been bleeding on it' (p. 550). The narrator uses the word 'uncanny' of the scene, and this effect is communicated to the reader as the story is full of masks and doubles, from the clown-like appearance of the travellers to the disconcerting nature of both the woman at the store and the narrator.

The woman is described, before the riders arrive at the store, as having blue eyes and yellow hair, but when she appears she is not a stereotypical blonde charmer: 'Certainly her eyes were blue, and what hair she had was yellow, but ugly. She was a figure of fun. Looking at her, you felt there was nothing but sticks and wires under that pinafore—her front teeth were knocked out, she had red, pulpy hands and she wore on her feet a pair of dirty Bluchers' (pp. 552–3). The enticing woman from European folk stories, who lures through her half-open door the innocent traveller passing along a remote road at twilight, is brutally transmogrified; the fact that this toothless siren is ' "female flesh" ' and knows ' "one hundred and twenty-five different ways of kissing" ' (p. 556) is not a headily erotic prospect.[14] The transformation of her from a ' "barmaid down the Coast—as pretty as a wax doll" ' (ibid.) is explained by the new railway; until it opened, coaches used to come past the store but now only ' "Maoris and sundowners" ' go by. The narrator too has a ghostly double, in that she seems for the larger part of the story to be a man, travelling with two men whose language suggests an all-male camaraderie; their journey is unexplained but apparently work-related. It is only when the unprepossessing 'kid' says: ' "I looked at her" ' (p. 557) when she was bathing in the creek that the narrator's sex is revealed and assumptions about the relationship between the two men and the narrator have to be reconstructed. There are two different versions of the woman's husband: according to the woman he has gone droving, but the 'kid had drawn the picture of the woman shooting at a man with a rook rifle and then digging a hole to bury him in' (p. 561). The whole story can be read as a feminist rewriting

14 Pamela Dunbar, *Radical Mansfield: Double Discourse in Katherine Mansfield's Short Stories* (London: Macmillan, 1997), 44–9, offers an astute reading of the story.

of the Australian Henry Lawson's classic tale of bush life 'The Drover's Wife', in which the husband really has gone droving and the wife heroically fights off marauding strangers and snakes, but is only identified through her relationship to the drover and their plucky children. In Mansfield's story however both the woman and the kid are deranged because of their impossible situation in the pioneers' patriarchy:

'It's six years since I was married, and four miscarriages. I says to 'im, I says, what do you think I'm doin' up 'ere? If you was back at the Coast I'd 'ave you lynched for child murder. Over and over I tells 'im— you've broken my spirit and spoiled my looks, and wot for—that's wot I'm driving at . . . When the coach stopped coming, sometimes he'd go away days, sometimes he'd go away weeks, and leave me ter look after the store. Back 'e'd come—pleased as Punch. "Oh, 'allo," 'e'd say. "'Ow are you gettin' on? Come and give us a kiss."' (p. 558)

This may have been a terrible revenge for his wife's experiments, presumably with a variety of experts, in kissing techniques, but the man's neglect of his wife and children is replicated as the woman's obsessive neurosis about her own situation results in cruelty to her one surviving child, who is repeatedly offered variants on ' "Shut yer lies" ' when she tries to enter the conversation. Her 'extraordinary and repulsively vulgar' drawings (p. 559), her delight at having seen the narrator naked, and the way in which 'she worked herself up into a mad excitement' (ibid.) as she shows the visitors the drawings imply that the child is already an abject, depraved by precocious sexual knowledge. That her name is Else is not surprising; all the female characters are something else, other than what they seem. Else is concealed and muted; when she first appears she hides behind her mother, then 'gave us the benefit of one eye from behind the woman's pinafore—then retired again' (p. 552). These are the silences and suppressed histories that Mansfield became aware of as she travelled in the bush. The child tells the story of her father's murder at the hands of her mother indirectly, but she puts it in a diagrammatic letter that is not fully received in that no one responds directly to her, and the travellers will clearly do nothing about it. Indeed the entire episode seems to be erased in the last line: 'A bend in the road, and the whole place disappeared' (p. 562). The brutal laconic humour of the story, more sardonic than Lawson's but comparable with the work of another writer for the *Bulletin*, Barbara Baynton, plays on gendered expectations and disappoints them; the narrator is indifferent to the plight of the desperate woman and child, and her narrative and dialogue are indistinguishable from those of her male companions. Both woman and child are left in their liminal state, failing to communicate, between the borders of town life and male mateship, both in a state of abjection.

A very different but equally disconcerting liminality, this time a rite of passage, is portrayed in the story that was originally called 'Autumn II' when first published in 1915 in the *Signature*, a short-lived magazine written entirely by Mansfield, Murry, and D. H. Lawrence. The story was then revised as 'The Wind Blows' for publication in the *Athenaeum* in 1920 and also included in *Bliss and Other Stories*: 'As to The Wind Blows I put it in because so many people had admired it. (Yes its Autumn II but a little different.) Virginia, Lytton [Strachey]—and queer people like Mary Hamilton [Clive Bell's lover] & Bertie [Bertrand Russell] all spoke so strongly about it I felt I must put it in.'[15] Mansfield was adamant that she 'couldn't have The Woman at the Store reprinted'.[16] Compared with 'The Woman at the Store', 'The Wind Blows' is inconclusive and closer to her mature style, using the piano and the sea antithetically to suggest Matilda's mood and her transitional state. Matilda Berry was Mansfield's pseudonym in *Signature* and the brother in the story is called Bogey, which was her brother Leslie's nickname, implying that the story arises from a memory of New Zealand; this was perhaps triggered by her brother's arrival to spend his last leave with her at Acacia Road in the autumn of 1915. She told Brett in 1921:

[A]t dusk an old ancient wind sprang up and it is shaking now and complaining. A terrible wind—a wind that one always mercifully forgets until it blows again. Do you know the kind I mean? It brings nothing but memories—and by memories I mean those that one cannot without pain remember. It always carries my brother to me.[17]

That the story is told in the present tense communicates the mental and emotional turmoil of Matilda, whose perspective is used throughout. Her resistance to her mother's instructions and her

---

[15] KMCL iii. 273–4, 6 Apr. 1920.   [16] Ibid. 210, 8 Feb. 1920.
[17] KMCL iv. 341, 19 Dec. 1921.

affinity with her brother, whose voice is breaking, suggest that she is adolescent; though she never refers directly to anxiety about her sexuality it is implicit in her heightened observation of the world around her, and in what she notices. The opening of the story links being in bed with a sense of impending disaster: 'Something dreadful has happened. No—nothing has happened. It is only the wind shaking the house, rattling the windows, banging a piece of iron on the roof and making her bed tremble' (p. 106). The see-saw quality of adolescent experience is conveyed instantly and economically, blurring the boundaries between what happens in the body and in the outside world. Matilda receives two contrasting impressions of female experience, as her mother grumbles about the servant who has left her washing to be torn to ribbons by the wind, and the girl next door tries to rescue her chrysanthemums from the same fate:

Her skirt flies up above her waist; she tries to beat it down, to tuck it between her legs while she stoops, but it is no use—up it flies. All the trees and bushes beat about her. She picks as quickly as she can, but she is quite distracted. She doesn't mind what she does—she pulls the plants up by the roots and bends and twists them, stamping her foot and swearing. (ibid.)

Though the text rushes on to the next impression, the reader is left with a vivid image of this confused gendered behaviour. One girl observes another who is so distracted by the embarrassment of the wind revealing her underwear and attacking her that she behaves trangressively, destroying the flowers that she came out to save, and cursing. Again there is a sense of sexual anxiety; one girl feels it and the other registers it. The wind seems to generate hysteria in Matilda; she rejects the rules of the Angel in the House who tells her to change her hat, and hurries towards a man whose priorities are artistic rather than domestic: 'she can hear the sea sob: "Ah! . . . Ah! . . . Ah-h!" But Mr Bullen's drawing-room is as quiet as a cave' (p. 107). The sea expresses Matilda's distress but the music teacher's masculine retreat calms her. Here a girl plays 'To an Ice-berg', a woman is depicted with her skirt in the right place and her legs decorously crossed, and the chrysanthemums are sedately placed in a vase on the mantelpiece, not wrenched from the ground by a desperate girl:

She likes this room. It smells of art serge and stale smoke and chrysanthemums . . . there is a big vase of them on the mantelpiece behind
the pale photograph of Rubinstein . . . *à mon ami Robert Bullen*. . . .
Over the black glittering piano hangs 'Solitude'—a dark tragic woman
draped in white, sitting on a rock, her knees crossed, her chin on her
hands.   (ibid.)

Though Matilda is comforted by the room, its associations may
disconcert the reader: the stale smells and odour of chrysanthemums, and the ghostly image of Rubinstein, suggest death;
one master of music communicates with another; solitude is
gendered as female. This unease is confirmed by Mr Bullen's
behaviour—is it paternal or not? The perception is Matilda's,
and she is contemptuous of the-girl-before-her who blushes when
Mr Bullen leans over her and puts his arms over her shoulders
to play a passage for her, but the reader may not be so sanguine
when Matilda, without mentioning them, is self-conscious about
her breasts: 'And her heart beats so hard she feels it must lift
her blouse up and down. Mr Bullen does not say a word. The
shabby red piano seat is long enough for two people to sit side
by side. Mr Bullen sits down by her' (p. 108). Her awareness
of her appearance and the way in which the text dwells on
Mr Bullen's silence and his hands ('his fresh hand with the ring
on it'; 'it is a very nice hand and always looks as though it
had just been washed') combine to intensify the unease, and the
suggestion of neurotic anxiety in the Pilate-like hand-washing.
The unease develops further when he takes her hands and she
rests her cheek on his shoulder; as he mouths sinister platitudes
about ' "that rare thing, a woman" ' the girl whose skirt flew
up in the wind comes in, and he 'gets up and begins to walk
up and down again' (p. 109). His reiterated phrase 'little lady'
hints at a perverse pleasure in his relationship with adolescent
girls. All three piano pupils are girls; Mr Bullen opens the work
of ' "the old master" ', Beethoven. The music lesson pivots on
mastery and control, both emotionally and physically.

Matilda, back in her bedroom, retains a heightened awareness of her surroundings that suggests hysteria, particularly
because it focuses on her bed: 'It's frightening to be here in her
room by herself. The bed, the mirror, the white jug and basin
gleam like the sky outside. It's the bed that is frightening'
(ibid.). One critic refers to this paragraph as an example of 'cute

sweetness',[18] but Matilda's image of 'all those stockings knotted up on the quilt like a coil of snakes' which her mother wants her to darn, seems to point to a terrified but suppressed awareness of sexual menace, with which the Angel in the House is perceived to be complicit. Liberation comes through another male character, Matilda's brother, who is portrayed as an aspect of herself and not a sexual threat. At the beginning of the story she dared not look in the glass but now she does: 'Her face is white, they have the same excited eyes and hot lips' (ibid.). Both are aroused, but not by each other; they complement and touch each other not as lovers but as doubles. They wear identical coats: 'Their heads bent, their legs just touching, they stride like one eager person through the town' (ibid.).

Now there is no self-consciousness about womanly behaviour, and earlier impressions are repeated in the new context as if the brother and sister together, standing by the sea, can heal the psychic damage inflicted earlier in the day. The brother's voice embodies for his sister both the music lesson and the torn washing: 'Bogey's voice is breaking. When he speaks he rushes up and down the scale. It's funny—it makes you laugh—and yet it just suits the day. The wind carries their voices—away fly the sentences like little narrow ribbons' (p. 110). That the windy day has been an initiation, a voyage of discovery, is indicated by the big black steamer that they watch; the wind which has frightened Matilda all day is now powerless as the ship puts out to sea: 'The wind does not stop her; she cuts through the waves, making for the open gate between the pointed rocks that lead to . . .' (ibid.). Because of the gendering of the ship, it is identified with Matilda and her rite of passage. Abruptly, almost cinematically, the perspective changes and brother and sister are on the ship, 'leaning over the rail arm in arm' and watching the town, unnamed but with Wellington's landmarks, disappear. The timescale shifts as the sister remembers how ' "I cried at my music lesson that day—how many years ago! Good-bye, little island, good-bye . . ." ' The final paragraph is enigmatic, as if the adults may lose sight of their adolescent doubles, and forget those moments when life is most urgent and most disturbing:

[18] Hermione Lee, *Virginia Woolf* (London: Chatto & Windus, 1996), 392.

Now the dark stretches a wing over the tumbling water. They can't
see those two any more. Good-bye, good-bye. Don't forget . . . But the
ship is gone, now.
   The wind—the wind.

The story itself is an act of memory, responding to the injunction 'Don't forget', but the atmosphere becomes menacing again.
The tumbling sea into which the ship sails suggests the dangerous
freedom which any adventurer encounters. The heightened, dis-
torted vision of the story reflecting Matilda's perception is like
an Expressionist painting; the reader's constant awareness of the
wind makes it expressive of Matilda's adolescent disorientation,
an inner turmoil and urgency reflected in a natural force. The
fusing of brother and sister implies not resolution of difference,
but Kristeva's attack on the symbolic order's binary opposites 'in
order that the struggle, the implacable difference, the violence be
conceived in the very place where it operates with the maximum
intransigence, in other words, in personal and sexual identity
itself, so as to make it disintegrate in its very nucleus.'[19]
   Though Rachel Vinrace, in Woolf's *The Voyage Out*, is 24, much
older than Matilda, she seems naïve enough to be still adolescent,
and it is her voyage of discovery that is traced in the novel. She
is a pianist, and from the opening of the novel the piano's agency
in her life is evident. Like the piano in 'Weak Heart', her piano is
visualized as something that can kill: ' "[M]y aunts said the piano
would come through the floor, but at their age one wouldn't
mind being killed in the night" ' (p. 15). Her piano is also seen
as an obstacle to what should be her business in life, according
to her aunts; though they do not object to being killed by the
piano, they do not want it to hamper her marriage prospects:

'I heard from Aunt Bessie not long ago,' Helen stated. 'She is afraid
that you will spoil your arms if you insist upon so much practising.'
   'The muscles of the forearm—and then one won't marry?'
   'She didn't put it quite like that,' replied Mrs Ambrose.
   'Oh, no—of course she wouldn't,' said Rachel with a sigh.   (p. 15)

This exchange anticipates Terence's interest in silence, and aspects
of women's lives that are hinted at but not addressed directly.
Its implication is that Rachel's music may offer her an alternative

[19] Julia Kristeva, *The Kristeva Reader* (Oxford: Basil Blackwell, 1986), 209.

to marriage, but there seems to be no question of her becoming a professional musician; ' "You see, I'm a woman" ' (p. 79) Rachel reminds Mr Dalloway, and his response is to kiss her as if that is the inevitable reaction to ' "female flesh" '. She seems imprisoned by patriarchy; Helen is aware that Rachel's father has appropriated her dead mother and turned her into an absent saint, which is not how Helen remembers her. Rachel's education has been non-existent: 'Her mind was in the state of an intelligent man's in the beginning of the reign of Queen Elizabeth; she would believe practically anything she was told, invent reasons for anything she said' (p. 31). The only hint of any kind of intellectual fulfilment for Rachel is in the metaphors the text uses for her playing, but they are to an extent ironic. As she plays, Rachel creates a shape: 'an invisible line seemed to string the notes together, from which rose a shape, a building' (p. 58). Here she is playing Bach, but she is interrupted by Mrs Dalloway and the 'shape of the Bach fugue crashed to the ground' (p. 59). Mr Dalloway is even more destructive: 'Richard sat upon Bach' (p. 78). Rachel's duty as her father's host supervenes; always her domestic duties come before her artistic aspirations, and it is she who has to write letters full of clichés in response to the clichés she has received on her engagement, while Terence reads. He has interrupted her: 'Up and up the steep spiral of a very late Beethoven sonata she climbed, like a person ascending a ruined staircase' (p. 339). Only partly humorously she says: ' "No, Terence, it's no good; here am I, the best musician in South America, not to speak of Europe and Asia, and I can't play a note because of you in the room interrupting me every other second" ' (p. 340). It is a repeated motif in the text for the reader to see her interrupted as she plays. The only time that this does not happen is when she plays for dancing at the hotel, and goes on playing to herself when the dancers are exhausted: 'They sat very still as if they saw a building with spaces and columns succeeding each other rising in the empty space' (p. 187). Yet she, like Matilda, is playing the works of the old masters, and recreating their buildings; she can interpret the musical patriarchs but she is not the architect. She cannot speak for herself, musically or verbally.

In a curious parallel to 'The Wind Blows', Rachel and Helen confront the wind as Bogey and Matilda do, and they look over the ship's rail together:

Leaning over the rail, side by side, Helen said, 'Won't you be cold?'
Rachel replied, 'No . . . How beautiful!' she added a moment later. Very
little was visible—a few masts, a shadow of land here, a line of brilliant windows there. They tried to make head against the wind.

'It blows—it blows!' gasped Rachel, the words rammed down her
throat. Struggling by her side, Helen was suddenly overcome by the
spirit of movement, and pushed along with her skirts wrapping themselves round her knees. (p. 13)

There is however a significant difference between this voyage
and the voyage suggested in 'The Wind Blows', as the patriarchs
accompany the women on the voyage and leave them in liminal territory; when Rachel and Helen look for somewhere to
escape the wind they peep through the blinds of the dining-room
and see that they cannot enter: 'In the dry yellow-lighted room
Mr Pepper and Mr Ambrose were oblivious of all tumult; they
were in Cambridge, and it was probably about the year 1875.'
All that remains as a refuge for the women is an in-between space
' "more like a landing than a room." ' The wind offers Rachel
a kind of initiation, a rite of passage, but it is eventually a one-
way journey that she makes, into death rather than fuller experience. It is the wind that blows her and Mr Dalloway into her
room; the ship lurches and he kisses her. ' "You tempt me," he
said. The tone of his voice was terrifying' (p. 80).

Rachel's fear is so profound because she is an only child,
brought up by aunts who suppress discussion of feelings of any
kind and have no language for sexual experience. When she asks
about how fond they are of each other her aunt's reply is: ' "If
one cares one doesn't think 'how', Rachel" ' (p. 34). This leads
Rachel to the deduction that there is safety only in her piano:
'To feel anything strongly was to create an abyss between oneself and others who feel strongly perhaps but differently. It was
far better to play the piano and forget all the rest. The conclusion was very welcome' (ibid.). Her aunts of course eschew
any approach to sexual matters so she 'groped for knowledge in
old books, and found it in repulsive chunks' (p. 32). She hints to
Terence of the effect of these furtive attempts to find out about
her own body, and of her speculations about what the women in
Piccadilly are doing, but she cannot tell him directly because she
has no language to express it; ' "There are terrors and agonies,"
she said, keeping her eye on him as if to detect the slightest hint

of laughter' (p. 247). Helen quickly recognizes her ignorance, and the extent to which patriarchal control is responsible for it: 'Helen could hardly restrain herself from saying out loud what she thought of a man who brought up his daughter so that at the age of twenty-four she scarcely knew that men desired women and was terrified by a kiss' (p. 86). Rachel, because of her unnaturally protracted adolescence, cannot recover from her fear as her moods no longer swing like Matilda's; the new view that Helen gives her of the relationship between the sexes causes a trauma from which she does not recover. Her perception is that her existence is by definition, and permanently, liminal:

By this new light she saw her life for the first time a creeping hedged-in thing, driven cautiously between high walls, here turned aside, there plunged in darkness, made dull and crippled for ever—her life that was the only chance she had—a thousand words and actions became plain to her.
   'Because men are brutes! I hate men!' she exclaimed.
   'I thought you said you liked him?' said Helen.
   'I liked him, and I liked being kissed,' she answered, as if that only added more difficulties to her problem.   (p. 87)

This image for her life, as a creeping creature driven between high walls, is starkly opposed to the 'building with spaces and columns' that she creates for others with her music. Her dreams insistently reveal that her unconscious accepts the hedged-in interpretation of being, possibly in a horrific and abject vision of her own body, with the tunnel as the cervix and the vault as the womb; she has this dream the night after she has been kissed by Richard Dalloway, and it recurs when she is dying, shortly after she has become engaged to Terence:

She dreamt that she was walking down a long tunnel, which grew so narrow by degrees that she could touch the damp bricks on either side. At length the tunnel opened and became a vault; she found herself trapped in it, bricks meeting her wherever she turned, alone with a little deformed man who squatted on the floor gibbering, with long nails. His face was pitted and like the face of an animal. The wall behind him oozed with damp, which collected into drops and slid down.
(p. 81)

The dream may stem partly from a conversation with Dalloway which conveyed an image of the material world as a live thing 'with drains like nerves, and bad houses like patches of diseased skin' (p. 88), though here the metaphor is reversed, and the oozing of the damp bricks represents bodily secretions, with Rachel's full self confined within her reproductive organs. Her conversation with Dalloway was about London; her diseased and dying dream takes place in a tunnel under the Thames, with the culminating horror being the oozing secretions from the walls: 'while the bricks of which the wall was made oozed with damp, which collected into drops and slid down the wall' (p. 386). The repetition of the word 'wall' insists on her horror of entrapment, but the walls' clammy moisture suggests membranes rather than bricks; she suffers an abjected disgust with her own body.

Rachel tells Terence that she is happiest when she is seeing but unseen, like the narrator of Mansfield's 'Vignette', and like the night when Rachel and Helen watched the inhabitants of the hotel without their knowledge: ' "I like seeing things go on— as we saw you that night when you didn't see us—I love the freedom of it—it's like being the wind or the sea" ' (p. 248). Playing the piano offers escape from speculation about the complexities of human feeling, and from political choice; when Terence asks Rachel if she thinks the franchise for women will do her any good she replies: ' "Not to me . . . But I play the piano" ' (p. 240). Becoming the wind or the sea, however, involves a dangerous freedom. In retrospect, an early description of the ship can be seen as a figure for Rachel herself, launching herself on the freedom and hazards of leaving her life with her aunts, which is encapsulated by her in the terse remark: ' "I've fed rabbits for twenty-four years" ' (p. 241). As the ship leaves London and sails into the open sea it is described in anthropomorphic terms that anticipate Rachel's story: 'The sea might give her death or some unexampled joy, and none would know of it. She was a bride going forth to her husband, a virgin unknown of men; in her vigour and purity she might be likened to all beautiful things, for as a ship she had a life of her own' (p. 30). But the ship and Rachel are controlled by Mr Vinrace. The reader is given the illusion that Rachel and Terence are driven by an ungovernable natural force which must carry them on; Terence 'was drawn on and on away from all he knew, slipping over barriers and past landmarks into unknown waters' (p. 311) and Rachel feels 'happiness swelling and breaking in one vast wave' (p. 331).

As readers of a *bildungsroman* we know what to expect, but it does not happen because the 'tunnels' of the unconscious are too powerful for Rachel. When she and Terence are together she feels that she can control the sea:

To be flung into the sea, to be washed hither and thither, and driven about the roots of the world—the idea was incoherently delightful. She sprang up, and began moving about the room, bending and thrusting aside the chairs and tables as if she were indeed striking through the waters. He watched her with pleasure; she seemed to be cleaving a passage for herself, and dealing triumphantly with the obstacles which would hinder their passage through life. (p. 347)

Yet this assertiveness seems punished when Rachel shows signs of illness as Terence reads her the invocation to Sabrina from Milton's *Comus*; Sabrina is sitting 'Under the glassy, cool, translucent wave' (p. 381) prefiguring what is about to happen to Rachel as she surrenders to the semiotic and goes under the water, rather than cleaving a path through it. As her fever mounts, her dreams of entrapment recur, and she is engulfed by the waters, not 'cleaving a passage for herself', not exploring the roots of the world, but a passive and helpless victim of tides and other people:

[S]he fell into a deep pool of sticky water, which eventually closed over her head. She saw nothing and heard nothing but a faint booming sound, which was the sound of the sea rolling over her head. While all her tormentors thought that she was dead, she was not dead, but curled up at the bottom of the sea. There she lay, sometimes seeing darkness, sometimes light, while every now and then someone turned her over at the bottom of the sea. (pp. 397–8)

She fleetingly comes 'to the surface of the dark, sticky pool, and a wave seemed to bear her up and down with it' (p. 404) but she goes under again and dies, leaving Terence looking out on the moon's 'long silver pathway upon the surface of the waves' (p. 412). The voyage was a journey of self-enlightenment, but what it revealed was the power of patriarchy and the symbolic order rather than the power to escape from abjection and the semiotic. An oblique link is made with the situation of colonial subjects, such as those that haunt the margins of the novel, in that their encounter with representatives of the metropolis creates a sense of exclusion and mystification. In her delirium

Rachel cannot recover because her terror of sexuality haunts her dreams, and the doctor resembles the gibbering man with the face of an animal from her first dream in that he 'had—it was the chief thing she noticed about him—very hairy hands' (p. 383). Her piano-playing cannot save her because in the end it reinforces patriarchy rather than offering empowerment; she interprets the works of great male composers and so uses the piano's language as a way of avoiding self-expression within the symbolic order.

Patriarchy and colonialism collaborate to marginalize female experience in the text, what Terence calls ' "this curious silent unrepresented life" ' (p. 245). Part of the power of patriarchy is to divide women against themselves; as Rachel says, her aunts 'built up the fine, closely woven substance of their life at home' and yet all 'her rages had been against them' (p. 246). Helen has betrayed her children for the sake of accompanying her husband on the voyage, and is haunted by guilt. Her life is organized round her husband's scholarship; the ironic tone suggests the narrator's gender: 'Mr Ambrose in his study was some thousand miles distant from the nearest human being, who in this household was inevitably a woman' (p. 191). Empire-building and masculine control are shown, unobtrusively but constantly, to dominate the ordinary domestic life of the women in the text. Centres of empire are linked; as Helen stands weeping at the separation from her children beside the Thames the narrator remarks: 'Sometimes the flats and churches and hotels of Westminster are like the outlines of Constantinople in a mist' (p. 4). Her husband, embarrassed by her tears, quotes the sabre-rattling opening of Macaulay's *Lays of Ancient Rome*; he is 'either a Viking or a stricken Nelson' (p. 6) in his gait, depending on what he is quoting. Though he is a scholar he identifies with heroic constructions of imperialism, as the conservative politician Richard Dalloway does. The malicious wit of the narrator implies an attitude to his activities: 'He ran his mind along the line of conservative policy, which went steadily from Lord Salisbury to Alfred, and gradually enclosed, as though it were a lasso that opened and caught things, enormous chunks of the habitable globe' (p. 51). At the ball in the hotel, St John Hirst, who claims to be one of the three most distinguished men in England, tyrannizes over Rachel by expressing his horror at her innocence of the imperial project for she has ' "reached the age of twenty-four without reading Gibbon" ' (p. 172); he lends her the first volume of *The Decline and Fall of the Roman Empire* and she reads that northern Europe 'scarcely deserved the expense and labour of conquest' (p. 196). She does not perceive that she is implicated in this process by being where she is, but the narrator has already suggested it by describing the way in which Santa Marina had been colonized by the British, Spaniards, and Portuguese in different waves of invasion and was now being recolonized:

The reasons which had drawn the English across the sea to found a small colony within the last ten years are not so easily described, and will never perhaps be recorded in history books. Granted facility of travel, peace, good trade, and so on, there was a kind of dissatisfaction among the English with the older countries and the enormous accumulations of carved stone, stained glass, and rich brown painting which they offered to the tourist.   (p. 97)

The exploitative undertones of this are clear, and the material incentive is shown in the Flushings' venture to the interior. Because Helen, Rachel, Mrs Dalloway, and most of the other women go along unquestioningly with their menfolk's projects, they do not see the link between their own marginalization and that of colonized people. Helen, who is intelligent, is shown in an absurd position, trying unsuccessfully to maintain two roles and caricaturing indigenous people as they are caricatured in *Heart of Darkness*. She sits between her embroidery frame and her volume of philosophy:

She was working at a great design of a tropical river running through a tropical forest, where spotted deer would eventually browse upon masses of fruit, bananas, oranges, and giant pomegranates, while a troop of naked natives whirled darts into the air. Between the stitches she looked to one side and read a sentence about the Reality of Matter, or the Nature of Good.   (p. 30)

The deer are presumably antelope, but the native dart-whirling seems to be one of those quaint habits of which 'savages' are so notoriously fond. Helen's 'great design' is a visual equivalent of Dalloway's lassoing 'enormous chunks of the habitable globe', but she would disown any such purpose. The implication of the narrative is that the colonial process, and women's acquiescence in it, may not be as harmless as it seems to those who take the trip up the river: 'Every year at this season English people made parties which steamed a short way up the river, landed, and looked at the native village, bought a certain number of things from the natives, and returned again without damage done to mind or body' (p. 308). This time crucial damage is done to Rachel's mind and body. The violation of invasion is only hinted at by a powerful evocation of a place previously untouched by colonialism:

The time of Elizabeth was only distant from the present time by a moment of space compared with the ages which had passed since the water had run between those banks, and the green thickets swarmed there, and the small trees had grown to huge wrinkled trees in solitude. Changing only with the change of the sun and the clouds, the waving green mass had stood there for century after century, and the water had run between its banks ceaselessly, sometimes washing away earth and sometimes the branches of trees, while in other parts of the world one town had risen upon the ruins of another town, and the men in the towns had become more and more articulate and unlike each other. (p. 308)

What Rachel's voyage out demonstrates to her and to the reader resembles what Mansfield's experience taught her, that patriarchy has colonized the territory. Colonized subjects, like the Amerindian people in *The Voyage Out* or the Maoris that Mansfield describes in *The Urewera Notebook*, cannot communicate with the colonizer in their own language; similarly for women music, in 'The Wind Blows', 'Weak Heart', and *The Voyage Out*, is a male language which can be interpreted but not composed by women. In the personal writings of Woolf and Mansfield as well as in their fiction, women are often represented as enablers of male discourse but as excluded from it; Helen creates the domestic circumstances in which her husband can converse with other scholars, as Mrs Ramsay does in *To the Lighthouse*. The piano, like the men, is silent until it is played by female pianists in the texts discussed here; the men in the novels mentioned, like Peacock in 'Mr Reginald Peacock's Day' or Stanley in 'At the Bay', have to be harmonized and set going by women. The piano which is the vehicle of the interpretation is an icon of Western culture which all three texts, like *The Piano*, associate with danger and death for the female pianist. Women like the woman at the store are the victims of the masculinist ethos of pioneering life, but are divided by their collusion with patriarchy from recognizing their own situation; the woman at the store still attempts to be the object of the male gaze. Helen and Rachel are complicit with the exploitation of the Amerindian people because they do not allow themselves to think what they are doing in going on a sightseeing tour down the river, and so do not dissociate themselves from the inanities of Mr Bax's sermon:

The argument of the sermon was that visitors to this beautiful land, although they were on a holiday, owed a duty to the natives . . . It rambled with a kind of amiable verbosity . . . observing that very small things do influence people, particularly natives; in fact, a very dear friend of Mr Bax's had told him that the success of our rule in India, that vast country, largely depended upon the strict code of politeness which the English adopted towards the natives. (p. 267)

Woolf's ironic subversion of English liberalism indicates that she and Mansfield were likely to laugh at the same things when they eventually met.

Mansfield reissued 'The Wind Blows' in *Bliss and Other Stories* because Woolf, among others, liked it; Mansfield and Woolf met partly because Mansfield's admiration of *The Voyage Out* was reported to Woolf:

Lytton met her, and—as he had with Leonard—it was he who whetted Virginia's interest, reporting back to her that Katherine was 'decidedly an interesting creature . . . very amusing and sufficiently mysterious' with 'an ugly impassive mask of a face—cut in wood, with brown hair and brown eyes very far apart; and a sharp and slightly vulgar-fanciful intellect sitting behind it.' She had been enthusiastic about *The Voyage Out* and said she wanted to meet Virginia more than anyone.[20]

When the friendship between Woolf and Mansfield was established they had a rapport that, at its best, created its own medium of exchange. Woolf describes having tea with Mansfield while 'Murry sat there mud-coloured & mute':

The male atmosphere is disconcerting to me. Do they distrust one? despise one? & if so why do they sit on the whole length of one's visit? The truth is that when Murry says the orthodox masculine thing about Eliot for example, belittling my solicitude to know what he said

[20] Lee, *Virginia Woolf*, 388.

of me, I dont knuckle under; I think what an abrupt precipice cleaves asunder the male intelligence, & how they pride themselves upon a point of view which much resembles stupidity. I find it much easier to talk to Katherine; she gives & resists as I expect her to; we cover more ground in much less time.[21]

In the same month Mansfield writes to Woolf to say that she has read her essay which was later collected as 'Modern Fiction' in *The Common Reader*: 'You write so *damned* well, so *devilish* well . . . To tell you the truth—I am *proud* of your writing. I read & I think *"How* she beats them" '.[22] This chapter will conclude by considering two stories that were written after the relationship between Woolf and Mansfield was established, which both focus on gardens: 'Kew Gardens', which embodies the writer's own rite of passage, and 'The Garden Party' in which a short journey symbolizes a major shift in the consciousness of the protagonist, Laura.

Antony Alpers has argued that 'Katherine Mansfield in some way helped Virginia Woolf to break out of the mould in which she had been working hitherto.'[23] He bases his case on the strange correlation between a letter from Mansfield to Ottoline Morrell, and Woolf's 'Kew Gardens'. At this time, August 1917, Woolf had not yet been to Garsington, but Mansfield was familiar with the house and gardens. She wrote what appear to have been two similar letters about it, one which has not survived to Woolf and the other to Ottoline Morrell:

Your glimpse of the garden—all flying green and gold made me wonder again *who* is going to write about that flower garden. It might be so wonderful—do you see *how* I mean? There would be people walking in the garden—several *pairs* of people—their conversation their slow pacing —their glances as they pass one another—the pauses as the flowers 'come in' as it were—as a bright dazzle, and exquisite haunting scent, a shape so formal and fine, so much a 'flower of the mind' that he who looks at it really is tempted for one bewildering moment to stoop & touch and make *sure*. The 'pairs' of people must be very different and there must be a slight touch of enchantment—some of them seeming so extraordinarily 'odd' and separate from the flowers, but others quite related and at ease. A kind of, musically speaking—conversation *set* to flowers.[24]

---

[21] VWD i. 265, 17 Apr. 1919.   [22] KMCL ii. 311, 10 Apr. 1919.
[23] Antony Alpers, *The Life of Katherine Mansfield* (New York: Viking, 1980), 251–2.   [24] KMCL i. 325, 15 Aug. 1917.

She says that, when she has time, she will 'have a fling at it' but the description fits the story that Woolf seems to have written as a result of receiving her letter. The weekend after she wrote the letters Mansfield stayed at Asheham, Woolf's house in Sussex; in her letter to Woolf thanking her for her hospitality she writes: 'Yes, your Flower Bed is *very* good. Theres a still, quivering, changing light over it all and a sense of those couples dissolving in the bright air which fascinates me'.[25] There is an ease about the letter, with a casual quotation from Wordsworth and a confidence that they are 'after so very nearly the same thing', that contrasts with the self-conscious and effusive tone of her letters to Ottoline Morrell. There seems to be no implication that Woolf had in any way plagiarized Mansfield's sketch for the story, but rather that Woolf's version, transposed from Garsington to Kew, demonstrated their affinity and may have been written as an experiment to be discussed during Mansfield's visit. Murry adds a footnote to his 1928 edition of Mansfield's letters saying that the 'Flower Bed' refers to Woolf's 'Kew Gardens'. At this time, Woolf was recovering slowly from a long period of mental illness, and her diary takes a new form when it recommences after two and a half years, in August 1917, two weeks before Mansfield's visit. She records brief but detailed observations of the countryside she walks through, with a hint that she has recently been beset by horror, a reminder of the way in which the liminar sees with startling clarity the familiar world to which she has returned. This observation was made while Mansfield was staying with her: 'Sat in the hollow; & found the caterpillar, now becoming a Chrysalis, wh. I saw the other day. A horrid sight: head turning from side to side, tail paralysed; brown colour, purple spots just visible; like a snake in movement. No mushrooms.'[26]

To transform this kind of naturalist's personal notebook into a piece of modernist fiction was clearly an imaginative leap for the writer, as was the movement from chronologically consecutive narrative to an impression with no narrative coherence. 'Kew Gardens' should perhaps be described as a post-impression as it has more in common with Van Gogh than Monet; the texture of the prose is something that Roger Fry recognized in

---

[25] Ibid. 327, 23 Aug. 1917.   [26] VWD i. 43, 19 Aug. 1917.

her writing, as she shows when she replies to him in response to his letter about 'The Mark on the Wall': 'I'm not sure that a perverted plastic sense doesn't somehow work itself out in words for me. I spent an hour looking at pots and carpets in the museums the other day, until the desire to describe them became like the desire for the lusts of the flesh.'[27] The plastic sense, and the density and texture of paint, are evident for the reader of 'Kew Gardens'; figures, grass, and flowers become colours:

Yellow and black, pink and snow white, shapes of all these colours, men, women and children, were spotted for a second upon the horizon, and then, seeing the breadth of yellow that lay upon the grass, they wavered and sought shade beneath the trees, dissolving like drops of water in the yellow and green atmosphere, staining it faintly with red and blue.[28]

A narrative version of this would state that, on a hot afternoon in the gardens, people avoid the sun-drenched expanses of grass and walk or sit under the trees, but that gives no visual sense of the scene, perceived perhaps by eyes dazzled by bright sunlight. The intensity of the focus is Expressionist; the colour is heightened and the object seen, for instance in the first paragraph of the story, is almost human, with veins, flesh, and heart- or tongue-shaped leaves. The sense of immanence is strong ('one expected them to burst'), as it is in Van Gogh's and sometimes in Cézanne's paintings:

The light fell either upon the smooth grey back of a pebble, or the shell of a snail with its brown circular veins, or, falling into a raindrop, it expanded with such intensity of red, blue and yellow the thin walls of water that one expected them to burst and disappear. Instead, the drop was left in a second silver grey once more, and the light now settled upon the flesh of a leaf, revealing the branching thread of fibre beneath the surface, and again it moved on and spread its illumination in the vast green spaces beneath the dome of the heart-shaped and tongue-shaped leaves.   (p. 90)

The snail's-eye view is maintained as one perspective but, as Mansfield says in her outline of the story, the people are 'separate from the flowers'. Readerly expectations point to a

---

[27] VWL ii. 285, 21 Oct. 1918.

[28] Virginia Woolf, *The Complete Shorter Fiction of Virginia Woolf* (London: Hogarth, 1989), 95. All future page refs. included in the text are to this edn.

convergence of the snail and the human view, but there is none. Nor do the human pairs link to make some kind of comment on life or gardens; as E. M. Forster says in his appreciative review of the story: 'It has no moral, no philosophy, nor has it what is usually understood by Form.'[29] Contemplation of the flower bed triggers memories or expectations in the people who look at it, four pairs, but their experiences are not linked in any other way; the only narrative concerns the snail's progress. Like Gulliver in Brobdignag, the snail is in an overpowering landscape, which to the human eye is composed of raindrops, grass blades and a dead leaf; liminal experience of being dazzled by a return to the known world pervades the writing, as Woolf tentatively recovers from severe disturbance: 'Brown cliffs with deep green lakes in the hollows, flat blade-like trees that waved from root to tip, round boulders of grey stone, vast crumpled surfaces of a thin crackling texture—all these objects lay across the snail's progress' (pp. 91–2). While the snail is perceived as having a human sense of purpose ('Before he had decided whether to circumvent the arched tent of a dead leaf', p. 92), the humans are described as if they were insects or flowers: 'They were both in the prime of youth, or even in that season which precedes the prime of youth, the season before the smooth pink folds of the flower have burst their gummy case, when the wings of the butterfly, though fully grown, are motionless in the sun' (p. 94). A deranged old man places the day in time by referring to 'this war', which explains the two women whose conversation seems to concern rationing: ' "Sugar, sugar, sugar" ' (p. 93). In her positive review of the story for the *Athenaeum*, Mansfield says: 'Anything may happen; her world is on tiptoe.'[30] The mood that is communicated could be seen as darker than this, in the context of the First World War: 'It seemed as if all gross and heavy bodies had sunk down in the heat motionless and lay huddled upon the ground' (p. 95) does not sound like people enjoying themselves in a park. The shift of perspective at the end is also, in an indefinable way, ominous; the lens of vision moves back from the sharp perception of the snail and

[29] Robin Majumdar and Allen McLaurin (eds.), *Virginia Woolf: The Critical Heritage* (London: Routledge & Kegan Paul, 1976), 69.
[30] Clare Hanson (ed.), *The Critical Writings of Katherine Mansfield* (London: Macmillan, 1987), 53.

from more familiar human observation to a panoramic shot which reduces individual human voices to sound, just as individual clothes have become part of a wash of colour:

Voices, yes, voices, wordless voices, breaking the silence suddenly with such depth of contentment, such passion of desire, or, in the voices of children, such freshness of surprise; breaking the silence? But there was no silence; all the time the motor omnibuses were turning their wheels and changing their gear; like a vast nest of Chinese boxes all of wrought steel turning ceaselessly one within another the city murmured; on the top of which the voices cried aloud and the petals of myriads of flowers flashed their colours into the air.   (ibid.)

This shifts from the texture of paint to a Constructivist image of machines within machines, noise within noise, reducing the incoherent but emotive sound of individual voices to part of the city's hum. It is a radical experiment in prose, a transition from the form of the two early novels to the mobile method of *Jacob's Room*.

The rite of passage in 'The Garden Party' is not the writer's but the character's; Laura's experience bewilders her, as Mansfield says in the letter quoted earlier (pp. 25–6): 'She feels things ought to happen differently. First one and then another. But life isn't like that. We haven't the ordering of it. Laura says, "But these things must not happen at once." And Life answers, "Why not? How are they divided from each other." And they *do* all happen, it is inevitable.'[31] The contradictory puzzle that Laura experiences is conveyed to the reader through the flexible, polyphonic narrative voice which expresses Laura's consciousness. Laura is adolescent, deeply influenced by the society of which she is a part and yet alert to other ways of seeing, with a voice of her own that occasionally asserts itself. Although one critic describes Laura's family as 'crass and disunited',[32] they in fact combine to protect their garden party from Laura's horrified feeling that it should be cancelled because a young carter who lived in the lane below the house has been killed. This is only reported halfway through the story. At first Laura's excitement is conveyed to the reader; we arrive, as so often in Mansfield's stories, *in medias res*, as if we know that the weather for the

---

[31] KML ii. 196, 13 Mar. 1922.
[32] Claire Tomalin, *Katherine Mansfield: A Secret Life* (London: Viking, 1987), 221.

garden party has been anxiously discussed: 'And after all the weather was ideal. They could not have had a more perfect day for a garden-party if they had ordered it' (p. 245). This family is in the habit of ordering what it wants, as we see later when two trays of canna lilies arrive and Laura has an almost orgasmic reaction to them: 'She crouched down as if to warm herself at that blaze of lilies; she felt they were in her fingers, on her lips, growing in her breast' (p. 249). Though the perception in the opening paragraph is Laura's, the language has been learned from her mother; the emphatic repetition and exaggeration are characteristic of Mrs Sheridan's speech when we meet her, though at this stage all the reader registers is the overblown prose: 'As for the roses, you could not help feeling they understand that roses are the only flowers that impress people at garden-parties; the only flowers that everybody is certain of knowing. Hundreds, yes, literally hundreds, had come out in a single night' (p. 245).

Laura's malleability gives the impression that she is about 16, constantly testing her own sense of the world against parental teaching: 'Laura's upbringing made her wonder for a moment whether it was quite respectful of a workman to talk to her of bangs slap in the eye' (p. 247). The narrative, full of questions, exclamations, and excited uncertainty is mirrored in her behaviour: ' "Good morning," she said, copying her mother's voice. But that sounded so fearfully affected that she was ashamed, and stammered like a little girl, "Oh—er—have you come—is it about the marquee?" ' (p. 246). She decides that she has 'silly boys' instead of workmen for friends because 'of these absurd class distinctions. Well, for her part, she didn't feel them. Not a bit, not an atom . . .' (pp. 247–8). The story so far has demonstrated that the reverse is true; she is so aware of social class that she is surprised that the workmen have ordinary human responses, like smelling lavender. The fluent revelation of Laura's consciousness anticipates the much more sombre conclusion to the story, where Laura reacts to the death of the carter.

Within the house, Laura listens to all the noises that convey bustle and anticipation. Her heightened consciousness transposes adjectives ('running voices') and comes to concentrate on a strange quasi-human sound:

She was still, listening. All the doors in the house seemed to be open. The house was alive with soft, quick steps and running voices. The green baize door that led to the kitchen regions swung open and shut with a muffled thud. And now there came a long, chuckling absurd sound. It was the heavy piano being moved on its stiff castors.

(p. 249)

The piano's self-importance is confirmed when Jose 'the butterfly' plays it, looking 'mournfully and enigmatically' at her mother and Laura and singing 'This Life is Weary':

But at the word 'Good-bye,' and although the piano sounded more desperate than ever, her face broke into a brilliant, dreadfully unsympathetic smile.
    'Aren't I in good voice, mummy?' she beamed.
    This Life is *Wee*-ary
    Hope comes to Die.
    A Dream—a *Wa*-kening. (p. 251)

As it does in 'Weak Heart' and *The Voyage Out*, the piano seems complicit with bourgeois hypocrisy; the despondent words of the song anticipate Laura's encounter with the carter's widow, her goodbye to her young husband, and desolation about her future, while Laura can only offer left-overs from the garden party. The frivolous snobbery of the Sheridan house is accentuated again when the cook, whose class is represented in her speech, invites the girls to have a cream puff and the girls snub her and have one:

'Have one each, my dears,' said cook in her comfortable voice. 'Yer ma won't know.'
    Oh, impossible. Fancy cream puffs so soon after breakfast. The very idea made one shudder. All the same, two minutes later Jose and Laura were licking their fingers with that absorbed inward look that only comes from whipped cream. (p. 252)

Everything about the Sheridan house is light and opulent, whipped cream and silver, in comparison with the lane in which the carter's family live; the Sheridan garden has roses and a lily-lawn, whereas garden patches in the lane sprout cabbage stalks and tomato cans. The description in the narrative of the houses in the lane is clearly the Sheridan view, exaggerated and supercilious with an implicit emphasis that sounds like Mrs Sheridan's voice:

True, they were far too near. They were the greatest possible eyesore and they had no right to be in that neighbourhood at all. They were mean little dwellings painted a chocolate brown. In the garden patches there was nothing but cabbage stalks, sick hens and tomato cans. The very smoke coming out of their chimneys was poverty-stricken. Little rags and shreds of smoke, so unlike the great silvery plumes that uncurled from the Sheridans' chimneys. (p. 254)

Laurie and Laura have walked through this forbidden territory because 'one must go everywhere' but they are repelled by it; again Mrs Sheridan's voice is audible in the terse sentence: 'Children swarmed.' The horror of the working class breeding like rabbits is inherent in this, and indeed the young carter proves his improvidence by accidentally getting killed and leaving a wife and five small children. Jose, whose eyes harden as she asserts her sympathy for the carter's family, immediately assumes that he was drunk, and therefore responsible for his own death, though the report of his death only mentioned that he had been thrown from his horse.

Tension between the two views of life, that have coexisted peacefully within Laura's mind at the beginning, arises when she hears of the carter's death and wants to cancel the party. Her mother's view of the loss of a party, and the expense that has gone into it, is evident when she misuses the term 'sacrifice': ' "People like that don't expect sacrifices from us" ' (p. 255). Her mother astutely plays on the aspect of family life that has been clear from the beginning, the image of themselves that the Sheridans project. She gives Laura her new hat; Laura returns to her bedroom: 'There, quite by chance, the first thing she saw was this charming girl in the mirror, in her black hat trimmed with gold daisies and a long black velvet ribbon' (p. 256). She is reclaimed by the material pleasures of the Sheridan world, its gold and velvet; her mother plays on adolescent vanity, and utilizes the 'duckling into swan' dimension for her own purposes, as Laura does not recognize herself at first in the charming girl in the mirror. She gives herself to the dream-like pleasures of the party, and to praise of her appearance: ' "I've never seen you look so striking" ' (p. 257). After the party, when Laura's father reminds them all of the dead carter ('Really, it was very tactless of father . . .', p. 258) her mother constructs another bourgeois role for Laura, by sending her off with a basket of scraps from the party in her party dress and new hat. She is aware of her image as she passes men in tweed caps and women in shawls.

Once she is in this unfamiliar territory she loses her middle-class control; other conventions take over and she cannot refuse to pay her respects to the dead, as the women in the carter's house assume she will do. She invokes mother, but that is powerless as other, rather voyeuristic, clichés overwhelm her: ' "You'd like a look at 'im, wouldn't you? . . . 'e looks a picture" ' (pp. 260–1). As Laura herself did earlier in the day, he does look a picture, and Laura constructs a narrative for him that reverses the fairy tale of Sleeping Beauty, except that the reader knows that this young man cannot be woken by a kiss:

There lay a young man, fast asleep—sleeping so soundly, so deeply, that he was far, far away from them both. Oh, so remote, so peaceful. He was dreaming. Never wake him up again. His head was sunk in the pillow, his eyes were closed; they were blind under the closed eyelids. He was given up to his dream . . . He was wonderful, beautiful . . . Happy . . . happy . . . All is well, said that sleeping face. This is just as it should be. I am content.   (p. 261)

This is evidently a rite of passage: a girl seeing a corpse for the first time and being surprised by its apparent tranquillity. Though she invents a fairy story to explain it to herself, and does not register the finality of what she is seeing, she recognizes to some extent her own betrayal of the dead man when she sobs child-ishly, ' "Forgive my hat" ' (ibid.). She is poised on the edge of a greater revelation when she meets her brother; as she cries and he comforts her, she tries to explain what has happened:

'It was simply marvellous. But, Laurie—' She stopped, she looked at her brother. 'Isn't life,' she stammered, 'isn't life—' But what life was she couldn't explain. No matter. He quite understood.

'*Isn't* it, darling?' said Laurie.   (ibid.)

This could be read as a significant transition for Laura from her mother's limited and class-bound view of the world to a release from boundaries, but Laura's assumption that Laurie quite understands is undercut for the reader by his response, which echoes so accurately what Mrs Sheridan would have said in the circumstances. We are taken back to the tone of the opening, with a perception that rites of passage are not easily achieved.

The fiction by Woolf and Mansfield concerning journeys and rites of passage explores what Kristeva describes as being strangers to ourselves, our own foreignness. It may arise from an extreme state; in Mansfield's case a horrified guilt that she invited her own penetration by tuberculosis, in Woolf's fear and shame about insanity. Extreme anxiety is evident in the fictional female pianists referred to in this chapter, in that they are the subjects of a prescribed and masculine musical language which might be described as a foreigner within, causing inner conflict. The voice of patriarchy speaks through them, despite their desire to escape it. They are tuned by a culture of patriarchy and reson-ate it, just as the piano itself is the product of a particular Western musical and industrial history. It is perhaps significant, fol-lowing the implicit link made between women and colonized subjects in some of the fictions discussed, that the piano is the one instrument not really absorbed and reworked by colonized people, possible because it is too strict, regulated, and expensive, too much a product of what is prized by patriarchy. The search for a form and narrative voice which will embody awareness of the foreigner within, and of the disintegration of a stable sense of identity, is described in the next two chapters.

6

A Single Day: 'At the Bay' and *Mrs Dalloway*

> They do not seek to imitate form, but to create form; not to imitate life, but to find an equivalent for life.[1]

IN a subtle article written in 1927 for the *Dial*, a Chicago magazine which published fiction by Mansfield and Woolf, the American poet Conrad Aitken observes that, in *Mrs Dalloway* and *To the Lighthouse*, Woolf writes 'as if she never for a moment wished us to forget the *frame* of the picture, and the fact that the picture *was* a picture.'[2] This insistence on the frame that draws attention to itself is of course familiar in the work of earlier modernist writers, in the narrator's introduction of Marlow's narrative in *Heart of Darkness* and in the title and structure of *A Portrait of the Artist as a Young Man* for example, but Woolf and Mansfield worked out their relationship to their own art very specifically through painters and painting. In 1921 Mansfield wrote to her young brother-in-law, Richard, who was about to become a student at the Slade School of Art, exploring the difference between art and life, and commenting on the upheavals that both art and life had experienced in recent years. Her emphasis is on a longing for technical knowledge which she sees as a 'deep sign of the times—rather the Zeitgeist—thats the better word.'[3] The implication is that the First World War has its parallel in the arts, though it began before 1914, and that, as Woolf says in her essays, the realism that was dynamic in the fiction of Dickens[4] has become an exhausted convention in both

---

[1] Roger Fry, *Vision and Design* (Harmondsworth: Penguin, 1937), 195.

[2] R. Majumdar and A. McLaurin (eds.), *Virginia Woolf: The Critical Heritage* (London: Routledge & Kegan Paul, 1975), 208.

[3] KMCL iv. 173, 3 Feb. 1921.

[4] Mansfield comments in a letter: 'Doesn't Charley Dickens make our little men smaller than ever—and such *pencil sharpeners!*', KMCL iv. 331, no date.

painting and writing in the early twentieth century. Having said that she has 'a passion for technique' Mansfield uses a curiously modern phrase to elucidate the difference between art and life: 'An aesthetic emotion is what we feel in front of *a work of art*— one doesn't feel an aesthetic emotion about a thing, but about its artistic representation.'[5] Here as elsewhere, she like Woolf is preoccupied by artistic representations of lived experience, but also by the search for forms which evoke an aesthetic emotion in the viewer, not a preconditioned response to familiar stereotypes. What Sydney Janet Kaplan writes of Mansfield resembles Aitken's observation about Woolf: 'Mansfield's practice . . . is deconstructive, in that it insists on interpreting all *constructions* as finally arbitrary, not as representations of the real.'[6] Linking her feeling about the impact of the First World War with the need for a shift in artistic perception and practice to accommodate it, which had to some extent begun before the war in the texts of Chekhov and Conrad, Mansfield complains to Murry in 1919 that she cannot tolerate Woolf's *Night and Day*, which she is attempting to review for the *Athenaeum*, and that novels like it 'will not do . . . Its not in the least a question of material or style or plot. I can only think in terms like "a change of heart". I cant imagine how after the war these men can pick up the old threads as tho' it had never been.'[7] The war transforms, through tragic knowledge, familiar reality, as the liminar's experience of the rite of passage transforms the things of ordinary life: 'they are intensified, they are illuminated.'[8]

The transformation of ordinary things that Mansfield felt was brought about by the war had been anticipated by seismic shifts in late nineteenth- and early twentieth-century painting; because of the professional involvement of Vanessa Bell and Roger Fry, Woolf was acutely aware of this. She asserts in her essay 'Mr. Bennett and Mrs. Brown' that human character changed 'in or about December, 1910.'[9] What altered was perception; the British public was able to see, for the first time in London,

---

[5] Ibid. 173, 3 Feb. 1921.
[6] Sydney Janet Kaplan, *Katherine Mansfield and the Origins of Modernist Fiction* (Ithaca, NY: Cornell University Press, 1991), 158.
[7] KMCL iii. 97, 16 Nov. 1919. [8] Ibid.
[9] Virginia Woolf, *The Captain's Death Bed and Other Essays* (London: Hogarth, 1950), 91.

the paintings Roger Fry brought together and called 'Manet and the Post-Impressionists'. Raymond Mortimer describes the exhibition as having

a success comparable to that of a knock-about farce. Rubicund clubmen in tall hats flocked to guffaw at the masterpieces of Cézanne; in front of paintings by Van Gogh and Matisse ladies in feather boas brandished angry parasols or broke into peals of carefully silvery laughter. Eminent physicians diagnosed the types of ophthalmia or insanity from which the painters must suffer; learned critics vied with ingenuous Academicians in the virulence of their abuse. But to a few young artists the show was a revelation.[10]

Among these young artists were Vanessa Bell, Woolf's sister, and Bell's partner, Duncan Grant. The kind of discussion the pictures provoked, and the writers' involvement in it, are indicated by a passage from Woolf's diary in 1918, when Maynard Keynes bought a painting by Cézanne:

There are 6 apples in the Cézanne picture. What can 6 apples *not* be? I began to wonder. Theres their relationship to each other, & their colour, & their solidity. To Roger & Nessa, moreover, it was a far more intricate question than this. It was a question of pure paint or mixed; if pure which colour: emerald or veridian; & then the laying on of the paint; & the time he'd spent, & how he'd altered it, & why, & when he'd painted it—We carried it into the next room, & Lord! how it showed up the pictures there, as if you put a real stone among sham ones; the canvas of the others seemed scraped with a thin layer of rather cheap paint. The apples positively got redder & rounder & greener.[11]

Woolf's bemused query about the significance of the apples shows the speculative imagination and intelligence that were later to reject the idea of one symbolic meaning for the lighthouse when Fry questioned her about *To the Lighthouse*, and it also suggests that she, at least, experiences Cézanne's modernism as a state of liminality, with his shapes hovering between the canvas surface and an illusory three dimensional reality and solidity. Woolf's fascination with her friends' responses to the painting stems from their obsession with their craft: with the texture of the picture and the density of the paint, the brushwork, and the time and

---

[10] Raymond Mortimer, *Duncan Grant* (Harmondsworth: Penguin, 1944), 5.
[11] VWD i. 140–1, 18 Apr. 1918.

meticulous care taken to realize the potential of six apples. Her image of the picture as a real stone suggests her sense of the painting's *gravitas* and presence in spite of its ephemeral subject. What obsessed Fry, Grant, and Bell about Cézanne's picture was its form: that the Post-Impressionist painters, especially perhaps Cézanne and Van Gogh, moved away from what Fry calls 'descriptive imitation' to something new, just as such poets as T. S. Eliot were fragmenting what had come to seem 'natural' poetic forms and, in Eliot's phrase, dislocating them into meaning. In the preface to the Catalogue of the second Post-Impressionist Exhibition, in 1912, Fry defines the assertive 'thisness' of the paintings: 'They do not seek to imitate form, but to create form; not to imitate life, but to find an equivalent for life . . . In fact, they aim not at illusion but at reality.'[12] This is not realism but a heightening of people or objects to give an experience equivalent to the impact made by people or objects in life. That was precisely how Van Gogh's paintings affected Mansfield; remembering the first Post-Impressionist Exhibition, eleven years later, she writes of it to her painter friend, Brett:

Yellow flowers—brimming with sun in a pot . . . That picture seemed to reveal something that I hadn't realised before I saw it. It lived with me afterwards. It still does—that & another of a sea captain in a flat cap. They taught me something about writing, which was queer—a kind of freedom—or rather, a shaking free . . . It is—literally—years since I have been to a picture show. I can *smell* them as I write.[13]

That Mansfield experienced the picture as she would something out of doors, and says that she can smell Van Gogh's sunflowers as she writes, makes Fry's point about this art as an equivalent for life, appealing to the viewer's imagination with the vividness of lived experience. The sense of liberation resonates in Mansfield's prose a decade after the event, conveying the power the exhibition had for those who did not feel inclined to brandish their parasols.

John Middleton Murry and Leonard Woolf were both actively involved with the exhibitions, Woolf as secretary to the second exhibition, Murry as critic and defender through his magazine

---

[12] Fry, *Vision and Design*, 195.
[13] KMCL iv. 333, 5 Dec. 1921.

Rhythm. Murry and Mansfield also befriended and supported the young French sculptor Henri Gaudier-Brzeska, who rejected the lack of engagement with the stone involved in using casts, the lost-wax technique, and returned to the classical practice of sculpting in stone; Fry argues that the Post-Impressionist painters are also in a classical rather than a romantic tradition. Gaudier put his creative energy into carving the object which became the equivalent of life; so much so that, when Gaudier turned against Murry, he said that he was going to ' "knock Murry's block off" '[14] but smashed the head of Murry that he had been working on by throwing bricks at it. Many of Virginia Woolf's most intimate relationships were with painters, especially Vanessa Bell, Duncan Grant, and Roger Fry; she and Vanessa Bell 'appeared as "indecent" Gauguin girls at the Post-Impressionist Ball, half-dressed in brightly coloured stuffs'.[15] The painters' constant debates about form and texture influenced her thinking, as their artefacts surrounded her. Her house in Sussex was full of their paintings as well as pottery, furniture, and fabrics from the Omega Workshops, founded by Roger Fry in 1913. Similarly some of Mansfield's most vibrant relationships were with painters: Dorothy Brett, a friend and contemporary at the Slade of Mark Gertler and Dora Carrington; Anne Estelle Rice, an Irish-American who painted Mansfield's portrait; and J. D. Fergusson, the Scottish painter who was a witness at Mansfield and Murry's wedding. Mansfield's account of a visit to Fergusson's studio in 1918 is almost like a description of a painting by him; he was an impressionable painter and had a cubist phase: 'The sun came full through the two windows, dividing the studio into four—two quarters of light and two of shadow, but all those things which the light touched seemed to float in it, to bathe and to sparkle in it as if they belonged not to land, but to water; they even seemed, in some strange way, to be moving.'[16] Cézanne is not far off: 'Very beautiful, O God! is a blue tea-pot with two white cups attending; a red apple among oranges addeth fire to flame'.[17] Similarly in 1917 Mansfield writes to Brett about her painting: 'What can one do, faced with this wonderful tumble

---

[14] A. Alpers, *The Life of Katherine Mansfield* (New York: Viking, 1980), 159.
[15] H. Lee, *Virginia Woolf* (London: Chatto & Windus, 1996), 291.
[16] KMJ 132, 25 Apr. 1918.   [17] Ibid.

of round bright fruits, but gather them and play with them—
and *become them*, as it were.'[18]

Gathering and playing with the fruits is a frisky, conversational indication of Mansfield's awareness of the significance
of form for Cézanne and the painters he influenced. In a long
letter to Brett written in Switzerland at the time that she was
writing 'At the Bay', Mansfield thanks her for lending her a book
on Cézanne: 'One of his men gave me quite a shock. He is the
spit of a man Ive just written about—one Jonathan Trout. To
the life. I wish I could cut him out & put him in my book.'[19]
In the same letter she criticizes in detail the composition of
one of Brett's paintings; Brett had sent her a photograph of it.
What Mansfield writes reveals as much about the aesthetic to
which she aspires in writing as it does about her understanding
of Post-Impressionism: 'All must be smooth. No *novelty*, no
appearance of effort. Thats the secret.'[20] The painstaking way
in which Cézanne composed his still lifes, for instance putting
a coin under a jug to place it at a tiny angle, destabilizing the
potential tranquillity of the composition, exemplifies a preoccupation with design that Mansfield and Woolf entirely understood and shared. This chapter focuses on 'At the Bay' and *Mrs
Dalloway*, because both take place in a single day and pivot
on liminal experience, requiring a structure that accommodates
the uncertainties of liminality. The writers' obsession with the
form of their fiction is explored in the context of changes in
the visual arts as, for both of them, looking at painting and
talking with painters provided routes into modernity. In writing, their expression of modernity was the form and narrative
voice that allowed the reader to experience the destabilizing of
the symbolic order, creating not imitating the life of human consciousness. Woolf's diary entry as she is coming to the end of
Mrs Dalloway shows an almost architectural but also musical
sense of shape:

[18] KMCL i. 330, 11 Oct. 1917.
[19] KMCL iv. 278, 12 Sept. 1921, Vincent O'Sullivan in the note to this letter
assumes that what 'KM has in mind is probably the figure on the right in Cézanne's
painting *The Card Players* (1892)'. However, I have an irrational conviction that
she was referring to the painting called both 'Man with Crossed Arms' and 'The
Clockmaker', *c*.1899, now in the Solomon Guggenheim Museum in New York.
[20] Ibid.

There I am now—at last at the party, which is to begin in the kitchen, & climb slowly upstairs. It is to be a most complicated spirited solid piece, knitting together everything & ending on three notes, at different stages of the staircase, each saying something to sum up Clarissa . . . Suppose one can keep the quality of a sketch in a finished and composed work?[21]

Mansfield's vehement response to a request from the publisher Michael Sadleir, at Constable, that she should alter the text of her story '*Je ne parle pas français*' is a measure of her ownership of the form of her stories. In a letter to Murry she indicates, in a vivid metaphor, that the story is a living entity for her:

No, I certainly won't agree to those excisions if there were 500000000 copies in existence. They can keep their old £40 & be hanged to them. Shall I pick the eyes out of a story for £40. Im *furious* with Sadler [*sic*]. No, Ill never agree. Ill supply another story but that is all. The *outline* would be all blurred. It must have those sharp lines.[22]

In a self-deprecating and poignant letter to Murry about their yearned-for but non-existent child she mocks her own obsession with structure: 'I hope I wont say to our darling little boy "As long as your mud-pies have *form*, darling, you can make them. But there must be no slopping over the mould." '[23]

One of the most striking aspects of the work of the Post-Impressionist painters exhibited in London in 1910 and 1912 was their practice of revisiting the same subject-matter in different lights. Whether he was painting still lifes, portraits, landscapes, or imaginary scenes, Cézanne returned to the same subjects: apples and jugs; his wife; Mont Sainte-Victoire; the bathers. Yet the apples are never the same; they are sometimes vibrant and glowing, like those Woolf describes, but at other times are muted, in subdued light, the paint scraped thinly. Sometimes the table seems tipped and the fruit about to topple; sometimes the domestic scene is stable and full of repose. The paintings communicate a mood to the viewer; objects are not just replicated but, as Fry says, these painters 'make images which by the clearness of their logical structure, and by their closely-knit unity of texture . . . appeal to our disinterested and

---

[21] VWD ii. 312, 7 Sept. 1924. [22] KMCL iii. 273, 6 Apr. 1920.
[23] Ibid. 7, 4 Oct. 1919.

contemplative imagination with something of the same vividness as the things of actual life appeal to our practical activities.'[24] 'Still-life' passages in the fiction of Mansfield and of Woolf are similarly charged, conveying both an image of the fruit and the mood of the perceiver. In 'Bliss', Bertha is preparing for a dinner party, placing fruit in a glass bowl and a blue dish:

There were some tangerines and apples stained with strawberry pink. Some yellow pears, smooth as silk, some white grapes covered with a silver bloom and a big cluster of purple ones . . . When she had finished with them and had made two pyramids of these bright round shapes, she stood away from the table to get the effect—and it really was most curious. For the dark table seemed to melt into the dusky light and the glass dish and the blue bowl to float in the air.[25]

These fruits are the equivalent of Cézanne's apples and oranges that are about to topple; their sensuous colour and disembodied intensity convey a sense that something is about to happen to the woman creating a picture by making a composition of the fruit. When Mrs Ramsay looks at the fruit bowl at her dinner party in *To the Lighthouse* her own middle-aged pilgrimage is suggested by 'take one's staff', but the fruit can also be seen as Rose's tribute to her mother's fecundity, and to her mother's role in creating a world for the children to inhabit. That Mrs Ramsay views it as a trophy from the seabed hints at the pre-Oedipal bond between mother and daughter, which can only be represented emblematically. There are eight children, as there are eight candles, all flickering into sexual and social awareness:

Now eight candles were.stood down the table, and after the first stoop the flames stood upright and drew with them into visibility the long table entire, and in the middle a yellow and purple dish of fruit. What had she done with it, Mrs Ramsay wondered, for Rose's arrangement of the grapes and pears, of the horny pink-lined shell, of the bananas, made her think of a trophy fetched from the bottom of the sea . . . Thus brought up suddenly into the light it seemed possessed of great size and depth, was like a world in which one could take one's staff and climb up hills, she thought, and go down into valleys.[26]

[24] Fry, *Vision and Design*, 195.   [25] CS 92–3.
[26] Virginia Woolf, *To the Lighthouse* (Oxford: Oxford University Press, 1992), 131.

Roger Fry, in a review of an exhibition in 1919 for the *Athenaeum* when John Middleton Murry was its editor, makes a direct comparison between Woolf's writing and contemporary developments in painting. Having described a French painting he writes: 'I see, now that I have done it, that it was meant for Mrs Virginia Woolf—that Survage is almost precisely the same thing in paint that Mrs Virginia Woolf is in prose.'[27] Language in the fiction of both Mansfield and Woolf is used to convey texture; Woolf describes a conversation about writing and painting that she had with Roger Fry: 'Roger asked me if I founded my writing upon texture or upon structure; I connected structure with plot, & therefore said "texture". Then we discussed the meaning of structure & texture in painting & in writing.'[28] Woolf says of Mansfield that she had 'the most amazing *senses* of her generation so that she could actually reproduce this room',[29] and refers enviously to 'that direct flick at the thing seen which was her gift'.[30] The 'flick at the thing' is what Mansfield experiences as 'the moment when you are *more* duck, *more* apple . . . than any of these objects could ever possibly be, and so you *create* them anew.'[31] The moment of identification, for writer or reader, painter or viewer, is paradoxically one of a heightened sense of the self, and of the inwardness but essential otherness of the thing perceived, its inscape, to use Gerard Manley Hopkins's word.

The literary equivalent of the painting Woolf and Mansfield admired was not, for them, to be found among anglophone writers; both complain in their letters and diaries, and less overtly in their reviews and essays, of the tedium of the fiction they have to review. The enigmatic quality of Cézanne's and Gauguin's painting finds its counterpart, for Woolf and Mansfield, in the Russian fiction that appeared in translation when they were in the closest phase of their friendship. Mansfield was reviewing Dostoevsky's stories at the same time as she reviewed *Night and Day*; both she and Woolf were friends of Koteliansky and collaborated with him in translating Russian texts. In a note added to a letter Mansfield sent to Woolf in May 1919 she writes: 'Tchekhov has a very interesting letter published in next week's

[27] Majumdar and McLaurin (eds.), *Virginia Woolf: The Critical Heritage*, 71.
[28] VWD i. 80, 22 Nov. 1917.   [29] VWL iii. 59, 30 July 1923.
[30] VWD iv. 315, 26 May 1935.   [31] KMCL i. 330, 11 Oct. 1917.

A . . . what the writer does is not so much to *solve* the question but to *put* the question.'[32] Cézanne, Van Gogh, and Gauguin put questions partly by eschewing both realism and the emphasis on narrative that was characteristic of Victorian and Edwardian British painting, from the Pre-Raphaelites, Frith, and Augustus Egg to Leighton, Sargent, and Beardsley.

The avoidance of closure in Chekhov's stories tantalized and intrigued both Woolf and Mansfield; Woolf asks, in her essay entitled 'Tchekhov's Questions', whether he found no connecting link which would provide a harmonious arrangement in his stories: 'It is difficult not to ask that question, and the very fineness and delicacy of Tchekhov's mind make it unusually difficult to be sure of an answer. He seems able with one tap to split asunder those emotions that we have been wont to think whole and entire, leaving them scattered about in small disconnected splinters.'[33]

In her essay 'Modern Fiction' Woolf comments on 'the inconclusiveness of the Russian mind. It is the sense that there is no answer, that if honestly examined life presents question after question which must be left to sound on and on after the story is over'.[34] During their intense discussions of fiction and new forms for new perceptions Woolf and Mansfield recurred to the question of the question, related to the form of fiction; Woolf's account of one of these conversations (referred to on p. 61) suggests the awareness and energy required to become either the apple or the question: 'I said how my own character seemed to cut out a shape like a shadow in front of me. This she understood . . . & proved it by telling me that she thought this bad: one ought to merge into things.'[35] Both writers constantly repeat in different ways in their journals, letters, essays, and reviews, the theme that art is not about solving problems but of finding an equivalent for life, as Mansfield does in a letter to Brett:

Tchekhov *said* over and over again, he protested, he begged, that he had no problem . . . And, when you come to think of it what was

---

[32] Ibid. ii. 320, 27 May 1919.
[33] Andrew McNeillie (ed.), *The Essays of Virginia Woolf* (London: Hogarth, 1987), ii. 246–7.
[34] Virginia Woolf, *The Common Reader* (London: Hogarth, 1962), i. 195.
[35] VWD ii. 61–2, 25 Aug. 1920.

Chaucer's problem or Shakespeare's? The 'problem' is the invention of the 19th century. The artist takes a *long look* at Life. He says softly, 'So this is what life is, is it?' And he proceeds to express that.[36]

The influence on Woolf of her relationship with Mansfield is evident not only from the ways in which she records their meetings, but also from the major shift in her fiction at the time when she is in regular contact with Mansfield and her work, including typesetting 'Prelude'. She remembers her own dissatisfaction with the form of her fiction at that time in a letter written in 1930 to the composer Ethel Smyth quoted earlier; she wrote *Night and Day* in a state of terror 'tremblingly afraid of my own insanity',[37] and so she 'made myself copy from plaster casts', presumably conventional forms of Edwardian fiction. She describes how she wrote 'The Mark on the Wall' 'all in a flash, as if flying, after being kept stone breaking for months'; this was the story that Mansfield told her she liked tremendously. The sense of discovery and revelation is relived in the letter to Smyth: 'The Unwritten Novel was the great discovery, however. That—again in one second—showed me how I could embody all my deposit of experience in a shape that fitted it'.[38] After the old stable ego, as D. H. Lawrence terms it, of the characters in Woolf's early stories such as 'Phyllis and Rosamond' and 'The Journal of Mistress Joan Martyn', where furniture and clothes are adjuncts to character, the mark on the wall, like the flowers in 'Kew Gardens', takes on the role traditionally assigned to a character. It is the pivot of the story, but all the conventional narrative developments suggested by it are considered by the narrator and rejected, implicitly also rejecting her earlier stories: 'But how dull this is, this historical fiction! It doesn't interest me at all.'[39] The story moves on to speculate about the construction of the self, the fictions that we create for ourselves to look into so that we are not simply 'that shell of a person which is seen by other people'; if we are only what is seen by others 'what an airless, shallow, bald, prominent world it becomes!' The narrator suggests that the business of fiction is to enquire into our images of ourselves, multiple selves as she implies in 'depths':

[36] KMCl iv. 317, 11 Nov. 1921.   [37] VWL iv. 231, 16 Oct. 1930.
[38] Ibid.
[39] Virginia Woolf, *Complete Shorter Fiction of Virginia Woolf* (London: Hogarth, 1989), 85.

And the novelists in future will realise more and more the importance of these reflections, for of course there is not one reflection but an almost infinite number; those are the depths they will explore, those the phantoms they will pursue, leaving the description of reality more and more out of their stories, taking a knowledge of it for granted.[40]

By reality she suggests she means that ordered regime by which bourgeois life was paced, 'Sunday afternoon walks, Sunday luncheons, also ways of speaking of the dead, clothes and habits . . . real standard things'. These things had imposed a pattern on fiction that curtailed imaginative freedom; another way of saying it might be that realism had fossilized into a modality that prevented it from finding an equivalent for reality, for life. 'The Mark on the Wall' signals a new fictional direction for Woolf, in which external reality is not subsumed by character but is a marker of difference: 'Thus, waking from a midnight dream of horror, one hastily turns on the light and lies quiescent, worshipping the chest of drawers, worshipping solidity, worshipping reality, worshipping the impersonal world which is proof of some existence other than ours.'[41]

Writing a few weeks before her suicide, Woolf recalls one of the few anglophone writers whose work seemed to her and to Mansfield indecent but significant; Woolf and her husband had been offered for publication the manuscript of Joyce's *Ulysses*: 'One day Katherine Mansfield came, & I had it out. She began to read, ridiculing: then suddenly said, But theres something in this'.[42] Woolf was reading *Ulysses* while she wrote *Mrs Dalloway*, after Mansfield's death, in 1923, and was interested as well as snobbishly repelled by it; it is not surprising that she was stimulated by it as both novels search for a form which provides an equivalent for, rather than an imitation of, life, pursuing the inner lives of a group of people on an ordinary day. Woolf's excited description of having found her method as she writes *Mrs Dalloway* indicates her interest in the interaction between surface reality and the psyche: 'how I dig out beautiful caves behind my characters; I think that gives exactly what I want; humanity, humour, depth. The idea is that the caves shall connect, & each comes to daylight at the present moment'.[43]

[40] Ibid. 85–6.   [41] Ibid. 88.   [42] VWD v. 353, 15 Jan. 1941.
[43] Ibid. ii. 263, 30 Aug. 1923.

What this may mean is that linguistic motifs link several of the characters, suggesting psychic comparisons within social, situational, and gender difference, such as the phrase from *Cymbeline* that echoes in the minds of both Septimus Warren Smith and Mrs Dalloway, 'Fear no more.' Similarly the day after Mansfield finished 'At the Bay' she wrote to Brett about the recreation of remembered sensuous experience but at the same time 'one tries to go deep—to speak to the secret self we all have'.[44] Again, the secret selves of the characters in 'At the Bay' are revealed on an ordinary day, and the revelation comes, as it does with Joyce's and Woolf's characters, through a constant interplay between past and present. Using the same cave metaphor as Woolf, in a review of Dorothy Richardson's *The Tunnel*, Mansfield describes what she sees in 1919 as the quasi-moral function of memory:

Life is sometimes very swift and breathless, but not always. If we are to be truly alive there are large pauses in which we creep away into our caves of contemplation. And then it is, in the silence, that Memory mounts his throne and judges all that is in our minds . . . putting this one to shine in the light and throwing that one into the darkness.[45]

In a letter in which she comments on having finished the proofs of her new book, which contained 'At the Bay', 'The Voyage', and 'The Garden Party', Mansfield uses images of metamorphosis: 'Its been like getting back into the skin one had sloughed off. Not at all the skin I thought it, either.'[46] The trope is suggestive of her writing process, getting into the skin of the past, not just remembering it nostalgically. In the same letter she remarks that she wants 'to live in the past, present and future all at one and the same time'.[47] That interaction, and its formal representation, preoccupied Woolf as she wrote *Mrs Dalloway*, groping for a structure that would express the interplay of past and present, and of the conscious and the unconscious mind: 'I think the design is more remarkable than in any of my books . . . It took me a year's groping to discover what I call my tunnelling process, by

---

[44] KMCL iv. 278, 12 Sept. 1921.
[45] C. Hanson (ed.), *The Critical Writings of Katherine Mansfield* (London: Macmillan, 1987), 12.   [46] KMCL iv. 328, 3 Dec. 1921.
[47] Ibid.

which I tell the past by instalments, as I have need of it . . . One feels about in a state of misery—. . . & then one touches the hidden spring.'[48] The language of sexual frustration and fulfilled desire reveals the significance of the process for her; often in the diaries at this stage in her life she uses tropes that suggest male probing and exploration of virgin land, but she casts herself in the male role, as the agent of penetration, a parallel to Mansfield's trope of the caves inhabited by seaweed gatherers and the controlling 'masculine' self apart in the carriage. 'The Hours' was the working title for what became *Mrs Dalloway*:

> I'm working at The Hours, & think it a very interesting attempt; I may have found my mine this time I think. I may get all my gold out . . . And my vein of gold lies so deep, in such bent channels. To get it I must forge ahead, stoop & grope. But it is gold of a kind I think.[49]

Mining for deep deposits of gold is, of course, a dangerous process; in writing 'At the Bay' and *Mrs Dalloway* the two writers were in rich but precarious territory. Working on 'At the Bay' Mansfield tells Brett that she 'feels *possessed*', and that, in recreating the lost world of childhood, 'I efface myself so that you [her family] may live again through me'.[50] The story enacts the ordinary story of extraordinary childhood terror: the recognition of parental betrayal. Within a couple of months of finishing 'At the Bay', during which she was in a state of collapse and only pretending to write, Mansfield sent a letter to her father apologizing for and explaining her long silence. It suggests what her state of mind has been, as a result of getting into the skin of the children in 'At the Bay' who felt they had been abandoned by their fathers. She had described her own role as masculine and Christlike: 'It is so strange to bring the dead to life again.'[51] Now, in reaction to her own temerity, she writes to Harold Beauchamp as if he were God the Father. The words of the General Confession from *The Book of Common Prayer*, which would have been deeply familiar to Mansfield as a child, seem to underpin the letter, with an ominously literal interpretation for her of the metaphorical phrase 'there is no health in us'. The prayer reads like this:

---

[48] VWD ii. 272, 15 Oct. 1923.
[50] KMCL iv. 278, 12 Sept. 1921.

[49] Ibid. 292, 9 Feb. 1924.
[51] Ibid.

Almighty and most merciful Father; We have erred, and strayed from thy ways like lost sheep. We have followed too much the devices and desires of our own hearts. We have offended against thy holy laws. We have left undone those things which we ought to have done; And we have done those things which we ought not to have done; And there is no health in us. But thou, O Lord, have mercy upon us, miserable offenders. Spare thou them, O God, which confess their faults. Restore thou them that are penitent.[52]

Mansfield's prayer for forgiveness acknowledges her father's power, and that she is not fit to approach him; the parable of the Prodigal Son, returning and asking forgiveness while admitting that he is no longer worthy to be called his father's son also underlies her plea, which encodes abjection. She is caught in a rejection of her writing self; as Kristeva describes it, with an antipodean simile, in abjection 'like an inescapable boomerang, a vortex of summons and repulsion places the one haunted by it literally beside himself.'[53] Mansfield pleads:

I must get over this fear of writing to you because I have not written for so long. I am ashamed to ask for your forgiveness and yet how can I approach you without it? Every single day I think and wonder how I can explain my silence. I cannot tell you how often I dream of you. Sometimes night after night I dream that I am back in New Zealand and sometimes you are angry with me . . . My heart is full of you. But the past rises before me, when I have promised not to do this very thing that I have done [we have done those things which we ought not to have done].[54]

The terror induced by having reversed the biological role of the father, and created him and his family in her text, reduces her to infancy, or at least to adolescence. The overt subject of the letter concerns her father's allowance to her, and his reluctance to provide for her as she has a husband who should be doing it, but the thrust of it, with its warning that he has not got long to make up his mind, is that she wants to be forgiven and restored to her secure place in the love of the Father who should restore to grace them that are penitent:

---

[52] The Book of Common Prayer, order for Morning Prayer.
[53] Julia Kristeva, *Powers of Horror* (New York: Columbia University Press, 1982), 1.   [54] KMCL iv. 306, 1 Nov. 1921.

Of course I appreciate your great generosity in allowing me so much money. And I know it is only because I am ill in the way I am that you are doing so. But it is highly unlikely that I shall live very long and consumption is a terribly expensive illness. I thought that you did not mind looking after me to this extent. And to feel that you did— was like a blow to me—I couldn't get over it. I feel as though I didn't belong to you, really . . . One does turn to ones father however old one is. Had I forfeited the right to do so? Perhaps . . . There is no reason, Father dear, that you should go on loving me through thick and thin. I see that. And I have been an extraordinarily unsatisfactory and disappointing child.[55]

The letter ends with overtly biblical language, as the writer says that 'it seemed to me my sin of silence was too great to beg forgiveness' but that now 'I must come to you and at least acknowledge my fault. I must at least tell you . . . that never for a moment, in my folly and my fear, have I ceased to love you and to honour you.' The impression that she has entered liminal space, abjection, is strong in this. Mansfield's own creativity in bringing the dead back to life has challenged her father's role but that temerity in turn reduces her to fever and helplessness. The sense of being haunted in the phrase 'the past rises before me' has none of the joy of ' "you are not dead, my darlings" '. In another image that suggests being shut in alien territory she says that what she has done is 'like a wall that I cant see over', again seeming to picture herself as a small child.

In an entry in her diary in which she describes being 'in the thick of the mad scene in Regents Park',[56] which was obviously one of the most dangerous parts of *Mrs Dalloway* for her to write as it drew on her own most terrifying experiences, Woolf comments:

I meant to record for psychological purposes that strange night when I went to meet Leonard & did not meet him. What an intensity of feeling was pressed into those hours! It was a wet windy night; & as I walked back across the field I said Now I am meeting it; now the old devil has once more got his spine through the waves. (but I cannot re-capture really). And such was the strength of my feeling that I became physically rigid. Reality, so I thought, was unveiled . . . I battled . . . Saw men & women walking together; thought, you're safe & happy I'm an outcast.[57]

---

[55] Ibid. 306–7.   [56] VWD ii. 272, 15 Oct. 1923.   [57] Ibid. 270.

The image of being alone in the unlit dark, an abject, at the time that she is entering Septimus Warren Smith's skin reveals the cost of the fiction; Septimus in the park moves into the liminal space between the living, Rezia, and the dead, Evans, and is maddened by it. To enter his psyche Woolf has to relive the experience herself; she ends the passage with the comment that 'it became connected with the deaths of the miners, & with Aubrey Herbert's death the next day',[58] showing that she thinks of her encounter with the 'old devil' as a 'death-in-life' moment.

One of the formal experiments made by both Woolf and Mansfield was to substitute a story cycle for the novel form. Their reasons for doing it differed; Mansfield was too ill to withstand the physical strain of writing a novel and Woolf wanted to escape from the tyranny of the structure she chose for her first two novels. The reader is drawn into a different relationship with the texts from that established by a novel; the apparently random fact that Mrs Dalloway appears in a series of stories as she did in *The Voyage Out* surprises the reader and poses the kind of question that Woolf asked of Chekhov's stories: whether there is a connecting link between the stories which will provide a harmonious arrangement of them. As with Chekhov's stories, there is no one obvious answer, though several can be suggested, but the links lie in the reader's perception of them. There is no evident theme with variations as there is with paralysis in Joyce's *Dubliners*. Mansfield wrote two cycles, the first of which she hoped to turn into a novel, *Karori*; this focuses on the Burnell family and includes 'Prelude', 'At the Bay', and 'The Doll's House'. The second centres on the Sheridan family who appear in 'The Garden Party', 'Her First Ball', 'By Moonlight', and 'The Sheridans'. The painful word that Mansfield uses to describe the stories implies the physical stress she endured in writing them:

I must begin writing for Clement Shorter today 12 'spasms' of 2,000 words each. I thought of the Burnells, but no, I don't think so. Much better, the Sheridans . . . what I want to stress chiefly is: Which is the real life—that or this?—late afternoon, these thoughts—the garden —the beauty—how all things pass—and how the end seems to come so soon . . . What is it that stirs one so? What is this seeking—so joyful—ah, so gentle! And there seems to be a moment when all is to be discovered.[59]

The interaction between the glinting evanescence of the mortal world and the inner self on the verge of an epiphany comes close to Cézanne and Woolf, but does not provide a tidy thematic link; attempts to impose such a straitjacket on Mansfield's stories usually distort as much as they illuminate, as with this brisk account: 'Broadly speaking, the Burnell sequence is concerned with the difficulties of the child or young adult coming to terms with the brutal realities of life (the egotism and cruelty of other people, the pressures of sexuality and so on).'[60] Another attempt, describing 'Prelude', is even more skewed: 'it revolves around the Burnells' destructive marriage that turns the pastoral setting of the story into a battlefield for a sexual guerrilla war, scarcely apprehended by the maimed combatants for what it is.'[61]

What happens in 'At the Bay' is that constructions of human experience such as these are subjected to scrutiny and revealed as inadequate; like Chekhov in Woolf's description of his method, Mansfield 'seems able with one tap to split asunder those emotions that we have been wont to think whole and entire, leaving them scattered about in small disconnected splinters.' The story is full of contradictory representations of the self, several of which indicate the character's aspirations or fantasy life. The comic disconnection between Mrs Stubbs's actual appearance and her photograph foregrounds this for the reader. 'She looked like a friendly brigand'[62] when she comes to the door with her bacon knife in her hand; she runs a general store. However the style of the photograph she has had taken reveals that she has a romantic, and possibly imperial, notion of her own potentialities:

Mrs Stubbs sat in an arm-chair, leaning very much to one side. There was a look of mild astonishment on her large face, and well there might be. For though the arm-chair stood on a carpet, to the left of it, miraculously skirting the carpet border, there was a dashing waterfall.

---

[59] KMJ 313–14, 3 May 1922.
[60] C. Hanson and A. Gurr, *Katherine Mansfield* (London: Macmillan, 1981), 20.
[61] Kate Fulbrook, *Katherine Mansfield* (Brighton: Harvester, 1986), 85.
[62] CS 229. All future refs. in the text will be taken from this edn.

On her right stood a Grecian pillar with a giant fern tree on either side of it, and in the background towered a gaunt mountain, pale with snow.   (p. 230)

While Mrs Stubbs is portrayed as a kind of New Zealand equivalent of Queen Victoria, with a tree fern and waterfall to suggest nationality, the late Mr Stubbs appears in an even more startling manifestation. Husband and wife shared an admiration for size, and so his photograph is as large as he was:

'That's 'im!' said Mrs. Stubbs, and she pointed dramatically to the life-size head and shoulders of a burly man with a dead white rose in the button-hole of his coat that made you think of a curl of cold mutton fat. Just below, in silver letters on a red cardboard ground, were the words, 'Be not afraid, it is I.'   (p. 231)

Mr Stubbs seems to be resurrected from the dead as Christ, using the words spoken to the disciples when he walked on the water,[63] but this Good Shepherd has a macabre curl of mutton fat in his lapel. The disconnections between Mr Stubbs's meaty appearance and his spiritual aspirations, and between the substantial presence of the photograph and the absence that is relished by his widow, are part of the process of splitting asunder for the reader, showing gaps between scripting the self and a much more slippery reality. The analogy with the painting that influenced the writers' perception is clear; Picasso's cubist portraits at this period use a variety of masks and overlapping planes to represent the sitter.[64]

Colonial aspirations to gentility and status are mocked in both photographs, but these are comic exaggerations of social constructions that most of the characters are influenced by. Mr and Mrs Stubbs are choosing their parts, and playing them in circumstances which are licensed by colonial social convention, however grotesque. Running through the story, in its polyphonic narrative, are suggestions that characters have written their own scripts and are trying to play the parts they have devised for

---

[63] Matthew 14: 27.

[64] Anna Gruetzner Robins, *Modern Art in Britain 1910–1914* (London: Merrell Holberton, 1997), lists the paintings by Monet, Cézanne, Picasso, etc. shown in the two Post-Impressionist exhibitions and demonstrates their influence on British painting of the period. Picasso's *Woman and Mustard Pot*, for instance, was part of the Second Post-Impressionist Exhibition.

themselves. When we first meet Stanley Burnell he is rushing to the sea to bathe: 'Stanley Burnell waded out exulting. First man in as usual! He'd beaten them all again' (p. 208). The perspective is clearly his, but it is wrong; someone playing a comically rhetorical part has beaten him to it: ' "Hail, brother! All hail, Thou Mighty One!" ' (ibid.). This is in fact how Stanley thinks of himself, but his might has been undermined by not having beaten them all, and his swim is ruined. Alice, when she goes to visit Mrs Stubbs, dresses for the part: 'Of course she wore gloves, white ones, stained at the fastenings with iron-mould, and in one hand she carried a very dashed-looking sunshade which she referred to as her *perishall*' (p. 228). The transformation of 'parasol' into 'perishall' implies Alice's repressed awareness that her mimicry of gentility is doomed to failure. She feels unnerved when Mrs Stubbs moves out of the prescripted text and chuckles with joy over the freedom of widowhood, just as Beryl takes fright when the romantic melodrama she imagines herself participating in becomes a reality. In her bedroom at night she imagines two people: 'Her arms were round his neck; he held her. And now he whispered, "My beauty, my little beauty!" ' (p. 241). When the expected culmination almost comes about in reality, she experiences it as ' "vile, vile" ' (p. 244). All these are gender roles, from the Stubbses as matriarch and patriarch to the lovers in the garden, but the reality that breaks in disrupts the prescripted texts that the characters are trying to live out. Harry Kember is understandably confused that Beryl will not finish the seduction scene in the darkened garden; Kezia is seized with terror when a familiar story is defamiliarized by an unexpected element. The comfort of a family tale is split open:

'Well, what happened to him?' Kezia knew perfectly well, but she wanted to be told again.

'He went to the mines, and he got a sunstroke there and died,' said old Mrs Fairfield . . .

'*You're* not to die.' Kezia was very decided.

'Ah, Kezia'—her grandma looked up and smiled and shook her head—'don't let's talk about it.'

'But you're not to. You couldn't leave me. You couldn't not be there.' This was awful. 'Promise me you won't ever do it, grandma,' pleaded Kezia. (pp. 226–7)

Kezia's unthinking belief in the stability of her relationship with the grandmother who is her mother-substitute is suddenly eroded and the mould of the reassuring narrative fractures. Permeating the narrative voice are the conventional representations of the binary oppositions of masculinity and femininity created by the colonial society, with which the characters interact; the list in this sentence, part of the paragraph introducing Mrs Kember, catalogues her deficiencies in a gossiping whine, the growing sense of outrage indicated by the increasing unpunctuated length of the phrases: 'Her lack of vanity, her slang, the way she treated men as though she was one of them, and the fact that she didn't care twopence about her house and called the servant Gladys "Glad-eyes," was disgraceful' (p. 218). That *lack* of vanity is disgraceful reveals how deep was the imperative for women to see themselves as decorative adjuncts to their husbands.

The anxiety and questions about gender roles that permeate the consciousness of many of the characters are implicit in the title of the story. On one level it is informative: the story is about a group of families most of whom are on their summer holidays in seaside cottages. Only Stanley Burnell goes off to work. But a bay is an in-between place, an area of protection between the land and the open sea that is not entirely safe. The story opens with two men swimming, but of the women only the dubious Mrs Kember, looking 'like a horrible caricature of her husband' (p. 220), swims boldly out to sea; her behaviour is seen by her society as suspiciously masculine in that she is the only woman at the bay who smokes, and she plays bridge or sunbathes all day since she has no children to care for. The other women and girls can swim, but show a gendered apprehension of the water; the skinny little Trout boys live up to their name and plunge in, whereas Isabel and Kezia are reluctant swimmers and Lottie is terrified, as the shift of the narrative voice to her perspective reveals:

As for Lottie, she didn't follow at all. She liked to be left to go her own way, please. And that way was to sit down at the edge of the water, her legs straight, her knees pressed together, and to make vague motions with her arms as if she expected to be wafted out to sea. But when a bigger wave than usual, an old whiskery one, came lolloping along in her direction, she scrambled to her feet with a face of horror and flew up the beach again.   (p. 217)

Lottie's perception of the wave as masculine and hairy suggests her fear of male sexuality and domination which obliquely reflects her mother's horror of sex leading to conception; Lottie with the other children is later petrified by 'a black beard' (p. 235) at the window of the washhouse. That the bay is a threatening place for women and girls is suggested by the small rites of passage that are enacted by Lottie, Kezia, Alice, Linda, and Beryl in the course of the story.

The mists at the bay symbolize the processes of the human minds at work in the story; at the time that Mansfield was writing 'At the Bay' she indicates, in a letter to Ottoline Morrell, that the mists may become a narrative method in the story, though she does not refer to it directly:

How strange talking is—what mists rise and fall —how one loses the other & then thinks to have found the other—then down comes another soft final curtain . . . But it is incredible, don't you feel, how mysterious and isolated we each of us are—at the last. I suppose one ought to make this discovery once & for all but I seem to be always making it again.[65]

As with *Mrs Dalloway*, the narrative structure lifts the mist on one person and then drops it, so that the reader glimpses a consciousness and then loses sight of it; it may or may not loom out of the mist again. Moments of finding the other occur, as when Linda talks to Jonathan or Mrs Dalloway lives Septimus's suicide, but mostly the soft curtain drops; in the marriages between Linda and Stanley, and Clarissa and Richard, the secret self of each remains unrevealed to the other yet neither marriage is portrayed for that reason as a failure. The opening of 'At the Bay' indicates that boundaries exist but are hidden; features of the landscape, like the psychic experiences that have shaped the consciousnesses of the characters, are known to be there but cannot be seen:

Very early morning. The sun was not yet risen, and the whole of Crescent Bay was hidden under a white sea-mist. The big bush-covered hills at the back were smothered. You could not see where they ended and the paddocks and bungalows began. The sandy road was gone and the paddocks and bungalows the other side of it; there were no white dunes

---

[65] KMCL iv. 252, 24 July 1921.

covered with reddish grass beyond them; there was nothing to mark which was beach and where was the sea. (p. 205)

There is a strong sense of expectation and immanence in the opening passage, as in the Cézanne paintings where the apples and onions seem about to topple off their table: 'Big drops hung on the bushes and just did not fall' and 'there was the splashing of big drops on large leaves, and something else—what was it?—a faint stirring and shaking, the snapping of a twig and then such silence that it seemed someone was listening' (ibid.). The present participles are restless and dynamic though nothing can be clearly seen; the mood is very similar to the opening of *Mrs Dalloway*. Although that is set in Bond Street, the morning is 'fresh as if issued to children on a beach' in Clarissa's mind:

How fresh, how calm, stiller than this of course, the air was in the early morning; like the flap of a wave; the kiss of a wave; chill and sharp and yet (for a girl of eighteen as she then was) solemn, feeling as she did, standing there at the open window, that something awful was about to happen; looking at the flowers, at the trees with the smoke winding off them and the rooks rising, falling; standing and looking.[66]

The openings of both texts confirm Conrad Aitken's observation that the picture is framed, in each case by a heightened observation of place with the writer drawing attention to the frame. Once the mist has dissipated, the shore, the liminal in-between area in 'At the Bay', hides its own secrets which echo those shrouded in mist; the suggestion is that there are lurking hazards in apparently benign settings, just as the apparently trustworthy adults betray the children. The passage about rock-pools evokes this feeling, and also pictures the caves of the unconscious as the narrator gazes down into the pool:

Looking down, bending over, each pool was like a lake with pink and blue houses clustered on the shores; and oh! the vast mountainous country behind those houses—the ravines, the passes, the dangerous creeks and fearful tracks that led to the water's edge. Underneath waved the sea-forest—pink thread-like trees, velvet anemones, and orange berry-spotted weeds. Now a stone on the bottom moved, rocked, and there was a glimpse of a black feeler; now a thread-like creature wavered by and was lost. (p. 224)

---

[66] Virginia Woolf, *Mrs Dalloway* (Oxford: Oxford University Press, 1992), 3. All future refs. included in the text will be taken from this edn.

The immediacy of the threat of this unexplored country is suggested by the repetition of 'now' and the fact that the 'thread-like creature' seems to have met its fate, which is perhaps connected with the 'black feeler'; the leisurely routine of a seaside holiday is constantly interrupted by hints of another view of time, the dimension offered by the pool, part of the framing of the picture. The story takes place in a single day, but Jonathan Trout sees his whole lifetime as a day. He and Linda resemble each other in their longing to explore; she remembers how her father promised that they would sail up a river in China, and Jonathan expresses his frustration violently: ' "And all the while I'm thinking, like that moth, or that butterfly, or whatever it is, 'The shortness of life! The shortness of life!' I've only one night or one day, and there's this vast dangerous garden, waiting out there, undiscovered, unexplored" ' (p. 237).

Even the most homely scenes in the story are imbued with a hint of danger, and specifically of domestic violence; the threat is not that one member of the family *will* hurt another, but that some are licensed by their society to inflict habitual pain on others, and it is deeply resented. Linda thinks how she is 'broken, made weak, her courage was gone, through child-bearing' (p. 223); the compulsion to become involved in sexual relationships, and so to conform to gender roles, is imaged as oppression justifying murder, which suggests the violence of the resentment felt about it. Stanley makes a fuss about his missing stick before he leaves home; he accuses Alice, Linda, Beryl, and his little daughters of having lost it, and he obviously regards it as an emblem of patriarchal authority, of which his womenfolk conspire to deprive him. When he leaves for the town, Alice acts for all of them when 'she plunged the teapot into the bowl and held it under the water even after it had stopped bubbling, as if it too was a man and drowning was too good for them' (p. 213). Since the reader first meets Stanley and Jonathan when they are bathing, specific men come to mind. Linda does love Stanley but she also yearns for freedom, the freedom Mrs Stubbs exults in, her 'soft, fat chuckle sounded like a purr' (p. 231). Mrs Kember appears sexually ambivalent, flirting with Beryl and at the same time seeming obliquely to invite her into an affair with Harry Kember: 'Beryl felt that she was being poisoned by this cold woman, but she longed to hear' (p. 220). The women at the bay expect Mrs Kember to be murdered by her husband, probably because she does not play the role of wife decoratively: 'they saw her, stretched as she lay on the beach; but cold, bloody, and still with a cigarette stuck in the corner of her mouth' (p. 219).

Though in a sense nothing happens as the story traces the progress of ordinary minds on an ordinary day, there is a series of small epiphanies for the female characters as they negotiate the dangers of an ordinary gendering process which raises constant questions and shows memory interacting with the present. That the little girls live in a precarious landscape in spite or perhaps because of their bourgeois family is constantly suggested: as they walk to the beach they struggle 'up that sliding, slipping hill' looking 'like minute puzzled explorers' (p. 214). Kezia is the one who is least likely to conform to social pressure; her wish to mould the world to her own vision is indicated by the way she eats her porridge: 'She had only dug a river down the middle of her porridge, filled it, and was eating the banks away' (p. 211). Her moment of recognition that she cannot construct the world as she wants it to be comes when she is told the story of Uncle William's death again: 'Kezia blinked and considered the picture again . . . A little man fallen over like a tin soldier by the side of a big black hole' (p. 226). At this point she sees a picture out of a familiar story, like 'The Tin Soldier' by Hans Anderson; she lies on her bed drawing in the air and waggling her toes until she is seized by the apprehension that not just she but her grandmother must die. Her perception of it is one of betrayal; she wants her grandmother to promise that she will never die, and her grandmother remains silent.

That betrayal is confirmed later in the day when all the children are playing in the washhouse; Kezia insists that her part must be ' "a ninseck" ' at the same time as her uncle is telling her mother that ' "I'm like an insect that's flown into a room of its own accord. I dash against the walls, dash against the windows, flop against the ceiling, do everything on God's earth, in fact, except fly out again" ' (p. 237). The link between them is temperamental rather than situational; both are humane, imaginative, and intelligent, and want to escape the confines of gendered expectations. Jonathan has ' "two boys to provide for" ' (p. 238) though he tries to believe that he is free; Kezia is sceptical about Pip's aggressive masculinity and his definitions of treasure. However, even Pip is terrified of the sudden arrival of darkness when they are playing in the washhouse, and Grandma, whose lamp in 'Prelude' was a symbol of security and home-coming, now seems, after Kezia's earlier experience, the embodiment of hypocritical betrayal:

And now the quick dark came racing over the sea, over the sand-hills, up the paddock. You were frightened to look in the corners of the washhouse, and yet you had to look with all your might. And some-where, far away, grandma was lighting a lamp . . . Oh, those grown-ups, laughing and snug, sitting in the lamp-light, drinking out of cups! They'd forgotten about them. No, not really forgotten. That was what their smile meant. They had decided to leave them there all by themselves. (pp. 234-5)

What happens next is an even worse example of the defamil-iarization of the familiar than the story about Uncle William; Kezia's Uncle Jonathan turns into a whiskery vampire, a reminder of Lottie's wave, confirming the children's suspicions of the adults' cynical cruelty:

Suddenly Lottie gave such a piercing scream that all of them jumped off the forms, all of them screamed too. 'A face—a face looking!' shrieked Lottie.

It was true, it was real. Pressed against the window was a pale face, black eyes, a black beard.

'Grandma! Mother! Somebody!'

But they had not got to the door, tumbling over one another, before it opened for Uncle Jonathan. (p. 235)

Though they do not know it, their mistrust is appropriate in that Jonathan does long to abandon his boys, and only fails to do so from inertia, not love.

The fact that Linda has spent the morning lying in a steamer chair while her children are at the beach indicates where she would like to be: on a ship, sailing away from her family. She gazes up at the beautiful little flowers of the manuka tree, which occasionally fall on her: 'Why, then, flower at all? Who takes the trouble—or the joy—to make all these things that are wasted, wasted . . . It was uncanny' (p. 221). The perception is very clearly hers; the statement 'she was alone' indicates her negation of her baby son, who is lying on the grass beside her. She acknowledges to herself her indifference to all her children, caused by her terror of childbirth: 'No, it was as though a cold breath had chilled her through and through on each of those awful journeys' (p. 223). She smiles unexpectedly at the baby when he beams at her, though she tells him she does not like babies; her transformation is signalled by the implicit comparison with the manuka flowers: 'Linda dropped off her chair on to the grass.' At this moment she flowers into love for the baby, though she does not recognize what it is, and becomes involved in the trouble and the joy, like the creator of the flowers, of an emotion she cannot yet name. The baby sees his own toes waving in front of him and tries to catch them: 'He made a tremendous effort and rolled right over' (p. 224). This links him with other agents of change in the story. Kezia 'rolled over quickly' (p. 227) when she realized that her grandmother might die; Jonathan 'rolled over on the grass' (p. 237) as he told Linda how constricted he felt, and Mrs Kember 'suddenly turned turtle' (p. 220) as she urged Beryl to enjoy herself. Unobtrusive repetitions suggest psychic similarities that transcend age and gender.

Beryl's epiphanic moment comes when a reality and a cultural construction from popular fiction intersect, in an episode where the phrase 'at the bay' is repeated. She is looking at the moonlit garden, imagining the advent of a dark stranger 'who will find the Beryl they none of them know, who will expect her to be that Beryl always' (p. 242). Just at this moment Harry Kember calls to her; he who is 'so incredibly handsome that he looked like a mask or a most perfect illustration in an American novel rather than a man' (p. 218). The two stereotypes complement each other, but Beryl suddenly begins to feel like Jonathan, imprisoned; the garden is harsh and menacing, and her hand is not held but appropriated: 'now she was here she was terrified and it seemed to her everything was different. The moonlight stared and glittered; the shadows were like bars of iron. Her hand was taken' (p. 244). As Kezia saw her Uncle William beside a black hole, Beryl sees the object of her walk with Kember, the fuschia bush, as having 'a little pit of darkness beneath', suggestive of death, hell, and the loss of the self; in her terror, she wrests herself free and gets away. Kember's irruption into the text playing the part of the vile seducer, since he has only been the subject of gossip until this point, shifts Beryl's perception of time from the timeless world of fantasy to an urgent present.

Similarly Stanley alters the experience of his household. When Stanley meets Jonathan in the sea he asserts that he has no time to fool about and wants to get his swim over; the third section of the story is paced by Stanley saying that he has twenty-five minutes before the coach passes, then twelve and a half, then the coach is due. When he leaves, his whole household feels released from the pressure of time: his 'little girls ran into the paddock like chickens let out of a coop' and the voices of the women 'were changed as they called to one another; they sounded warm and loving and as if they shared a secret' (p. 213). The secret they share is participating in a perception of time that differs from Stanley's. He experiences time as apocalyptic and linear, moving towards deadlines, and the ultimate closure, whereas they measure in seasons and cycles, suggested by the sea's tides and the changes in light and temperature during the story's one day. The opposition is suggested by what seems a verbal version of a painting of Mrs Fairfield by Van Gogh, and Stanley's interruption of it:

The old woman paused, her hand on the loaf of bread, to gaze out of the open door into the garden. The sea sounded. Through the wide-open window streamed the sun on to the yellow varnished walls and bare floor. Everything on the table flashed and glittered. In the middle there was an old salad bowl filled with yellow and red nasturtiums. She smiled, and a look of deep content shone in her eyes.

'You might *cut* me a slice of that bread, mother,' said Stanley. 'I've only twelve and a half minutes before the coach passes.' (p. 211)

Everything mentioned in the passage associates Mrs Fairfield with the cycles of traditional domestic life, the bread, the open door and window, the gleaming room and the flowers, and with the rhythm of the seasons suggested by the sound of the sea.

As a reiterated motif in the story the pattern of cyclical time being disrupted by a man repeats itself, as it does with Beryl and Harry Kember. The image of Mr Stubbs as divine messenger fails to spoil his wife's tea-party, but it prefigures Linda's experience after she has fallen in love with her baby son; she is in the garden talking to Jonathan as the sun sets and beams of light shine through the clouds. The two versions of a sunset simultaneously hint at alternative selves and remind the reader of painters' skies; Van Gogh's menacing *Crows over Wheatfield* was part of the Post-Impressionist exhibition of 1910:

Sometimes when those beams of light show in the sky they are very awful. They remind you that up there sits Jehovah, the jealous God, the Almighty, Whose eye is upon you, ever watchful, never weary. You remember that at His coming the whole earth will shake into one ruined grave-yard; the cold, bright angels will drive you this way and that, and there will be no time to explain what could be explained so simply . . . But to-night it seemed to Linda there was something infinitely joyful and loving in those silver beams. And now no sound came from the sea. It breathed softly as if it would draw that tender, joyful beauty into its own bosom. (pp. 238–9)

The watchful, never weary eye is a reminder of Mr Stubbs overseeing Mrs Stubbs with the warning, 'It is I', and of Stanley surveying his womenfolk critically as they fail to pay sufficient attention to his lost stick. God the Father is presented from Linda's perspective as being as unreasonable and impatient as Stanley, incapable of seeing that there are different ways of looking at things, and moving inexorably to the deadline that he has decreed. Opposed to this is the image of the breathing sea drawing beauty to its bosom, its tides now in tune with the woman who has accepted her motherhood of her son: 'she breathed in a small whisper to the boy, "Hallo, my funny!"' (p. 223). When Stanley returns, he brings into the bay the sounds and language of his masculinist business world: 'Presently there sounded the rumble of the coach, the crack of Kelly's whip. It came near enough for one to hear the voices of the men from town, talking loudly together' (p. 240). Immediately Linda is plunged into demands and urgency, accompanied by icons of clock-time and a reference to God the avenging Father: ' "Good God! You can't have forgotten," cried Stanley Burnell. "I've thought of nothing else all day. I've had the hell of a day. I made up my mind to dash out and telegraph, and then I thought the wire mightn't reach you before I did. I've been in tortures, Linda" ' (p. 240).

Stanley's bullying managerial style, inflicted on his family, is replicated among the children as Pip has a system for finding what is buried in the sand; his resolute searching for treasure and organizing the other children, with its failure to discriminate between a 'nemeral' and an old boot, suggests that he, like Stanley, makes an issue of hunting for what is on the surface if only he could see it. Stanley's treasure is his domestic situation, but he is so busy worrying about it that he cannot look at the nasturtiums and the sunlight. Pip makes a slave of his little brother, Rags, and tries to silence Kezia with superior male wisdom: ' "You can't be a bee, Kezia. A bee's not an animal. It's a ninseck" ' (p. 232). Male control of the script by which all the characters live is as evident as the suggestion that there is another rhythm that could be heard, if it were not drowned out by narratives that privilege heroic action and demand closure. Linda contemplates her marriage:

There were glimpses, moments, breathing spaces of calm, but all the rest of the time it was like living in a house that couldn't be cured of the habit of catching fire, or a ship that got wrecked every day. And it was always Stanley who was in the thick of the danger. Her whole time was spent in rescuing him, and restoring him, and calming him down, and listening to his story. (p. 222)

These are seen as gendered narratives, which the self-reflexive text avoids; its time is cyclical rather than apocalyptic, and its movement conveys rhythms rather than a narrative imperative.

The form of the story used for 'At the Bay' is the same as that for 'Prelude' and 'The Daughters of the Late Colonel'; Ian Gordon has defined it as the twelve-cell story, 'multi-cellular like living tissue',[67] in that it has an organic shape, rather than that it contains self-enclosed units. Some of the opening lines of sections signal the story's preoccupation with natural rhythms: 'Very early morning'; 'As the morning lengthened'; 'The tide was out; the beach was deserted; lazily flopped the warm sea'; 'The sun was still full on the garden'; 'Light shone in the windows of the bungalow.' Other openings focus on particular characters, but the tidy division suggested by the appearance of the story is belied by the content. The sections almost seem to draw attention to the fact that divisions are impossible, just as the passage of chronological time is undermined by the characters' movements into their own past: 'Did it make her sad? To look back, back. To stare down the years, as Kezia had seen her doing. To look after *them* as a woman does, long after *they* were out of sight' (p. 226). The mists rise and fall erratically, but different parts of the story mirror each other; Kezia, Linda, Beryl, and

---

[67] I. Gordon, *Undiscovered Country* (London: Longman, 1974), p. xix.

the children together experience rites of passage but each is private and the reader cannot tell how significant it seems to the character. The children's fear is of their grown-ups, but they only express a fear of spiders; the other characters do not quite formulate what has happened to them. Gendered consciousness is conveyed to the reader through the rhythms of the prose rather than through more overt methods. The fertility and life of the natural world is communicated through lively present participles and a sentence form that flows in the same pattern, and is interrupted repeatedly like the water it describes: 'And from the bush there came the sound of little streams flowing, quickly, lightly, slipping between the smooth stones, gushing into ferny basins and out again; and there was the splashing of big drops on large leaves' (p. 205). Stanley's driven speed is conveyed quite differently, through a series of abrupt monosyllabic verbs, indicating that he does everything as if it is a competition, going through rather than round obstacles: 'A few moments later the back door of one of the bungalows opened, and a figure in a broad-striped bathing-suit flung down the paddock, cleared the stile, rushed through the tussock grass into the hollow, staggered up the sandy hillock, and raced for dear life over the big porous stones' (p. 208). The reader experiences it as heightening to provide an equivalent for life, in Roger Fry's phrase; this passage is strenuous, the earlier one is pleasurable.

Stanley's blundering irruption into the sea and into the world of the text is seen by his sensitive but unsuccessful brother-in-law, Jonathan, as absurd: 'There was something pathetic in his determination to make a job of everything' (p. 209). He respects the rhythms that Stanley wants to deny: 'To take things easy, not to fight against the ebb and flow of life, but to give way to it' is his response to the sea, though he stays in too long and turns blue. The opposition between successful men who accept the masculinist imperative of their society and men whose sensitivity prevents them from conforming to it surfaces constantly in *Mrs Dalloway* as it does in 'At the Bay', often with a similar muted comedy. After Septimus Warren Smith's terrible and reluctant suicide, his widow is given a narcotic by Dr Holmes, whose arrival had caused Septimus to jump out of the window on to the area railings:

'Let her sleep,' said Dr Holmes, feeling her pulse. She saw the large outline of his body dark against the window. So that was Dr Holmes.

One of the triumphs of civilization, Peter Walsh thought. It is one of the triumphs of civilization, as the light high bell of the ambulance sounded. (p. 197)

The first impression the reader receives is that Walsh is commenting on Dr Holmes as a triumph of civilization; though it becomes clear that Walsh admires the ambulance service in London after living in India, the initial impact of his comment remains as part of the reading experience. Holmes and the Harley Street psychiatrist Sir William Bradshaw do, of course, see themselves as the triumphs of civilization; this is suggested through the kinds of paintings that are associated with them. 'Lady Bradshaw in ostrich feathers hung over the mantelpiece' (p. 132) again causes the reader a double-take, but presumably refers to a society portrait such as those produced by Sargent; when the Bradshaws arrive at Mrs Dalloway's party they are linked with Sir Harry whose pictures 'were always of cattle, standing in sunset pools absorbing moisture, or signifying, for he had a certain range of gesture, by the raising of one foreleg and the toss of the antlers, "the Approach of the Stranger"—all his activities, dining out, racing, were founded on cattle standing absorbing moisture in sunset pools' (p. 229). The representation of soggy cows, or deer since they have antlers, and its approval by an art establishment, gives the artist the power to drink, gamble, and regale his friends with anecdotes about chorus girls, but an attitude is only suggested by a recurrent irony in the narrative voice, amused here and much more savage in the apparent comment on Dr Holmes. The disturbing question of what civilization is resonates through *Mrs Dalloway*, because the issue of the war to end all wars is not avoided here, as Katherine Mansfield felt it was in *Night and Day*, and it is linked to the artistic representation of reality. It is no accident that Lady Bradshaw, when not hanging over the mantelpiece, replicates reality: 'if there was a church building, or a church decaying, she bribed the sexton, got the key and took photographs, which were scarcely to be distinguished from the work of professionals, while she waited' (pp. 123–4). This description of the way in

which she waits for the great man, and fills in her time by recording its passage, suggests a contempt for professional photo-
graphers as artists, and a linear attitude to the passing of time,
with civilization represented by decaying monuments.

Just as Stanley Burnell harasses the women in his household
with his obsession with the clock, so Sir William Bradshaw and
Dr Holmes measure time and health as if they were grocers
weighing sugar. Part of Sir William's resentment of Septimus stems
from suspicion of someone who has made time for what he
values; Septimus is shabby but his passion for reading shows
in his capacity for irony and 'there was in Sir William, who had
never had time for reading, a grudge, deeply buried, against
cultivated people who came into his room and intimated that
doctors, whose profession is a constant strain upon all the
highest faculties, are not educated men' (p. 127). The reader is
invited to think, 'Psychiatrist, heal thyself,' but Sir William is
interested only in categories and preconceived ideas, not in his
own or anyone else's deeply buried psychic experiences; he has
already written the script before he sees the patient, and wants
nothing to do with the particular pain of an individual case.
In entering his consciousness the narrator exposes him through
his rational, common-sense language which reveals a mechanical and obtuse desire to straitjacket his patients, mentally if not
physically:

To his patients he gave three-quarters of an hour; and if in this exact-
ing science which has to do with what, after all, we know nothing
about—the nervous system, the human brain—a doctor loses his sense
of proportion, as a doctor he fails. Health we must have; and health
is proportion; so that when a man comes into your room and says he
is Christ (a common delusion), and has a message, as they mostly have,
and threatens, as they often do, to kill himself, you invoke proportion;
order rest in bed; rest in solitude; silence and rest; rest without friends,
without books, without messages; six months' rest; until a man who
went in weighing seven stone six comes out weighing twelve.   (p. 129)

Rest without books is central to this, literal, prescription; the
individuality of the patient is negated in the prescribed plot,
and recovery hinges on the lack of books and physical solidity.
Sir William's monomania makes him quite as insane as his patient; he 'made England prosper, secluded her lunatics, forbade
childbirth, penalized despair, made it impossible for the unfit to

propagate their views' (ibid.). Yet his fascist programme of control and will to power are sanctioned by his society because they maintain a national fiction that is crucial to the society's view of itself. That Septimus's response to trench warfare might be more fully human than Sir William's cannot be admitted because it would undermine the significance of British civilization. Septimus's guilt, disgust, and horror at having survived pivot on the question of manliness. He had lived a series of pre-scripted stories; he left home leaving a note 'such as great men have written, and the world has read later when the story of their struggles has become famous' (p. 110). As he volunteered for active service in the war 'he developed manliness; he was promoted' (p. 112). But manliness means, in this context, an inhuman denial of feelings. When his close friend and superior officer Evans was killed, Septimus 'congratulated himself upon feeling very little and very reasonably' (pp. 112–13). Yet this is deeply unreasonable, a denial of the self, and it drives Septimus mad; no one in his society is prepared to acknowledge that the 'manly' ethic of war requires the repression of those feelings, such as love and loyalty, that are most prized in peace. He is left with the conviction that he is a monster 'so pocked and marked with vice that women shuddered when they saw him in the street' (p. 119), yet knowing also that Holmes, 'the repulsive brute, with the blood-red nostrils' (p. 120) and Bradshaw are the real monsters who accuse him of being in a funk, and 'scour the desert. They fly screaming into the wilderness. The rack and the thumbscrew are applied' (p. 127). That fear is a proper and necessary response to the suppression of feeling needed for survival in trench warfare becomes clear to the reader who inhabits Septimus's mind as he tries to confront Holmes and Bradshaw. The drive to move on to the next part of the societally prescribed narrative, promotion in his job and the birth of children, is a chronological sequence that Septimus's inner rhythms reject. He is given no space or time, even by Rezia, to examine what has happened to him; Rezia thinks 'it was cowardly for a man to say he would kill himself, but Septimus had fought; he was brave; he was not Septimus now' (p. 29). The foreigner within him has become so evident that Rezia can see him. Septimus's suicide is caused by the sound of Holmes coming up the stairs to put Bradshaw's timed programme into action; it is no accident that his name is a reminder of the railway timetable, *Bradshaw's Monthly Railway Guide*. Up till the last moment Septimus enjoys the unprogrammed cycles of the seasons, the light in the room, and the sun on his skin.

The form of *Mrs Dalloway* is itself an implicit rejection of the Bradshaw prescription for life and art. Like the form of 'At the Bay', the structure of *Mrs Dalloway* draws attention to itself. There are no chapters; the inference must be that it cannot be divided into the tidy chronologically arranged parcels so admired by Sir William. Motifs are woven through the text, making unexpected links between unlikely characters. One of the most persistent of these is the British empire,[68] in defence of which Septimus had fought. That there might be different ways of thinking about it is suggested from the beginning of the novel by the narrative voice, which does not limit itself to Mrs Dalloway's perspective. The car with the important unidentified personage in it leaves a ripple behind it that makes strangers look at each other and think 'of the dead; of the flag; of Empire. In a public-house in a back street a Colonial insulted the House of Windsor, which led to words, broken beer glasses, and a general shindy' (p. 22). This becomes more complex in retrospect, when the reader is aware of Septimus's resistance to the equation of the dead, the flag, and empire. The imperatives of a national script have prevented him from thinking of the dead at the time when he needed to mourn, and he and the unnamed Colonial are linked in resistance. Throughout the novel there are passing references to what is happening in India, that is to the politics of resistance to the Raj; though most of the characters regret this development, the text does not necessarily endorse their view. In considering Sir William Bradshaw's bigotry, the narrator's persona loses its chameleon quality and attacks the destruction of indigenous beliefs and cultures:

But Proportion has a sister, less smiling, more formidable, a Goddess even now engaged—in the heat and sands of India, the mud and swamp of Africa, the purlieus of London, wherever, in short, the climate or the devil tempts men to fall from the true belief which is her own

---

[68] The historical context of the novel is well explored in Jeremy Tambling, 'Repression in Mrs Dalloway's London', in Su Reid (ed.), *New Casebooks: Mrs Dalloway and To the Lighthouse* (London: Macmillan, 1993), 57–70.

—is even now engaged in dashing down shrines, smashing idols, and setting up in their place her own stern countenance. Conversion is her name. (p. 130)

This of course accepts a view of the empire constructed by other texts rather than by enquiry; 'the mud and swamp of Africa' sounds more like *Heart of Darkness* than like an idea of locality. But the wreckers of shrines and idols can be construed as the agents of imperialism, asserting the same masculinist power that destroys Septimus. When Septimus thinks about his situation, he remembers visiting the Tower, the Victoria and Albert Museum and watching the King going to open Parliament, all emblematic of imperial power; this makes him realize that he cannot bring children into the world he inhabits where the powerful

hunt in packs. Their packs scour the desert and vanish screaming into the wilderness. They desert the fallen. They are plastered over with grimaces . . . In the streets, vans roared past him; brutality blared out on placards; men were trapped in mines; women burnt alive; and once a maimed file of lunatics being exercised or displayed for the diversion of the populace (who laughed aloud) ambled and nodded and grinned past him, in the Tottenham Court Road, each half apologetically, yet triumphantly, inflicting his hopeless woe. (p. 117)

The powerless, including women, the poor, the mad, and colonial subjects, are helpless to represent themselves; they are constructed and given their parts by the powerful, and driven to destruction, like Septimus, or, like Lady Bradshaw, to a lifetime of subservience: 'Fifteen years ago she had gone under' (p. 131).

The sinister and repressed narrative of imperialism is explored with most complexity in the character of Peter Walsh. He is in some senses a failure and a rebel who meets with disapproval in the Conservative political circles in which Richard and Clarissa Dalloway move; he has contempt for Clarissa's conventionality and yet constantly writes conventional narratives himself in his mental scripting of events. Though he despises the evidence of status and class that characterize the Dalloways' marriage, he privileges work over domesticity as Stanley Burnell does. He constantly clutches his knife when he feels intimidated by Dalloway's success, in personal and public terms:

And this has been going on all the time! he thought; week after week; Clarissa's life; while I—he thought; and at once everything seemed to radiate from him; journeys; rides; quarrels; adventures; bridge parties; love affairs; work; work, work! and he took out his knife quite openly—his old horn-handled knife which Clarissa could swear he had had these thirty years—and clenched his fist upon it.   (p. 56)

This overt symbol of masculine power suggests the ambivalence of Walsh's radicalism, just as what radiates from him is rooted in traditionally masculine competition and aggression. He seems to have been sent down from Oxford for being a socialist and yet his politics are as confused and compromised as everything else about him; his conception of civilization, seen in the following passage, is perilously close to that which destroys Septimus:

A splendid achievement in its own way, after all, London; the season; civilization. Coming as he did from a respectable Anglo-Indian family which for at least three generations had administered the affairs of a continent (it's strange, he thought, what a sentiment I have about that, disliking India, and empire, and army as he did), there were moments when civilization, even of this sort, seemed dear to him as a personal possession; moments of pride in England.   (p. 71)

In isolation, this can seem the rather endearing muddle of a middle-aged man whose memories are stirred by being back in London, but Walsh's story is intertwined with Septimus's last day, and one comments obliquely on the other. As he walks up Whitehall Walsh hears a regular thudding: 'Boys in uniform, carrying guns, marched with their eyes ahead of them, marched, their arms stiff, and on their faces an expression like the letters of a legend written round the base of a statue praising duty, gratitude, fidelity, love of England' (pp. 65–6). Such statues are all too familiar in the aftermath of the war, and this construction of boyish heroism is so sentimental in a novel that also contains Septimus that it implicates Walsh in Bradshaw's values: nationalism and proportion. As the boys pass him, on their way to lay a wreath on the tomb of the unknown warrior, the trope used for their movement becomes even more macabre, but still Peter fails to recognize the implications of what he perceives: 'on they marched, past him, past everyone, in their steady way, as if one will worked legs and arms uniformly, and life, with its varieties, its irreticences, had been laid under a pavement of monuments and wreaths and drugged into a stiff yet staring corpse by discipline. One had to respect it' (p. 66). One only has to respect its machine-like draining of the life from the boys if one in some way condones its objectives. Peter gazes at statues of Nelson, Gordon, and Havelock, imperial heroes who died respectively in the Battle of Trafalgar, at Khartoum, and at the relief of Lucknow. He thinks particularly sympathetically of Gordon but he identifies with the leaders, not the cannon fodder, and with the colonizers rather than the colonized. It becomes clear that gendered narratives of conquest are what drive him; that he is much closer to Stanley Burnell and Bradshaw than to Jonathan Trout and Septimus. He is in London to see his lawyers about the divorce of Daisy, yet it is evident that he wants to possess her, like territory; he does not really want to marry her, but wants to prevent anyone else from doing so. It is a story about the exercise of power rather than love, like his pursuit of a woman who crosses Trafalgar Square towards him. As she passes Gordon's statue she seems 'to shed veil after veil, until she became the very woman he had always had in mind' (p. 68). The narrative that he is creating about her is obviously based in orientalism; she is 'black, but enchanting', like Salome in her shedding of veils. She seems to say 'you' to him as he follows her, 'stealthily fingering his pocket-knife' into, unsurprisingly, Cockspur Street. He continues to imagine her as an oriental enchantress 'with a lizard's flickering tongue' (p. 69), and he fantasizes about his own role: 'he was an adventurer, reckless, he thought, swift, daring, indeed (landed as he was last night from India) a romantic buccaneer, careless of all these damned proprieties' (p. 69). He wants to believe this a harmless fling, in that nothing comes of it, but the gendered and imperialist narrative that underpins it suggests how culturally powerful are myths of racial and sexual subordination in this society.

Woven through the novel are portraits of women that confirm these myths. Clarissa thinks of politics and masculinity as inextricable; she wishes she had been 'like Lady Bexborough, slow and stately; rather large; interested in politics like a man' (p. 12). Such women are linked with men in recording the passage of chronological time: 'she feared time itself, and read on Lady Bruton's face, as if it had been a dial cut in impassive stone, the dwindling of life' (p. 38). Lady Bruton is part of the colonial project; the curious transitive use of 'emigrate' suggests the extent of her power: 'that fibre which was the ramrod of her soul, that essential part of her without which Millicent Bruton would not have been Millicent Bruton; that project for emigrating young people of both sexes born of respectable parents and setting them up with a fair prospect of doing well in Canada' (p. 141). Her name connects her with 'the repulsive brute', Holmes; though the narrator treats her with playful comedy she pervades the text as a sinister presence, deliberately snubbing Clarissa by inviting only Richard to lunch and, like Lady Bradshaw, linking the present with a past of monuments and effigies rather than a living art, as she does not read Shakespeare:

For she never spoke of England, but this isle of men, this dear, dear land, was in her blood (without reading Shakespeare), and if ever a woman could have worn the helmet and shot the arrow, could have led troops to attack, ruled with indomitable justice barbarian hordes and lain under a shield noseless in a church, or made a green grass mound on some primeval hillside, that woman was Millicent Bruton . . . she had the thought of Empire always at hand, and had acquired from her association with that armoured goddess her ramrod bearing, her robustness of demeanour, so that one could not figure her even in death parted from the earth or roaming territories over which, in some spiritual shape, the Union Jack had ceased to fly. To be not English even among the dead—no, no! Impossible!   (pp. 236–7)

Her flabby minion is Hugh Whitbread, who shuffles obsequiously in the corridors of power with his phallic substitute, a fountain pen, at the ready. Even he has his buccaneering story, for he kissed Sally Seton in the conservatory at Bourton to punish her for her aggressive feminism; because of his oppressive respectability no one believed her account of it.

What links all these characters, including Peter Walsh, is a willingness to categorize: to classify as Sir William Bradshaw does when he lists the symptoms he expects to find in Septimus. The implication of this is that the script is written in advance, in the binary oppositions of traditional patriarchy; everything is known and human experience fits a Procrustean bed. Mrs Dalloway's affinity with Septimus, for all her obvious differences, is that she allows things to happen to her: 'she would not say of Peter, she would not say of herself, I am this, I am that' (p. 10). She is in this way the antithesis of Sir William Bradshaw, because she loathes conversion, and the idea that anyone has the right to impose their own view of the world on anyone else. She is therefore not implicated in the imperialism of her society, except to the extent that she entertains those that are; after speaking to Miss Kilman she thinks: 'Had she ever tried to convert anyone herself? Did she not wish everybody merely to be themselves?' (p. 165). Like Septimus, she experiences fear because she is not protected by a narrative that enables her to file what happens to her in a preconstructed category; after Septimus's death she thinks that '(she had felt it only this morning) there was the terror . . . there was in the depths of her heart an awful fear' (p. 242). She and Septimus throughout the day of the novel have running through their heads the line from the dirge in *Cymbeline*, 'Fear no more the heat o' the sun', implying that death will be a relief from fear. The reader's exposure to Septimus's suicide comes more through Mrs Dalloway's response to it than from an account of the event in its own right; her vulnerability and negative capability are evident:

He had killed himself—but how? Always her body went through it, when she was told, first, suddenly, of an accident; her dress flamed, her body burnt. He had thrown himself from a window. Up had flashed the ground; through him, blundering, bruising, went the rusty spikes. There he lay with a thud, thud, thud in his brain, and then a suffocation of blackness. (p. 241)

The thudding reminds the reader of the boys' boots, marching in Whitehall; Septimus's vulnerability and theirs is an indictment of Walsh and Dalloway as well as Holmes and Bradshaw.

Mrs Dalloway inhabits the foreground of the text and to some extent identifies herself with imperial triumph as her husband does when he strolls through Green Park, gendering the palace: 'As for Buckingham Palace (like an old prima donna facing the audience all in white) you can't deny it a certain dignity, he considered, nor despise what it does, after all, stand to millions of people (a little crowd was waiting at the gate to see the King drive out) for a symbol' (pp. 152–3). She seems an ideal wife for a public figure, but the dominant image for her inner life is one of withdrawal, reflected in the way in which she leaves her party when it is at its height to stand alone looking out of the window.

The tropes used of her suggest liminality: a nun leaves the physical world in order to approach the spiritual, and as in *Jane Eyre*, *The Yellow Wallpaper*, and possibly in Woolf's own life with her half-sister, an attic traditionally houses members of families who cannot be ejected completely but are disgraceful secrets:

> Like a nun withdrawing, or a child exploring a tower, she went, upstairs, paused at the window . . . There was an emptiness about the heart of life; an attic room . . . The sheets were clean, tight stretched in a broad white band from side to side. Narrower and narrower would her bed be . . . And really she preferred to read of the retreat from Moscow. He knew it. So the room was an attic; the bed narrow; and lying there reading, for she slept badly, she could not dispel a virginity preserved through childbirth which clung to her like a sheet . . . She could see what she lacked. It was not beauty; it was not mind. It was something central which permeated; something warm which broke up surfaces and rippled the cold contact of man and woman, or of women together.   (pp. 39–40)

The fact that she is repeatedly imaged as being inside looking out from an attic window in a house which is apparently at the centre of things, visited by the Prime Minister, stresses her apartness. She is in a liminal space, mother but virgin, reading about imperial conquest but not part of it, unable to break down barriers in the most intimate relationships. Though she loves her husband she does not want him to cross boundaries into her isolation; visual images of Mrs Dalloway's solitary no man's land punctuate the text: 'The sheet was stretched and the bed narrow. She had gone up into the tower alone and left them blackberrying in the sun. The door had shut, and there among the dust of fallen plaster and the litter of birds' nests how distant the view had looked, and the sounds came thin and chill' (p. 60). She feels that she has been abandoned, but at the same time wants that abandonment, as if this in-between space is her element, a place of habitation, and enables her to avoid prescriptiveness. It also allows her to experience and not to condemn Septimus's suicide.

Similarly liminal images are used throughout the novel for Septimus, who is himself aware of being between sanity and insanity, and between life and death. For him the dead constantly invade the world of the living, showing the reader but not Septimus himself how much he felt about his friend's death:

But the branches parted. A man in grey was actually walking towards them. It was Evans! But no mud was on him; no wounds; he was not changed. I must tell the whole world, Septimus cried, raising his hand (as the dead man in the grey suit came nearer), raising his hand like some colossal figure who has lamented the fate of man for ages in the desert alone. (p. 91)

Behind Evans are 'legions of men'; Septimus is willing them back to life. The fact that he cannot tell the world of their resurrection, and that the world does not want to hear, isolates him in his obsession with his dead comrades; they wait lurking in the undergrowth of the park, causing him both joy and agonized terror and guilt. In Kristeva's terms he is an abject. He lives in a twilight world which accentuates where he has always to some extent been:

To look at, he might have been a clerk, but of the better sort; for he wore brown boots; his hands were educated; so, too, his profile —his angular, big-nosed, intelligent, sensitive profile; but not his lips altogether, for they were loose; and his eyes (as eyes tend to be), eyes merely; hazel, large; so that he was, on the whole, a border case.
(p. 109)

This is the categorizing language of the Bradshaws and Holmeses, with its grotesque pigeon-hole for educated hands; the narrative voice shifts its perspective constantly but the summarising 'border case' is telling. The passage is introduced by another liminal place; the narrator describes Septimus in the West End 'as if Portland Place were a room he had come into when the family are away, the chandeliers being hung in holland bags, and the caretaker, as she lets in long shafts of dusty light upon deserted, queer-looking armchairs, lifting one corner of the long blinds, explains to the visitors what a wonderful place it is' (p. 109). The house is haunted by absences, as Septimus's whole world is; he feels himself to be 'this last relic straying on the edge of the world, this outcast, who gazed back at the inhabited regions, who lay, like a drowned sailor, on the shore of the world' (p. 121). Again the language juxtaposes opposites to evoke Septimus's sense of his liminality. He is an object, a relic, that walks; an outcast outside the boundaries of the inhabited world who gazes though he is dead, a drowned sailor. Travel and transition recur in his own and the narrator's tropes for him, though what he wants more than anything is simply to inhabit his own house. His pleasure in the ordinary routines of his domestic life, when they are not disrupted by visions of the dead, is like Mrs Dalloway's, perhaps because both are so familiar with feeling excluded. When Mrs Dalloway comes home after shopping she feels that 'moments like this are buds on the tree of life, flowers of darkness' (p. 37) while Septimus 'had a sense, as he watched Rezia trimming the straw hat for Mrs Peters, of a coverlet of flowers' (p. 186); both experience the magic of the everyday, like Linda Burnell with her baby boy.

The connection between the caves of the unconscious of Mrs Dalloway and Septimus is shared by the text itself. It is haunted by a giant figure, rather like the looming presence of the eucalypt in the mist which recurs in 'At the Bay' and is first mentioned in the opening section: 'Then something immense came into view; an enormous shock-haired giant with his arms stretched out' (p. 206). In *Mrs Dalloway* the nurse who knits on a bench beside Peter Walsh as he dozes in the park becomes 'one of those spectral presences which rise in twilight in woods made of sky and branches. The solitary traveller, haunter of lanes, disturber of ferns, and devastator of great hemlock plants, looking up suddenly, sees the giant figure at the end of the ride' (p. 73). The unexplained figure, which may be in Peter Walsh's dream but seems to have more connection with the unconscious of the whole text than with him, haunts the margins of the novel when the characters are in a state of uncertainty; worshippers in Westminster Abbey saw Miss Kilman 'at the end of the row, praying, praying, and, being still on the threshold of their under-world, thought of her sympathetically as a soul haunting the same territory; a soul cut out of immaterial substance' (p. 175). When Walsh wonders what to do about Daisy he visualises 'a figure standing at the crossroads at dusk, which grows more and more remote' (p. 207). These advancing and receding figures resemble the horrors and awful ecstasies that inhabit Septimus's world, suggesting perhaps that the communal experience of the war reverberates in the nerves and psyches of London's inhabitants more traumatically than it seems to do on the sunny surface of a day in June.

The formal subtlety of the novel constantly implies that character and experience cannot be explored in a linear narrative;

simple events, such as the regal car, the vapour trail of the aero-
plane, or Mrs Dalloway's party, bring together disparate people
whose similarities are suggested to the reader through unobtrusive
mirroring. The way in which the rhythms of the body and of
domestic life are violated for Mrs Dalloway when Walsh bursts
in on her resembles Holmes's intrusion on Septimus, which pre-
cipitates his suicide. As she sews what Walsh later sees as her
mermaid's dress, in which she goes 'lolloping on the waves',
Mrs Dalloway's consciousness is not in tune with clock time.
The prose enacts different rhythms, rhyming 'all' and 'fall', with
the present participles and the shift to the present tense suggesting that it is happening now, that the body does not recognize
the past:

So on a summer's day waves collect, overbalance, and fall; collect and
fall; and the whole world seems to be saying 'that is all' more and
more ponderously, until even the heart in the body which lies in the
sun on the beach says too, that is all. Fear no more, says the heart.
Fear no more, says the heart, committing its burden to some sea, which
sighs collectively for all sorrows, and renews, begins, collects, lets fall.
And the body alone listens to the passing bee; the wave breaking, the
dog barking, far away barking and barking. (p. 51)

The soporific rhythm of the prose, possibly influenced by the
music of Tennyson's 'The woods decay, the woods decay and fall',[69]
enacts the tidal movement of the sea and of the breath in the
body; the image of a collective lament is not apocalyptic and
threatening here, as it is with the figure at the end of the ride,
but is soothing in its use of the Shakespearean song, until the
door bursts open. The body attunes itself to cyclic time until
it is disturbed by a man who comes in, grasps a penknife, and
opens the blade. The episode prefigures Septimus's interlude of
peace before Holmes comes pounding up his staircase:

Outside the trees dragged their leaves like nets through the depths of
the air; the sound of water was in the room, and through the waves
came the voices of birds singing. Every power poured its treasures on
his head, and his hand lay there on the back of the sofa, as he had
seen his hand lie when he was bathing, floating, on the top of the waves,
while far away on shore he heard dogs barking and barking far away.
Fear no more, says the heart in the body; fear no more. (p. 182)

[69] The opening line of 'Tithonus'.

This passage too is full of present participles, and it shifts into the present tense; the rhythm of the heart and the waves, with phrases repeated from the paragraph about Mrs Dalloway, signals the affinity between the two characters, and their obliviousness to the warning of the barking dogs. The same trope is used of Peter Walsh, but he uses it consciously himself; it is not the way in which the narrator represents his consciousness. Walsh is always ready to suppress his inner life in the interests of imperial imperatives, and pictures the waves rather than feeling their tidal movements:

For this is the truth about our soul, he thought, our self, who fish-like inhabits deep seas and plies among obscurities threading her way between the boles of giant weeds, over sun-flickered spaces and on and on into gloom, cold, deep, inscrutable; suddenly she shoots to the surface and sports on the wind-wrinkled waves; that is, has a positive need to brush, scrape, kindle herself, gossiping. What did the Government mean— Richard Dalloway would know—to do about India? (pp. 210–11)

The cadences of this passage do not lull the reader into a different dimension as those about Mrs Dalloway and Septimus do; this is the brisk prose of a man who wants to deny that he is ageing.

The two perceptions of time that pervade the novel are not polarized; clock or linear time is expressed in a metaphor that suggests ripples in a pool: 'The leaden circles dissolved in the air' (p. 122). But the regular irruption of the sound of clocks chiming invades the characters' space rather as Walsh bursts into Mrs Dalloway's drawing-room. Clocks seem to endorse Bradshaw's materialist view of the world and Walsh's dependence on his knife, and to erode Septimus's perspective: 'Shredding and slicing, dividing and subdividing, the clocks of Harley Street nibbled at the June day, counselled submission, upheld authority, and pointed out in chorus the supreme advantages of a sense of proportion' (p. 133). That there are rhythms that run counter to clock time, and moments that stand outside it, is implied by the constant tropes relating to tides and water, to flowering, and to biological cycles. Though she is nunlike, and has failed her husband, Mrs Dalloway remembers moments with women when 'she did undoubtedly then feel what men felt.' The orgasmic rhythm is perceived as being outside clock time, in tune with the fleeting moment when a crocus opens and reveals its golden pistil:

It was a sudden revelation, a tinge like a blush which one tried to check and then, as it spread, one yielded to its expansion, and rushed to the farthest verge and there quivered and felt the world come closer, swollen with some astonishing significance, some pressure of rapture, which split its thin skin and gushed and poured with an extraordinary alleviation over the cracks and sores. Then, for that moment, she had seen an illumination; a match burning in a crocus; an inner meaning almost expressed. But the close withdrew; the hard softened. It was over— the moment. (p. 41)

This is a kind of epiphany, like Linda's in 'At the Bay', linked like hers to living in the body and not dictated by external exigencies. The image of parched skin being flooded with healing fluid connects the body to dry ground, and to the regeneration of land that has been drought-stricken. It is gendered very differently from *The Waste Land* but has a similar yearning for fertility in a barren place.

This potent image of female sexuality experienced out of time is unique in the novel, as is the strange episode of the old crone singing an incomprehensible love song outside Regent's Park Tube Station. She erupts out of nowhere, but reverses the process of Walsh invading Mrs Dalloway's contemplation, confronting him in his turn with something alien. He is marching along clutching his penknife; as he reaches the crossing he also reaches a moment of transition from the dimension of timetabled arrangements to something else: a voice which is described in terms of a spring of water bubbling up 'from a tall quivering shape, like a funnel, like a rusty pump, like a wind-beaten tree' (p. 105) in a totally urban setting:

As the ancient song bubbled up opposite Regent's Park Tube Station, still the earth seemed green and flowery; still, though it issued from so rude a mouth, a mere hole in the earth, muddy too, matted with root fibres and tangled grasses, still the old bubbling burbling song, soaking through the knotted roots of infinite ages, and skeletons and treasure, streamed away in rivulets over the pavement and all along the Marylebone Road, and down towards Euston, fertilizing, leaving a damp stain. (p. 106)[70]

---

[70] There is an incisive Lacanian reading of this passage, and of *Mrs Dalloway*, in Makiko Minow-Pinkney, *Virginia Woolf and the Problem of the Subject* (Brighton: Harvester, 1987), 54–83.

The old woman's song seems to be issuing from her sexual organ, a hole matted with tangled grasses; she embodies primeval rhythms that predate language as her song can only be represented as 'ee um fah um so'. Yet there is no doubt that the song is a fertility rite; it leaves a damp stain all over the streets round the station, which represents timetables and contemporary communications. She is the antithesis of Sir William Bradshaw and Millicent Bruton; her language is indecipherable but is understood in the pulse of the body rather than the analysis of the reason. The cycles of procreation reduce the present to an insignificant blur in her ancient eyes: 'the passing generations—the pavement was crowded with bustling middle-class people—vanished, like leaves, to be trodden under, to be soaked and steeped and made mould of by that eternal spring' (p. 107).

The old woman is as disturbing to the reader as to Peter Walsh; she puts a question but it is left, like Chekhov's questions, reverberating in the reader's mind. The framing of both 'At the Bay' and *Mrs Dalloway* draws attention to itself; the picture is perceived to be a picture through the form of the narratives, where conventions of compartmentalizing the text are reformed, as in 'At the Bay', or ignored, in *Mrs Dalloway*. In both texts time seems to be prioritized, in that they record the passing of a single day, but it is then undermined by the effects of gender and exclusion on the characters' experience of temporality. To return to the Post-Impressionists, paint is applied differently here from the way in which other modernist novelists use it: it is no accident that, on the day that Woolf records in her diary that she has finished *Mrs Dalloway* she also comments: 'The thought of Katherine Mansfield comes to me . . . K. & I had our relationship; & never again shall I have one like it.'[71] The layers of paint occlude and occasionally reveal, and the texture of the prose always gestures towards psychic as well as physical landscapes. The heightened language gives the reader an experience that does not mimic life but is equivalent to a happening in life, as in this painterly moment in *Mrs Dalloway* that evokes the unseen presences of the night and the unconscious:

[71] VWD ii. 317, 17 Oct. 1924.

So a rocket fades. Its sparks, having grazed their way into the night, surrender to it, dark descends, pours over the outlines of houses and towers; bleak hillsides soften and fall in. But though they are gone, the night is full of them; robbed of colour, blank of windows, they exist more ponderously, give out what frank daylight fails to transmit —the trouble and suspense of things conglomerated here in the darkness; reft of the relief which dawn brings when, washing the walls white and grey, spotting each window-pane, lifting the mist from the fields, showing the red-brown cows peacefully grazing, all is once more decked out to the eye; exists again. (p. 30)

7

Vertigo in 'The Daughters of the Late Colonel' and *Jacob's Room*

> Why is life so tragic; so like a little strip of pavement over
> an abyss. I look down; I feel giddy; I wonder how I am
> ever to walk to the end.[1]

DURING the time that she was writing *Jacob's Room*, Virginia
Woolf was involved in the most intense phase of her friendship
with Katherine Mansfield. In an entry in her diary where she
says that she is planning to begin the book in the following week,
she remarks, 'I can wince outrageously to read K. M.'s praises
in the Athenaeum. Four poets are chosen; she's one of them.'
Though the choice has been made by Murry, and it is Mansfield's
friend J. W. N. Sullivan who describes her as a genius, 'you see
how well I remember all this—how eagerly I discount it.'[2] The
joint stimulus of jealousy and affinity acted as a spur, and Woolf
forged ahead with the new book at the same time as she said
what proved to be her final farewell in person to Mansfield, on
23 August 1920. She records in her diary her conflicting emotions
about the parting, wondering whether she feels sufficiently deeply
and 'then, after noting my own callousness, of a sudden comes
the blankness of not having her to talk to.'[3] The insecurity caused
by missing Mansfield and envying her literary success combines
with fear of T. S. Eliot's intellectuality and his admiration of James
Joyce's fiction, and Woolf's diary records that she has stopped
writing *Jacob's Room*; in one of her most powerful metaphors
she expresses the disconcerting experience of living happily
in her domestic space and at the same time inhabiting liminal
territory, walking on an ordinary piece of urban architecture over
nothingness:

[1] VWD ii. 72, 25 Oct. 1920.   [2] Ibid. 28, 10 Apr. 1920.
[3] Ibid. 61, 25 Aug. 1920.

Why is life so tragic; so like a little strip of pavement over an abyss. I look down; I feel giddy; I wonder how I am ever to walk to the end. . . . The fire burns; we are going to hear The Beggars Opera. Only it lies about me; I can't keep my eyes shut . . . Unhappiness is everywhere; just beyond the door; or stupidity which is worse. Still I dont pluck the nettle out of me . . . And with it all how happy I am—if it weren't for my feeling that its a strip of pavement over an abyss.[4]

The visual images evoked by this passage, of sitting beside the fire or in the opera house and at the same time walking a pavement plank over extinction, resemble the technique of *Jacob's Room*, where incongruous pictures jostle each other: they are described as 'these chasms in the continuity of our ways' which are as 'frequent as street corners in Holborn'.[5] It is what Kristeva describes as being both here and there,[6] an experience of liminality that is encoded in the distinctive vertiginous form of 'The Daughters of the Late Colonel', 'Pictures', and *Jacob's Room*.

A contemporary review of *Jacob's Room* in the *Yorkshire Post* defines Woolf's 'new way of writing a novel' as 'snapshot photography, with a highly sensitive, perfected camera handled by an artist. The result is a crowded album of little pictures.'[7] Other reviewers use the same metaphor, but it does not catch the swooping movement of the novel from one picture into another. Another contemporary art is hinted at in the *Yorkshire Post* review, when it comments on *Jacob's Room*'s lack of narrative; it has 'above all, no perspective: its dissolving views come before us one by one, each taking the full light for a moment, then vanishing completely . . . *Jacob's Room*, beautiful as much of it is, seems flickering, impermanent.'[8] The cinematic imagery reflects what Woolf seems to be aiming at when she is planning the novel: she writes in her diary that the new novel will be 'all crepuscular, but the heart, the passion, humour, everything as bright as fire in the mist.'[9] In her essay on the cinema, written in 1926, she anticipates films like Jean Cocteau's *La Belle et la Bête* (1946):

    [4] Ibid. 72–3, 25 Oct. 1920.
    [5] Virginia Woolf, *Jacob's Room* (Oxford: Oxford University Press, 1992), 130. All future refs. in the text are taken from this edn.
    [6] Julia Kristeva, *Powers of Horror* (New York: Columbia University Press, 1982), 12.
    [7] Robin Majumdar and Allen Mclaurin (eds.), *Virginia Woolf: the Critical Heritage* (London: Routledge & Kegan Paul, 1975), 107.   [8] Ibid.
    [9] VWD ii. 13–14, 26 Jan. 1920.

The most fantastic contrasts could be flashed before us with a speed which the writer can only toil after in vain; the dream architecture of arches and battlements, of cascades falling and fountains rising, which sometimes visits us in sleep or shapes itself in half-darkened rooms, could be realized before our waking eyes. No fantasy could be too far-fetched or insubstantial. The past could be unrolled, distances annihilated, and the gulfs which dislocate novels . . . could by the sameness of the background, by the repetition of some scene, be smoothed away.[10]

'Dream architecture' is an evocative phrase for what Woolf creates in her fiction, in spite of what she says about its inaccessibility to the writer, exploring as she does the caves of the psyche that are unreachable through rational processes. The gulfs which dislocate realistic novels are smoothed away in *Jacob's Room* by techniques very like this: whole paragraphs are repeated in new contexts; motifs, idiosyncratic links, and punctuation recur to obviate the need for sequential narrative. Similarly in 'The Daughters of the Late Colonel' Mansfield uses visual signifiers to create unstated links, and destabilizes the apparently tidy division of the story into parts by the illogicality of the story's juxtapositions. One part does not grow out of another as an organic narrative; the sequence of the parts expresses the dream architecture of the sisters' unconscious rather than a coherent plot. This chapter focuses on the ways in which the movement of the narrative voice in Mansfield's and Woolf's work expresses boundaries and overcrossings.

It is clear from Woolf's diaries that she went frequently to the cinema; Mansfield was at times an extra in films. Anne Estelle Rice gives an account of meeting her and commenting on her changed appearance; Mansfield replied that she had just jumped off Battersea Bridge to be rescued by the hero in a film.[11] In letters to Bertrand Russell in 1917 she writes: 'Tomorrow I am acting for the movies—an "exterior scene in walking dress." ' Her health suffered because of it: 'My last day with the "movies" —walking about a big bare studio in what the American producer calls "slap up evening dress" has laid me low ever since.'[12] There is no record of which films she appeared in, but her fiction,

---

[10] Virginia Woolf, *The Captain's Death Bed and Other Essays* (London: Hogarth, 1950), 170–1.
[11] Gillian Boddy, *Katherine Mansfield: The Woman and the Writer* (Ringwood: Penguin, 1988), 59.   [12] KMCL i. 293–4, 16 and 21 Jan. 1917.

like Woolf's, suggests a sensitivity to new cinematic editing techniques such as dissolves, montage, the cut, and the possibility of surreal juxtapositions, such as those in Buñuel and Dali's *Un Chien Andalou* (1928). A dissolve, fading one scene out as another fades in, and showing both simultaneously for a second or two, is literally impossible in writing, but Woolf comes very close to it in passages such as this, which focuses on Mrs Flanders' letter to Jacob when he uses the privacy of his room for an affair with the prostitute, Florinda. The verbal camera focuses initially on the letter, but invites the reader's imagination to dissolve in and out of what is happening in other rooms; physical objects acquire heightened significance as the reader, like them, is locked out. The letter, identified by Jacob as his mother's handwriting, becomes, in a surreal transformation brought about by a play on language, Mrs Flanders's hand which her son abandons in favour of his mistress; it is further transmuted to become her heart:

The letter lay upon the hall table; Florinda coming in that night took it up with her, put it on the table as she kissed Jacob, and Jacob seeing the hand, left it there under the lamp, between the biscuit-tin and the tobacco-box. They shut the bedroom door behind them.

The sitting-room neither knew nor cared. The door was shut; and to suppose that wood, when it creaks, transmits anything save that rats are busy and wood dry is childish. These old houses are only brick and wood, soaked in human sweat, grained with human dirt. But if the pale blue envelope lying by the biscuit-box had the feelings of a mother, the heart was torn by the little creak, the sudden stir. Behind the door was the obscene thing, the alarming presence, and terror would come over her as at death, or the birth of a child. Better, perhaps, burst in and face it than sit in the antechamber listening to the little creak, the sudden stir, for her heart was swollen, and pain threaded it. My son, my son—such would be her cry, uttered to hide her vision of him stretched with Florinda. (pp. 123–4)

The repetition of the significant phrase 'the little creak, the sudden stir' has the effect that Woolf imagines for repetition in her essay on film; it suggests the orgasm of the lovers without invasive curiosity.

Though the novel ostensibly has a male protagonist, the seeing eye in the text is that of the female narrator, who sometimes imitates the technique of cinematic montage to invite the reader to make connections which Jacob does not see. Eisenstein's theory of montage, applied in such films as *The Battleship Potemkin*, was that 'the result of juxtaposition is always qualitatively (that is, in dimension, or power, if you like) different from each of the components taken separately.'[13] In the following sequence from *Jacob's Room* the narrator accumulates a series of images, isolated by blank spaces on the page, which invite the reader to make connections that are entirely implicit in the pictures offered.[14] Jacob walks into London with his friend Timmy Durrant, thinking of Florinda who has made sexual advances to him:

However, as he tramped into London it seemed to him that they were making the flagstones ring on the road to the Acropolis, and that if Socrates saw them coming he would bestir himself and say 'my fine fellows', for the whole sentiment of Athens was entirely after his heart; free, venturesome, high-spirited . . . She had called him Jacob without asking his leave. She had sat upon his knee. Thus did all good women in the days of the Greeks.

At this moment there shook out into the air a wavering, quavering, doleful lamentation which seemed to lack strength to unfold itself, and yet flagged on; at the sound of which doors in back streets burst sullenly open; workmen stumped forth.

Florinda was sick.

Mrs Durrant, sleepless as usual, scored a mark by the side of certain lines in the *Inferno*.

Clara slept buried in her pillows; on her dressing-table dishevelled roses and a pair of long white gloves.

Still wearing the conical white hat of a pierrot, Florinda was sick.

(pp. 102–3)

The interpretation of this 'montage' sequence will depend on each reader, which is not what Eisenstein intended with his principle of dialectical montage; it is more like the filmic Impressionism of Jean Vigo's *L'Atalante* (1934). One possible way of reading this passage is to see the men at the beginning of it as linked by an ineluctable imperial bond. Jacob, as one of the officer class, marches into Athens/London, but the ideals of democratic government require that the 'fine fellows' must be ready to die

---

[13] Sergei Eisenstein, *Notes of a Film Director* (Moscow: Foreign Languages Publishing House, 1946), 64.

[14] John Mepham discusses this technique as freeze-framing and collage in *Virginia Woolf: A Literary Life* (London: Macmillan, 1991), 79.

for their country. The associations of Jacob's surname, Flanders, and the recurrent sound of marching boots in the novel, anticipate the conclusion, in which his mother asks his friend what to do with her dead son's shoes. Inextricably linked to the officers are the men who respond to a siren calling them to work, and also make their boots ring in the streets. There is no joy or eagerness in their reaction; they have no education, and cannot place themselves in a privileged tradition, as Jacob does. But the appearance of the text on the page, where individual sentences about the women are surrounded by blank space, suggests that the women are isolated both from the men and from each other. Florinda has been turned into a carnival figure, given a name 'by a painter who had wished to signify that the flower of her maidenhood was still unplucked' (p. 103). Her pierrot's hat implies that this is both unlikely and degrading; her illness seems more than physical when the phrase 'Florinda was sick' is reiterated. Mrs Durrant's sleeplessness suggests neurosis and associates her with a preoccupation with death, since she is reading Dante's *Inferno*. Her daughter seems to have been to a ball, and yet her dishevelled roses, and the fact that she is 'buried in her pillows', isolate her and hint that the time for gathering rosebuds is over. Mortal as they are, there is no bond between the women; mother and daughter are cut off from each other, and from the prostitute. The gloves and the pierrot hat imply that both young women have roles to play which are destructive to them.

Mansfield's story 'Pictures' is about a middle-aged woman who has to play a series of roles; she has been a singer but is now down on her luck and looking for a part as an extra. The first version of the story was a dialogue published in *New Age* in May 1917 entitled 'The Common Round'; when the story incorporating the dialogue was first published in *Art and Letters*, in 1919, it was called 'The Pictures', but it was reprinted as 'Pictures' in *Bliss and Other Stories* in 1920. The shift in title is significant as 'The Pictures' limits the meaning mainly to the movies, whereas there is a whole series of different interpretations of pictures within the story. It begins with uncharacteristically precise placing, like the intertitle of a silent film: 'Eight o'clock in the morning'.[15] The filmic technique is continued as

---

[15] CS 119.

Miss Moss gazes at the ceiling but sees what is in her mind: 'A pageant of Good Hot Dinners passed across the ceiling, each of them accompanied by a bottle of Nourishing Stout.' The capital letters imply that these have been central to Miss Moss's way of life, and that she clings to them as totems of sturdy physical comfort in an increasingly hostile and changing world. The characters' names have a cartoon quality that is alien to Mansfield's other mature work, again suggesting a link with the title: Miss Moss has to batten on her upstanding landlady, Mrs Pine; the companies that recruit extras are called 'Kit and Kadgit' and 'Beit and Bithems'; Miss Moss is rejected by the 'Backwash Film Company', which suggests both a backwater and the adage, ominous for Miss Moss as she can offer no exchange, 'if you wash my back, I'll wash yours.' Miss Moss's first attempt at acting is a failure; she pretends the letter the landlady brings in contains good news about a job, but the landlady is not deceived. The scene is one of claustrophobic entrapment. Miss Moss's privacy is invaded when: 'Suddenly, in bounced the landlady' (p. 119); the inversion of the sentence stresses the intrusion. Another unsuccessful attempt at playing a part is exposed when Miss Moss speaks bracingly to her reflection in the mirror: 'But the person in the glass made an ugly face at her' (p. 121). The alienation from the self, and the desperate attempt to inhabit the image that she is trying to present, which is itself pathetically at odds with the glamour required for the movies, are evident in the writer's presentation of her anonymous picture:

Ten minutes later, a stout lady in blue serge, with a bunch of artificial 'parmas' at her bosom, a black hat covered with purple pansies, white gloves, boots with white uppers, and a vanity bag containing one and three, sang in a low contralto voice:
'Sweet-heart, remember when days are forlorn
It al-ways is dar-kest before the dawn.'
But the person in the glass made a face at her, and Miss Moss went out. (p. 122)

Here she is doubly alienated, a stout lady singing a music-hall song and addressing herself as 'sweet-heart' but disconnected from the person in the glass, with the vanity bag an indicator of the hopelessness of her endeavour; stout ladies covered in artificial pansies and violets cannot compete in a world that idolizes Lilian Gish and Mary Pickford. The repetition of 'the person in the glass made a face at her' stresses Miss Moss's loneliness, defamiliarizing her own image and making it one of the text's many pictures.

The description of the street that Miss Moss steps into is surreal, and a reminder that both Woolf and Mansfield intensely admired T. S. Eliot's 'The Love Song of J. Alfred Prufrock'; Mansfield read it aloud to the other guests at Garsington, Ottoline Morrell's country house, in June 1917. *Prufrock and Other Observations* also contains 'Rhapsody on a Windy Night', with its 'cat which flattens itself in the gutter'. When Miss Moss goes out:

There were grey crabs all the way down the street slopping water over grey stone steps. With his strange, hawking cry and the jangle of cans the milk-boy went his rounds. Outside Brittweiler's Swiss House he made a splash, and an old brown cat without a tail appeared from nowhere, and began greedily and silently drinking up the spill. It gave Miss Moss a queer feeling to watch—a sinking, as you might say.

(p. 122)

The final phrase is Miss Moss's own; no wonder she is depressed in a world of surreal creatures, where humans become crabs: 'the char began crawling towards her' (p. 123). The sinister impact on the reader of the streets is reinforced by insistent contextual references; the landlady mentions the young Pine, ' "my poor dear lad in France" ' and the waitress tells the cashier that her boyfriend has just returned from France and is so ' "brahn" ' that she calls him ' "old mahogany" ', suggesting the felling of human timber. Miss Moss, covered as she is with false flowers which imply that her natural bloom is over, is intimidated by the implication of masculine power, and female empowerment through the women's link with serving soldiers. The idea is reiterated when Mr Bithem 'gave her a whole grin to herself and patted her fat back. "Hearts of oak, dear lady," said Mr Bithem, "hearts of oak!" ' (p. 125). The image of herself that Miss Moss is trying to sustain is dented twice; she is invisible to the waitress and the cashier in the ABC, and as she tries to cross the road, a taxi-driver yells at her: ' "Look out, Fattie; don't go to sleep!" ' She writes a series of scenes for herself, which are miniature film scripts resembling film narratives of the period, though the picture in the mirror undermines her attempts at cheerfulness: 'But the person in the pocket mirror made a hideous face at her, and that was too much for Miss Moss; she had a good cry' (p. 127). Her final sustained attempt at a script, to protect herself against all the parts she cannot play which require sand-dancing, buck-jumping, high-diving, and girlish glamour, provides the context for the story's climax. She contemplates entering the Café de Madrid:

'It's such a place for artists too. I might just have a stroke of luck . . . A dark handsome gentleman in a fur coat comes in with a friend, and sits at my table, perhaps. "No, old chap, I've searched London for a contralto and I can't find a soul. You see, the music is difficult; have a look at it." ' And Miss Moss heard herself saying: 'Excuse me, I happen to be a contralto, and I have sung that part many times. . . . Extraordinary! "Come back to my studio and I'll try your voice now." . . . Ten pounds a week.' (p. 127)

The reflection of this hopeful narrative in the mirror that the story itself provides is like the person in the glass who makes an ugly face. The man who sits opposite her is not dark and handsome, but stout, and he wears, not a fur coat, but 'a very small hat that floated on the top of his head like a little yacht' (p. 128). He is not looking for a contralto:

The stout gentleman considered her, drumming with her fingers on the table.
'I like 'em firm and well covered,' said he.
Miss Moss, to her surprise, gave a loud snigger.
Five minutes later the stout gentleman heaved himself up. 'Well, am I goin' your way, or are you comin' mine?' he asked.
'I'll come with you, if it's all the same,' said Miss Moss. And she sailed after the little yacht out of the café. (ibid.)

The sense that she is acting a part alien to the person in the mirror is sustained when she is surprised by her own snigger, which is a contradiction of her own affirmation, just before she goes into the café, that: ' "I'm a respectable woman—I'm a contralto singer." '

Miss Moss has no room of her own; her space can be repossessed by the landlady, and she has to act a series of parts to try to retain it; the final role, of prostitute, negates everything that she has tried to affirm about her own dignity. It is ironic that she cannot get a job as an extra, as life requires her to act to survive. In their own lives, as I have indicated, Woolf and Mansfield acted some parts voluntarily, but also felt that they were part of a way of life that demanded masks; in comparing E. M. Forster with Clive Bell, Woolf writes in her diary that 'Clive showed as gaslight beside Morgan's normal day—his day not sunny and tempestuous but a day of pure light, capable of showing up the rouge & powder, the dust & wrinkles, the cracks & contortions of my poor parrokeet. He makes me feel the foot-lights myself.'[16] Both were made to feel insecure by trying to write themselves into a position where they were perceived to be doing something new, not conforming to prescripted parts, to masculine or traditional imperatives about the nature of fiction. Woolf writes in her diary of her insecurity about what she is doing with *Jacob's Room*; her confidence has been sapped by a conversation with T. S. Eliot about James Joyce: 'He said nothing—but I reflected how what I'm doing is probably being better done by Mr Joyce. Then I began to wonder what it is that I am doing: to suspect, as is usual in such cases, that I have not thought my plan out plainly enough—so to dwindle, niggle, hesitate—which means that one's lost.'[17] At the same time she is planning a response to Arnold Bennett's view that men are intellectually and creatively superior to women, a contradictory situation to live out as she is at once cowed by Eliot's stance and mistrustful of it. Similarly the response to 'The Daughters of the Late Colonel' undermined Mansfield's confidence as it assumed malice in the writer. Mansfield describes her feelings about it in a letter to William Gerhardi, who had written to her to say how much he admired the story:

While I was writing that story I lived for it but when it was finished, I confess I hoped very much that my readers would understand what I was trying to express. But very few did. They thought it was 'cruel'; they thought I was 'sneering' at Jug and Constantia; they thought it was 'drab.' And in the last paragraph I was 'poking fun at the poor old things.'
Its almost terrifying to be so misunderstood.[18]

---

[16] VWD ii. 6, 10 Jan. 1920.   [17] Ibid. 69, 26 Sept. 1920.
[18] KMCL iv. 248–9, 23 June 1921.

Woolf and Mansfield are both inside and outside, here and there, asserting their place by writing their fiction and yet easily undermined, grateful for male approval and nervous without it, feeling their own creative energy and yet frightened that their contravention of the Father's Law will be punished in some way. The central focus of comparison for this chapter is between *Jacob's Room* and 'The Daughters of the Late Colonel'. Both writers refer to their characters in these works as ghostly: Woolf reports her husband's view that in *Jacob's Room* 'the people are ghosts'[19] and Mansfield reflects ruefully about 'The Daughters' that 'what seems to me even *lively* is ghostly glee.'[20]

The spectral quality in both works relates to the state of liminality experienced by Woolf and Mansfield as a result of their precarious health, their tenuous place in a male world of letters, and their relationships with their families, particularly with their fathers. Both works are about the death of the father; both begin with it, and the absent father is a palpably felt presence in both texts. In both, women, as Miss Moss does in 'Pictures', try to find a place for themselves in a world controlled by patriarchy.[21] Constantia and Josephine creep round their dead father's house wondering whether they can ask their servant for a cup of hot water, fearful of entering their father's room; in *Jacob's Room*, a powerfully rhetorical account of the dispossession of the uneducated, both male and female, in contrast to men of letters, sandwiches Jacob's authority between the homelessness of particular women who do not reappear in the text. Jacob visits St Paul's in an idle moment:

Tired with scrubbing the steps of the Prudential Society's office, which she did year in and year out, Mrs Lidgett took her seat beneath the great Duke's tomb, folded her hands, and half closed her eyes. A magnificent place for an old woman to rest in, by the very side of the great Duke's bones, whose victories mean nothing to her, whose name she knows not, though she never fails to greet the little angels opposite, as she passes out. (pp. 86–7)

The great Duke is Wellington, victor of Waterloo, at home in the national shrine; his power is a comment on Mrs Lidgett's

---

[19] VWD ii. 186, 26 July 1922.   [20] KMCL iv. 230, 19 May 1921.
[21] This is well explored in Kate Flint's introduction to the World's Classics edn. of *Jacob's Room*.

exclusion. She does not even get inside the Prudential Society's office, but only scrubs its steps; she, a weary old woman, is cut off from knowledge of her country's history and mystified by it. Jacob is linked with the great Duke by the book he carries; education makes him part of an élite, and his book is about empire, connecting the Greeks with the British empire which was established in all its expansive energy in the nineteenth century on the foundation of Wellington's victory over Napoleon:

> Only Jacob, carrying in his hand Finlay's *Byzantine Empire*, which he had bought in Ludgate Hill, looked a little different; for in his hand he carried a book, which book he would at nine-thirty precisely, by his own fireside, open and study, as no one else of all these multitudes would do. They have no houses. The streets belong to them; the shops; the churches; theirs the innumerable desks; the stretched office lights; the vans are theirs, and the railway slung high above the street. If you look closer you will see that three elderly men at a little distance from each other run spiders along the pavement as if the street were their parlour, and here, against the wall, a woman stares at nothing, boot-laces extended, which she does not ask you to buy.   (pp. 87–8)

It is partly the rhythm of this extraordinary passage which conveys its filmic quality; the repetition of 'carrying in his hand', 'in his hand he carried a book, which book' insists that we dwell on it as Jacob will do because he has his own space. The abrupt statement 'They have no houses' tersely shifts into the present tense and introduces the nomadic experience of most of the population, as the camera cuts off, looking from a distance and then coming in for a close-up on the three spider-running men, as weird as the crabs in Miss Moss's street. The figures move as they do in film projected too fast, or like shapes created by animation:

> Innumerable overcoats of the quality prescribed hung empty all day in the corridors, but as the clock struck six each was exactly filled, and the little figures, split apart into trousers or moulded into a single thickness, jerked rapidly with angular forward motion along the pavement; then dropped into darkness. Beneath the pavement, sunk in the earth, hollow drains lined with yellow light for ever conveyed them this way and that, and large letters upon enamel plates represented in the underworld the parks, squares, and circuses of the upper.   (p. 88)

The resonances of this passage are many and varied. It may remind the reader of the crowd flowing over London Bridge in

Eliot's *The Waste Land*, which was published in the same year as *Jacob's Room*, 1922. It also anticipates the Expressionist film directed by Fritz Lang, *Metropolis*, released in 1926. Partly because the novel culminates in Jacob's death in the First World War and this is constantly prefigured in the book, the little figures dropping into the darkness and tunnels may also bring to mind the newsreel footage of events such as the trench warfare in the Battle of the Somme (1916). All these mechanical people, enmeshed in the world of metropolitan work, are framed by a woman who is as wild and weird as the singer at the doorway to the underground station in *Mrs Dalloway*. She is the antithesis of Jacob holding his book which is both about authority and symbolizes Jacob's own authority; she seems to be outside patriarchy. She makes up and sings her own song of unfettered human passions, which are unlike all Jacob's experiences of lust or love. When he feels the hook in his side, and is caught by a woman, he has a classical backdrop, and visits the Acropolis with her after sunset; the repetition ('not for coppers', 'singing', 'wild', 'heart') in the description of the unnamed, blind singer in this after-sunset scene stresses her wildness, flouting conventions about child-rearing, as the long sentence of which the paragraph is composed indicates the flow of her emotion:

Long past sunset an old blind woman sat on a camp-stool with her back to the stone wall of the Union of London and Smith's Bank, clasping a brown mongrel tight in her arms and singing out loud, not for coppers, no, from the depths of her gay wild heart—her sinful, tanned heart—for the child who fetches her is the fruit of sin, and should have been in bed, curtained, asleep, instead of hearing in the lamplight her mother's wild song, where she sits against the Bank, singing not for coppers, with her dog against her breast. (p. 89)

Jacob has a room of his own; both Woolf and Mansfield indicate in their journals and letters the need for private space. Mansfield writes in Ospedaletti: 'My room is horrible. Very noisy: a constant clatter and a feeling as though it were *doorless*. French people don't care a hang how much noise they make.'[22] When Woolf was involved in writing *Mrs Dalloway* her sister-in-law Karin arrived with her daughter Ann:

[22] KMJ 197, 1 Feb. 1920.

There I was swimming in the highest ether known to me, & thinking I'd finish by Thursday; Lottie suggests to Karin we'd like to have Ann: Karin interprets my polite refusal to her own advantage & comes down herself on Saturday, blowing everything to smithereens . . . 'Disturbing the flow of inspiration?' she said this morning, having shouted outside the door till I had to fetch cotton wool. And its down in ruins my house; my wings broken; & I left on the bare ground . . . feeling that I ought to go in & be a good aunt—wh. I'm not by nature.[23]

Guilt about not playing the woman's role is mixed with a series of destructive images, of Karin exploding her sanctuary, both her quiet room and the house of fiction she creates in it, leaving her as a grounded bird unable to fly.

In her writing Woolf consistently links having a room of one's own in which to read and write, as Jacob has, with the house of fiction; her personal writing is full of architectural metaphors. She plans *Jacob's Room* thinking that 'one thing should open out of another' and that there will be 'no scaffolding; scarcely a brick to be seen'.[24] Once it is done, she writes to Hope Mirrlees that: 'Writing without the old bannisters, one makes jumps and jerks that are not necessary'.[25] The movement of the camera may have been sympathetic to her because film was a new form which had not yet been decisively shaped into gendered structures, whereas most literary forms were in male ownership: 'a book is not made of sentences laid end to end, but of sentences built, if an image helps, into arcades or domes. And this shape too has been made by men out of their own needs for their own uses.'[26] Mansfield and she think alike about the need to expand the limits of prose fiction, an area in which women have from its inception had some input into its design, according to Woolf. Crafting individual sentences to enact what is being expressed is crucial to both of them. Mansfield's response to a comment from Murry about her use of dashes makes the reader regret that his letters from these months were destroyed, though it is amusing to guess what he might have said:

About the punctuation in The Stranger. Thank you, Bogey. No, my dash isn't quite a feminine dash (certainly when I was young it was).

[23] VWD ii. 314–15, 29 Sept. 1924.   [24] Ibid. 13, 26 Jan. 1920.
[25] VWL iii. 3, 6 Jan. 1923.
[26] Virginia Woolf, *A Room of One's Own* (London: Hogarth, 1929), 115–16.

But it was intentional in that story. I was trying to do away with the three dots. They have been so abused by female & male writers that I fight shy of them—*much* tho' I need them. The truth is—punctuation is infernally difficult. If I had time Id like to write an open letter to the A. on the subject. Its boundaries need to be enlarged.[27]

In the works to be focused on in this chapter, boundaries are enlarged in both content and form, in that the writers concentrate on middle-aged women, figures who are on the margins of most texts, certainly male-authored ones. Though Jacob is ostensibly the subject of *Jacob's Room*, he is in fact the shadowy focus of the female gaze, including the narrator's; she says: 'Whether we know what was in his mind is another question. Granted ten years' seniority and a difference of sex, fear of him comes first; this is swallowed up by a desire to help . . . As for following him back to his rooms, no—that we won't do' (p. 128). The narrator is trapped between two roles, following her young hero wherever he goes as his creator, and fearing his masculine confidence so much that she wants to serve it in some way. The classic trap for the middle-aged woman novelist is articulated in the text: the narrator's exaggerated respect for the protagonist's privacy leaves readers aware of their own frustration in never understanding Jacob, and aware also of the position of the chorus of women in the text, whom they know much more intimately. Most of these women are, like the narrator, acting the part that their society has written for them, and at the same time we see them trying, in letters and diaries, to write an alternative script which gives them their own space.

Jacob's Room opens with a woman writing; Jacob's mother is writing a letter to Captain Barfoot. She is at the bay, the in-between place, writing of her position as a disempowered member of her society, a widow with three small boys. There is an intimate link between her writing and her emotion; the phrase 'slowly welling' suggests tears rather than ink, implying that for Betty Flanders there is a continuum between writing, feeling, and perception which may annihilate conventions of punctuation: 'Slowly welling from the point of her gold nib, pale blue ink dissolved the full stop; for there her pen stuck; her eyes

---

[27] KMCL iv. 118–19, 23 Nov. 1920.

fixed, and tears slowly filled them. The entire bay quivered; the lighthouse wobbled; and she had the illusion that the mast of Mr Connor's little yacht was bending like a wax candle in the sun' (p. 3). Like her author, she ignores the full stop, allowing the blot to spread, as the novel blurs one scene into another. At the same time she is the unconscious object of a male gaze, an artist who has a very precise view of her function: 'Here was that woman moving—actually going to get up—confound her! He struck the canvas a hasty violet-black dab. For the landscape needed it' (pp. 4–5). This is the view of imaginary critics of his painting; unlike Betty's letter, this artefact is produced from a sense of critical imperatives, not feeling. Yet her letters are valued by their recipients partly for their form; Mrs Flanders' letter rejecting Mr Floyd's proposal of marriage shows that she can create her own roles as a text which moves the recipient: 'it was such a motherly, respectful, inconsequent, regretful letter that he kept it for many years' (p. 23). There is also the implication that this is not the whole story, and that Mrs Flanders uses surrogates to express the secret self which is suppressed in her writing. She and her boys are given the red-haired Floyd's cat, Topaz: 'she smiled, thinking how she had had him gelded, and how she did not like red hair in men. Smiling, she went into the kitchen' (p. 25). She has also created her own enduring fiction about her husband; the narrator's sentence describing it moves from fact through local gossip to culminate, ungrammatically but decisively, in Mrs Flanders' view of the matter:

'Merchant of this city,' the tombstone said; though why Betty Flanders had chosen so to call him when, as many still remembered, he had only sat behind an office window for three months, and before that had broken horses, ridden to hounds, farmed a few fields, and run a little wild—well, she had to call him something. An example for the boys.
(p. 15)

The novel shows Mrs Flanders, Mrs Jarvis, Mrs Durrant, Mother Stuart, Clara, and Florinda writing letters 'for letters are written when the dark presses round a bright red cave' (p. 126), the recurrent image of female habitation; Jacob's are 'long letters about art, morality, and politics' (p. 127) but the others are 'the unpublished works of women, written by the fireside' (p. 123) which attempt, obliquely at least, self-definition. Some of these women are so constrained by the shape patriarchy has imposed on them that they can only replicate it. Clara attempts to express what she feels about Jacob in her Letts diary: 'But Mr Letts allows little space in his shilling diaries. Clara was not the one to encroach upon Wednesday' (pp. 94–5). Similarly Mrs Norman writes two mental scripts in quick succession when Jacob joins her carriage in the train to Cambridge; it is no accident that she is armed with a novel from Mudie's library. When she realizes that she is shut up with him for the whole journey: 'She would throw the scent-bottle with her right hand, she decided, and tug the communication cord with her left . . . it is a fact that men are dangerous' (p. 35). Almost immediately after this she feels maternal towards him: 'Should she say to the young man (and after all he was just the same age as her own boy): "if you want to smoke, don't mind me"?' (p. 36). The narrator plays with these archetypal roles, both undermining them and showing how women allow themselves to be entrapped by them. At Mrs Pascoe's austere but beautiful Cornish cottage: 'The picture papers were delivered punctually on Sunday, and she pored long over Lady Cynthia's wedding at the Abbey. She, too, would have liked to ride in a carriage with springs' (p. 70). In fictional terms, we think we know how to place her as a wholesome rustic, but are taken by surprise: 'Her face was assuredly not soft, sensual, or lecherous, but hard, wise, wholesome rather, signifying in a room full of sophisticated people the flesh and blood of life. She would tell a lie, though, as soon as the truth' (pp. 69–70).

Throughout the novel a chorus of named women reflect on the characters and events, rarely affecting the action but providing a series of seeing eyes through which the reader can observe the text's shadowy men, and inviting contemplation of gender roles. The narrator herself participates in this, in response to Mrs Flanders' sudden, uncensorious, reaction to her son Archer:

'What did I ask you to remember?' she said.
'I don't know,' said Archer.
'Well, I don't know either,' said Betty, humorously and simply, and who shall deny that this blankness of mind, when combined with profusion, mother wit, old wives' tales, haphazard ways, moments of astonishing daring, humour and sentimentality—who shall deny that in these respects every woman is nicer than any man?   (p. 9)

The impression given is that this is not an absolute judgement from the narrator, but an impulsive response to the fact that Mrs Flanders does not give the expected reply; the familiar interrogation of the wary child has a totally unpredictable and self-deprecatory outcome. Her roles are suggested by the way in which she is named: ' "Mrs Flanders"—"Poor Betty Flanders"—"Dear Betty" . . . Elizabeth Flanders' (p. 14).

Masculine domination of women and their roles is inscribed, often literally, on the landscape and architecture depicted by the text. In Scarborough, Mrs Barfoot is the daughter of James Coppard 'who was mayor at the time of Queen Victoria's jubilee, and Coppard is painted upon municipal watering-carts and over shop windows, and upon the zinc blinds of solicitors' consulting-room windows' (p. 29). In the reading room of the British Museum, the feminist Julia Hedge gazes at the names inscribed and gilded on the roof: 'And she read them all round the dome—the names of great men which remind us—"Oh damn," said Julia Hedge, "why didn't they leave room for an Eliot or a Brontë?" ' (p. 145). Imperial male power is manifest in the buildings the characters see, from the Roman fortress that Mrs Flanders and her children visit at the beginning to the Acropolis and the Parthenon at the end. The great statue of Athena is no longer there, and Jacob significantly stands where she used to stand, to identify landmarks, uninterested in personal associations: 'he seldom thought of Plato or Socrates in the flesh; on the other hand his feeling for architecture was very strong; he preferred statues to pictures; and he was beginning to think a great deal about the problems of civilization, which were solved, of course, so very remarkably by the ancient Greeks' (p. 207). He himself is consistently seen as a piece of monumental masonry, not of dream architecture, and compared to statues that manifest the power of their owners or of their society. At a party on Guy Fawkes' Night, itself a celebration of the preservation of the state, Jacob is wreathed in flowers and glass grapes 'until he looked like the figure-head of a wrecked ship' (p. 100). Florinda tells him that he is ' "like one of those statues" ' (p. 108) in the British Museum, and 'Fanny's idea of Jacob was more statuesque, noble, and eyeless than ever. To reinforce her vision she had taken to visiting the British Museum, where, keeping her eyes downcast until she was alongside of the battered Ulysses, she opened them and got a fresh shock of Jacob's presence' (p. 238). The eyelessness is significant, because Jacob cannot see the obvious human needs and desires that surround him; he thinks instead 'of Rome; of architecture; of jurisprudence' (p. 239). Sandra Wentworth Williams 'got Jacob's head exactly on a level with the head of the Hermes of Praxiteles. The comparison was all in his favour' (p. 200). All these statues are emblems of male power and domination, reminding their societies of narratives of masculine strength; the statues are much larger than life, and Jacob's interest in sculpture and architecture suggests his difference from the women in the text, including the narrator. He is not concerned with impulse, fluidity, and movement, the cinematic dimension of the novel, but with the monumental, the ancient, and the rational. The description of his room in London is repeated as if to suggest its permanence in a novel with no scaffolding and scarcely a brick to be seen; its balanced dimensions belong to the Age of Reason, though its ram's skull is a reminder of Jacob's childhood trauma when, at a moment of masculine triumph straddling the rock-pool, he was terrified by the apparition of the lovers and lost his way on the beach: 'The rooms are shapely, the ceilings high; over the doorway a rose, or a ram's skull, is carved in the wood. The eighteenth century has its distinction' (pp. 93–4).

The statues and buildings celebrate what ancient Greek and many subsequent European societies have prized: military prowess, masculine discipline, political stability, and intellectual distinction. Such stories are woven into the fabric of Jacob's society, so that a woman trying to assert a different perspective has to go against her own grain:

He was a man with a temper; tenacious; faithful. Women would have felt, 'Here is law. Here is order. Therefore we must cherish this man. He is on the Bridge at night,' and, handing him his cup, or whatever it might be, would run on to visions of shipwreck and disaster, in which all the passengers come tumbling from their cabins, and there is the captain, buttoned in his pea-jecket, matched with the storm, vanquished by it but by none other. 'Yet I have a soul,' Mrs Jarvis would bethink her, as Captain Barfoot suddenly blew his nose in a great red bandanna handkerchief, 'and it's the man's stupidity that's the cause of this, and the storm's my storm as well as his.' (p. 33)

Many of the women in the text are, like Ellen Barfoot, 'civilization's prisoner' (p. 29), existing in a world where their educated menfolk are answering essay questions such as Jacob's, ' "Does History consist of the Biographies of Great Men?" ' (p. 48). The life of the Duke of Wellington, mentioned casually as a book in Jacob's study, occurs as a significant repetition throughout the novel. The great Duke's tomb in St Paul's gives him quasi-divine power, as saviour of his nation; his story is written into the fabric of the building. His status as a father of the nation is constantly referred to:

'The Duke of Wellington was a gentleman,' said Timmy.
'Keats wasn't.'
'Lord Salisbury was.'
'And what about God?' said Jacob.   (p. 66)

The stories that the society tells itself and reinterprets are of male heroism: at Covent Garden 'Tristan was twitching his rug up under his armpits twice a week' (p. 90), a rather dismissive reference to Wagner's hero and his belief in his own ineffable power and self-sacrifice. The narrator envies masculine authority and wonders about it: 'doffing one's own headpiece, how strange to assume for a moment someone's—anyone's—to be a man of valour who has ruled the Empire' (p. 91). The most potent image of female exclusion from intellectual and imperial power is repeated twice on the same page, but without comment from the narrator; it focuses on Jacob walking from the British Museum to his room, both buildings bastions of male dominance:

In the street below Jacob's room voices were raised.
   But he read on. For after all Plato continues imperturbably. And Hamlet utters his soliloquy. And there the Elgin Marbles lie, all night long, old Jones's lantern sometimes recalling Ulysses, or a horse's head; or sometimes a flash of gold, or a mummy's sunk yellow cheek. Plato and Shakespeare continue; and Jacob, who was reading the *Phaedrus*, heard people vociferating round the lamp-post, and the woman battering at the door and crying, 'Let me in!' as if a coal had dropped from the fire, or a fly, falling from the ceiling, had lain on its back, too weak to turn over.   (p. 149)

The powerlessness and insignificance of the woman, and her inability to storm the male fortress, comment obliquely on the chorus of female voices in the text, and Jacob's security as a privileged reader. The marginalized chorus itself signals the writer's awareness that she still writes, to some extent, within the constraints of classical patriarchy. In the end however Jacob himself is sacrificed to the ideology he has collaborated with: 'sixteen gentlemen, lifting their pens or turning perhaps rather wearily in their chairs, decreed that the course of history should shape itself this way or that way, being manfully determined, as their faces showed, to impose some coherency upon Rajahs and Kaisers and the muttering in bazaars' (p. 241). Their manfulness admits of no female feeling, and they are watched 'with fixed marble eyes and an air of immortal quiescence' (ibid.) by statues of Pitt, Chatham, Burke and Gladstone. The narrator does not appear to acquiesce in this admiration of diplomacy in comparison with the 'frivolous fireside art' (p. 216) of writing fiction. She becomes a camera, recording like newsreel footage the sublime absurdity in which all this rationality culminates:

The battleships ray out over the North Sea, keeping their stations accurately apart. At a given signal all the guns are trained on a target which (the master gunner counts the seconds, watch in hand—at the sixth he looks up) flames into splinters. With equal nonchalance a dozen young men in the prime of life descend with composed faces into the depths of the sea; and there impassively (though with perfect mastery of machinery) suffocate uncomplainingly together. Like blocks of tin soldiers the army covers the cornfield, moves up the hillside, stops, reels slightly this way and that, and falls flat, save that, through fieldglasses, it can be seen that one or two pieces still agitate up and down like fragments of broken match-stick. (ibid.)

One can see why Woolf regretted that Mansfield did not live to read this book, and specifically this passage. The whole novel has shown women gazing helplessly at stony-eyed men who are sure they should exclude women from their deliberations, as Jacob wants to exclude women from King's College Chapel. This passage records the result, apparently dispassionately but inviting the reader to see it through the eyes of Mrs Flanders, Mrs Jarvis, and the narrator, with both horror and, possibly maternal, pity.

This supremely illogical, unreasonable outcome of sombre rational debate which excludes women reveals an anxiety that the narrator explores throughout the novel. She resists the kinds of generalizations that Jacob and his male companions make in their masculine confidence; when Jacob and Timmy are together: 'They were boastful, triumphant; it seemed to both that they had read every book in the world; known every sin, passion, and joy. Civilizations stood round them like flowers ready for picking' (p. 101). The narrator is much more hesitant: 'It is no use trying to sum people up. One must follow hints, not exactly what is said, nor yet entirely what is done' (p. 214). Indeed she says of Jacob that as far as she, the narrator is concerned, 'what remains is mostly a matter of guess work' (p. 98). This indirection is encoded in the novel, in the pages with blank gaps, for instance; this sentence appears isolated in the middle of a page: 'Jacob Flanders, therefore, went up to Cambridge in October, 1906' (p. 35). It seems logical, but 'therefore' relates to nothing as there is only a blank preceding it. Possibly it suggests some intuitive process in Mrs Flanders' mind, as the conversation that leads up to it is apparently about whether Captain Barfoot will stand for the council. Readers are left to follow hints, as they are when, after a blank, they read: ' "I shall go to Athens all the same," he resolved' (p. 204). Again this is a *non sequitur*, as 'all the same' must represent an argument in Jacob's mind rather than something that has been expressed in the text; the blanks seem to indicate what cannot be known about the characters. Mansfield speculates about this in a letter to her brother-in-law, in the month after she wrote 'The Daughters of the Late Colonel':

I suddenly thought of *a living mind*—a whole mind—with absolutely nothing left out. With *all* that one knows how much does one *not* know? I used to fancy one knew all but some kind of mysterious core (or one could). But now I believe just the opposite. The unknown is far far greater than the known. The known is only a mere shadow.[28]

The unknown is signalled in 'The Daughters of the Late Colonel', rather as it is in *Jacob's Room*, by blurring an apparently tidy surface.

'The Daughters of the Late Colonel' is a twelve-cell story; the reader probably expects that the twelve parts will alternate

---

[28] KMCL iv. 165, 17 Jan. 1921.

between the perspectives of the two sisters, Constantia and Josephine, or that some sections will be retrospective and some in the present, and that the division into parts will signal stages in the narrative. The parts often begin as if this is the case: the second section begins 'Another thing which complicated matters' (p. 264). But the reader asks what the first thing was, and there is no obvious answer. The wavering illogicality of the sisters' minds is caught as they try to believe that they are in control of their own lives: other sections begin with the lines: 'But, after all, it was not long now' (p. 266) and 'Well, at any rate, all that part of it was over' (p. 268). The first paragraph of the story begins briskly but then meanders off into ellipsis: 'their minds went on, thinking things out, talking things over, wondering, deciding, trying to remember where . . .' (p. 262). The sisters worry and try to decide what to do, so deeply familiar with each others' mental moves that the oddity of each seems normal to the other: ' "Speaking of Benny," said Josephine. And though Benny hadn't been mentioned Constantia immediately looked as though he had' (p. 273). Like 'Pictures' and *Jacob's Room*, the story concerns middle-aged women who are required to act parts prescribed for them by a male-dominated society; in *Jacob's Room* such women take over sections of the text though they are apparently on its margins, but here Constantia and Josephine are the central characters. Their bewilderment at being placed centre stage because of their father's death, instead of lurking in the wings, comments obliquely on the way in which drama and fiction usually privilege the young and beautiful; the sisters do not know what to say or how to dress for their parts. The unknown that is hidden within their consciousnesses signals its presence throughout, with a filmic dwelling on particular objects that suggest what the sisters are suppressing.

The title of the story was originally to have been 'The Non-Compounders', a term used at Queen's College when Mansfield was a pupil there for students who were not boarders but could attend classes in the school. It suggests a liminal state when it is applied to the story: people who do and at the same time do not belong. The title that was used when the story was published is more accessible to a general public; it places the characters in a world of genteel euphemism with 'the late colonel', and makes clear that their identity is entirely dependent on his status in society. 'The Daughters' casts them as perpetual dependants, and as permanent girls rather than women. Use of euphemism is carried into the opening line of the story: 'The week after was one of the busiest weeks of their lives' (p. 262). The reader is never told what the event that preceded the busy week was, though we guess that it was the death of the sisters' father; the fact that it cannot be articulated, and is not named until the final section of the story, may signify in a variety of ways. Polite society has difficulties in expressing the embarrassing fact of death; that this awkwardness may afflict the sisters is indicated in 'On the morning—well, on the last morning' (p. 264). They may also be so overwhelmed by grief that they cannot bear to speak of its source, or they may be feeling something that is not part of the script for bereaved daughters. This is hinted at when they are chatting, in bed at night in their shared bedroom:

And suddenly, for one awful moment, she nearly giggled. Not, of course, that she felt in the least like giggling. It must have been habit. Years ago, when they had stayed awake at night talking, their beds had simply heaved. And now the porter's head, disappearing, popped out, like a candle, under father's hat . . . The giggle mounted, mounted; she clenched her hands; she fought it down; she frowned fiercely at the dark and said 'Remember' terribly sternly. (p. 262)

The narrative perspective is Josephine's, and the sequence of thought is characteristically illogical; the implication is that they have always shared a room, so there is no reason why a childhood habit should reassert itself now. But perhaps there is, when we discover that their mother died when they were small children; possibly this reversion to infancy signals their joy that they are at last released from the patriarchal presence, though they try to invoke him by quoting the ghost of Hamlet's father. Josephine's response to the letters she has written about their bereavement could indicate that she is genuinely grief-stricken:

[T]wenty-three times when she came to 'We miss our dear father so much' she had broken down and had to use her handkerchief, and on some of them even to soak up a very light-blue tear with an edge of blotting-paper. Strange! She couldn't have put it on—but twenty-three times. Even now, though, when she said over to herself sadly 'We miss our dear father *so* much,' she could have cried if she'd wanted to.
(p. 263)

The phrase 'broken down' is obviously the standard one for the occasion, but Josephine does not actually seem to be experiencing uncontrollable grief; her tears are easily manageable, and she can cry when she wants to. It is the phrase 'We miss our dear father so much' rather than the fact of the death that moves her; the idea of being bereft is touching to her, acting the part of the orphaned daughter rather than experiencing the desolating wrench of loss. Josephine's foetal position at the end of the first section indicates a longing to return to infancy, before the Law of the Father had to be recognized by her and her sister.

That their father's tyranny over them has been replicated in others is clear from their reaction to Nurse Andrews and to their servant Kate; the syntax of the sentences about Kate expresses their fear of her and her abruptness with them. After long sentences in the narrative full of parentheses about the sisters, Kate enters:

And proud young Kate, the enchanted princess, came in to see what the old tabbies wanted now. She snatched away their plates of mock something or other and slapped down a white, terrified blancmange.
    'Jam, please, Kate,' said Josephine kindly.
    Kate knelt and burst open the sideboard, lifted the lid of the jam-pot, saw it was empty, put it on the table, and stalked off.   (pp. 265–6)

The series of monosyllabic finite verbs enacts the abruptness of Kate's actions, and 'mock something or other' shows her contempt for their euphemistic and apologetic way of life. The phrase 'the enchanted princess' alludes to the unfamiliarity of the narrative, where the traditional heroine is made marginal to what would normally themselves be peripheral figures. Again, conventional narratives haunt the story as the sisters remember their father's death, and how it failed to conform to their idea of a death-bed scene:

Then, as they were standing there, wondering what to do, he had suddenly opened one eye. Oh, what a difference it would have made, what a difference to their memory of him, how much easier to tell people about it, if he had only opened both! But no—one eye only. It glared at them a moment and then . . . went out.   (pp. 266–7)

The final phrase is again a euphemistic avoidance, possibly indicating that the sisters have not yet understood that their father's absence is permanent. His brutality to them is clear, as is their wish that he had been a loving father, if only in death. Their main overt preoccupation is with their role in telling the colonel's story; it is obviously hard to create a moving tale out of the demise of an angry Cyclops. Sometimes the sisters collaborate with and perceive the wonderful comedy of the story, but here they seem embarrassed and humiliated.

The sisters' secret selves show in half-conscious moments, opposing the power of the old tyrant without being aware that one script becomes another. In the scene with the vicar, two conventional phrases come together, but one subverts the other and reveals a hidden desire, the foreigner within, in Constantia. The vicar calls to ask what kind of funeral the sisters want for their father: ' "I should like it to be quite simple," said Josephine firmly, "and not too expensive. At the same time I should like—" "A good one that will last," thought dreamy Constantia, as if Josephine were buying a night-gown' (p. 268). Her reaction to thinking, though not expressing, her secret longing for her father to stay lastingly dead is that she feels the guilt of survival. Guilt and anxiety in relation to male authority dominate the sisters' conception of their role; they imagine a terrible resurrection for their father, a domestic Last Judgement, in which he has his revenge for the fact that they buried him. Their neurosis about having done it suggests how strong their desire to inter him is: 'What would father say when he found out? For he was bound to find out sooner or later. He always did. "Buried. You two girls had me *buried*!" She heard his stick thumping. Oh, what would they say? What possible excuse could they make? It sounded such an appallingly heartless thing to do' (pp. 268–9). They are clearly defined, by the father's 'girls' and their own wishing to make an excuse, as being trapped in permanent childhood; the thumping stick links to Kate's banging and reveals a pattern of oppression against which they have no resistance. Their anxiety about the cost of the funeral, with the colonel 'absolutely roaring' about it, mirrors the scene Woolf describes when she and her sister had to confront Leslie Stephen with the weekly accounts: 'There was a roar. His vein filled. His face flushed.'[29]

The two women's first attempt to stop playing the part of daughters, and to assert their own individuality, comes when

---

[29] Virginia Woolf, *Moments of Being* (St Albans: Triad/Panther, 1978), 145.

they enter their father's room, like Jacob's room a shrine to masculinity and patriarchy. The sisters whisper as if they were in a holy place, and they feel his presence everywhere, 'ready to spring' like a predatory animal: 'how could she explain to Constantia that father was in the chest of drawers?' (p. 271). The room is ice-cold and shrouded; the sisters seem to be confronting their father's power effectively to kill them. They feel a hallucinatory horror: they dare not look at the door and 'Constantia felt that, like the doors in dreams, it hadn't any handle at all' (p. 270). At this moment of crisis, Constantia paradoxically asserts the strength of weakness, affirming a feminine value, that it is not necessary to confront what one fears. In doing this, she does confront what she fears: ' "Why shouldn't we be weak for once in our lives, Jug? It's quite excusable. Let's be weak—be weak, Jug. It's much nicer to be weak than to be strong" ' (p. 272). Having privileged weakness, she locks the wardrobe and takes away the key, risking 'deliberately father being in there among his overcoats' (ibid.). Josephine expects the 'huge glittering wardrobe' to fall on her in retribution, as Constantia has symbolically locked father into his coffin, but nothing happens: 'Josephine followed just as she had the last time, when Constantia had pushed Benny into the round pond' (ibid.). Again, 'the last time' does not make logical sense in that there is no overt link between locking a wardrobe and pushing a brother into a pond, but we infer that the sisters have a private and unspoken record of their acts of revenge on the male despots in their family. As with *Jacob's Room*, there is an implicit link between domestic tyranny and the empire; we infer that the colonel served in the Colonial Service in Ceylon, and his son Benny, in Constantia's imagination, has all the conventional icons of expatriate exploitation: 'On the veranda, dressed all in white and wearing a cork helmet, stood Benny. His right hand shook up and down, as father's did when he was impatient. And behind him, not in the least interested, sat Hilda, the unknown sister-in-law. She swung in a cane rocker and flicked over the leaves of the *Tatler*' (p. 273). This time Josephine has an inspiration about revenge, but hers is wonderfully comic rather than heroic, like Constantia's; she imagines sending her father's gold watch to Benny in a corset box, and hints at her enjoyment of his outrage and embarrassment on receiving it. Her individuality emerges as she 'liked the idea of having to make a parcel such a curious shape that no one could possibly guess what it was' (p. 274). She and her sister are just beginning to send their own messages, albeit coded ones, rather than complying with the script that has been written in advance. She thinks that it 'would be almost too much of a surprise for Benny to open that and find father's watch inside' (ibid.). For father's watch to go to his son wrapped in a box that has held her most intimate clothing suggests that she wants to send them both a radical message that she is not a child, and that she has her own sexual adult body.

The impression that the sisters have been living the role of daughters and maiden aunts all their lives is confirmed in the only external view the reader is given of them, when the perspective is briefly that of their nephew, Cyril; though he is an adult Josephine behaves 'as though he and she were at the dentist's together' (p. 278). The final section of the story focuses the reader's attention on a series of objects that embody the possibility that the two sisters might develop their own adult and separate identities. It is done visually, filmically dwelling on objects, furniture, and light, because the sisters are unable to articulate what they feel. The possibility for release comes from the organ-grinder, a low form of street life in their father's view, but in theirs defying the military order that has been inflicted on them: 'A perfect fountain of bubbling notes shook from the barrel-organ, round, bright notes, carelessly scattered' (p. 282). For the first time they can think the forbidden phrase: 'A week since father died'. Constantia feels something close to sexual arousal as she looks at a statue of Buddha, though she cannot name the feeling:

And the stone and gilt image, whose smile always gave her such a queer feeling, almost a pain and yet a pleasant pain, seemed today to be more than smiling. He knew something; he had a secret. 'I know something that you don't know,' said her Buddha. Oh, what was it, what could it be? And yet she had always felt there was . . . something.   (ibid.)

The ellipsis indicates her tentative groping for something beyond her experience. Josephine looks at faded family photographs, but meanwhile the narrator's moving camera follows the sun: 'On the Indian carpet there fell a square of sunlight, pale red; it came and went and came—and stayed, deepened—until it shone almost golden' (ibid.). Josephine hears sparrows chirping on the window-sill but knows 'that queer little crying noise' is inside her, the suppressed self not able yet to express its grief about the wasted years but beginning to be audible. In a powerfully visualized trope of lives lived in liminal territory, a tunnel, Constantia almost brings the hidden self into the open, as she used to do when she reverted to the semiotic, escaping from masculine discourse, and sang beside the sea; the moonlight and the sea, as they do with Mrs Ramsay, link the rhythms of the female body with cyclic time. The passage again suggests cinematic images:

She remembered too how, whenever they were at the seaside, she had gone off by herself and got as close to the sea as she could, and sung something, something she had made up, while she gazed all over that restless water. There had been this other life, running out, bringing things home in bags, getting things on approval, discussing them with Jug, and taking them back to get more things on approval, and arranging father's trays and trying not to annoy father. But it all seemed to have happened in a kind of tunnel. It wasn't real. It was only when she came out of the tunnel into the moonlight or by the sea or into a thunderstorm that she really felt herself. (p. 284)

Here she recognizes her own and her sister's indecisiveness, and her role as a domestic slave to her father. The sea suggests the limitless possibilities that she has been on the edge of, as the thunderstorm implies that she was and perhaps still is capable of passion and fulfilment. When she turns to her sister to try to articulate what she has glimpsed, she and Josephine engage in a fatal moment of bourgeois politeness, an 'after you, no, after you' conversation; the flickering possibility of change evaporates with it: 'A pause. Then Constantia said faintly, "I can't say what I was going to say, Jug, because I've forgotten what it was . . . that I was going to say." Josephine was silent for a moment. She stared at a big cloud where the sun had been. Then she replied shortly, "I've forgotten too"' (p. 285). Again this has to be shown visually as they cannot articulate their loss; the cloud blotting out the sun represents it. Thomas Hardy sent Mansfield a message to say that she should write more about the two sisters, but he, in common with many other readers, must have misread the story for there is clearly no more to say.

As Mansfield wrote to William Gerhardi: 'All was meant, of course, to lead up to that last paragraph, when my two flower-less ones turned with that timid gesture, to the sun. "Perhaps *now*." And after that, it seemed to me, they died as truly as Father was dead."[30] Patriarchy triumphs, and their father's cold room closes on the sisters.

Their lives are ordinary tragedies, like those of Mansfield's Miss Moss and Miss Brill, and like the unfulfilled women in *Jacob's Room*; the delicate comedy with which they are treated acknowledges the problems of making middle-aged women the centre of a narrative. The sisters have fallen off Woolf's little strip of pavement over the abyss; their irrationality and uncertainty make their mental death poignant and absolute. Mansfield's surreal images evoking the dream architecture of the psychic life assert powerfully the sexuality, painful sacrifice, and perhaps masochism that a woman defined as a bourgeois spinster with no sexual experience has suppressed:

This time her wonder was like longing. She remembered the times she had come in here, crept out of bed in her night-gown when the moon was full, and lain on the floor with her arms outstretched, as though she was crucified. Why? The big, pale moon had made her do it. The horrible dancing figures on the carved screen had leered at her and she hadn't minded. (p. 284)

The narrative voices of *Jacob's Room* and 'The Daughters of the Late Colonel' suggest, in their sweeping movement, that the binary oppositions and structures of patriarchy, expressed so confidently by the dead colonel and Jacob, are undermined by a more flexible and tentative vision. Everything that is ex-cluded by respectable bourgeois life, both socially and psychic-ally, haunts both texts through the almost vertiginous camera movements of the hidden narrator. Virginia Woolf implies that she envies the clear lens of Mansfield's narrative eye when she writes to her at the time Woolf was feeling uncertain about the form of *Jacob's Room*:

What I admire in you so much is your transparent quality. My stuff gets muddy; and then in a novel one must have continuity, but in this one I'm always chopping and changing from one level to another.

[30] KMCL iv. 249, 23 June 1921.

I think what I'm at is to change the consciousness, and so to break up the awful stodge. Does this convey anything to you? And you seem to me to go so straightly and directly,—all clear as glass—refined, spiritual. But I must read them over again properly. I feel as if I didn't want just all realism any more—only thoughts and feelings—no cups and tables. When will your next book come out?[31]

---

[31] Joanne Trautmann Banks (ed.), *Congenial Spirits: The Selected Letters of Virginia Woolf* (London: Hogarth, 1989), 127–8, letter of 13 Feb. 1921.

8

Threshold People

Grey is the landscape; dim as ashes; the water murmurs
and moves.[1]

BECAUSE margins are dangerous they are also places of revelation. Mansfield and Woolf recur in their letters to the magnetism
as well as the terror of the overcrossing, of being on a landing
on strange stairs where the everyday consciousness becomes
aware of the foreigner within. This final chapter considers two
short stories, Woolf's 'An Unwritten Novel' and Mansfield's 'The
Stranger', in both of which a journey becomes the medium for
inner exploration. In each case the liminal experience is transitory, though one of the stories also implies that writing itself
offers what Turner describes as liminal *communitas*, a place
of habitation, where the bonds are egalitarian and direct, nonrational.

Looking back more than twenty years, Woolf describes writing 'An Unwritten Novel' as 'the great discovery . . . That—again
in one second—showed me how I could embody all my deposit
of experience in a shape that fitted it—not that I have ever reached
that end; but anyhow I saw, branching out of the tunnel I made,
when I discovered that method of approach, Jacob's Room, Mrs
Dalloway etc.'[2] The tunnel as an in-between place leads to sudden revelation, and the story itself involves tunnels; the writer-
narrator creates fictions about her fellow passengers as she travels
on a train from London to Eastbourne, an unusual subject for
Woolf whose narrative method is usually more mobile than her
fictional situation. The vertiginous form of the story enacts the
disintegration of fixed identity and asserts a play of difference;
as the writer observes her potential characters and imagines

---

[1] Virginia Woolf, *The Complete Shorter Fiction of Virginia Woolf* (London:
Hogarth, 1989), 121.   [2] VWL iv. 231, 16 Oct. 1930.

fictions focused on them she is not androgynous but a chameleon, shifting subject positions and gender identities. Eventually the title asserts fluidity rather than authority as the novel remains *unwritten*, and the rhythm of the prose reminds the reader that it all happens on a moving train, where what is seen through the window and what is imagined merge: 'The woods flit and fly—in summer there are bluebells; in the opening there, when Spring comes, primroses. A parting, was it, twenty years ago? Vows broken? Not Minnie's! . . . She was faithful. How she nursed her mother! All her savings on the tombstones—wreaths under glass—daffodils in jars. But I'm off the track' (p. 115).

Throughout the story there are references to mapping and reading: the passengers in the train hide from their knowledge of what life is like by reading or 'a fourth stares at the map of the line framed opposite' (p. 112). As the narrator gazes at the passenger whose story she is imagining, the woman spreads a handkerchief on her knees 'into which drop little angular fragments of eggshell—fragments of a map—a puzzle. I wish I could piece them together! If you would only sit still. She's moved her knees—the map's in bits again' (p. 117). The shifting, restless voice itself constantly transforms its subject, here from second to third person, and the map is repeatedly made and unmade. The narrator composes stories from existing maps; as she reads the face opposite her, she places her in class and narrative terms: 'She opened the door, and, putting her umbrella in the stand— that goes without saying: so, too, the whiff of beef from the basement; dot, dot, dot' (ibid.). This part of the encounter comes from fictional patterns and the realistic details accrue easily: 'this we'll skip; ornaments, curtains, trefoil china plate, yellow oblongs of cheese' (p. 114). At the same time she receives other messages; as the woman passenger rubs 'some indelible contamination' (p. 113) off the carriage window, the narrator takes her glove and rubs at her window, and she too begins to twitch as her companion does. It is an act of imaginative unselving, as she becomes her character's double, the foreigner within, in order to accomplish the birthing process while she discards other possibilities, 'the unborn children of the mind, illicit, none the less loved' (p. 118).

The narrator moves from the mapped patterns to the liminal space, beyond borders, underwater, where the familiar becomes strange: 'what a swirl these monsters leave, the waters rocking, the weeds waving and green here, black there, striking to the sand, till by degrees the atoms reassemble, the deposit sifts itself, and again through the eyes one sees clear and still' (p. 119). Her counterpart has her liminal experience which can only be imagined by the narrator moving about underwater where she can hear what cannot be said: '[W]hen the self speaks to the self, who is speaking?—the entombed soul, the spirit driven in, in, in to the central catacomb; the self that took the veil and left the world—a coward perhaps, yet somehow beautiful, as it flits with its lantern restlessly up and down the dark corridors' (p. 120). This is both part of the train journey and is the 'guilt-less maternity' that Kristeva links to literary creation, where a woman writer nourishes her society 'with a more flexible and free discourse'.[3] It is part of the fluid vitality of the story that the narrator's liminal experience, her loss of the self in the search for the other woman, is placed by 'Minnie's' motherhood. The narrator has seen her as a spinster aunt, but the woman's son meets her and she goes off with him, erasing the script that has been written for her. The narrator momentarily finds it 'untrue, it's indecent' (p. 121), and exclaims 'my world's done for!' As she recovers from the shock she retrieves herself and celebrates her literary maternity, and the revelations of desire and love that the overcrossing brings her:

Ivy in dark gardens. Milk carts at the door. Wherever I go, mysterious figures, I see you, turning the corner, mothers and sons; you, you, you. I hasten, I follow. This, I fancy, must be the sea. Grey is the landscape; dim as ashes; the water murmurs and moves. If I fall on my knees, if I go through the ritual, the ancient antics, it's you, unknown figures, you I adore. (ibid.)

The sea the narrator reaches is both the English Channel on the beach at Eastbourne and her own amniotic fluid; her birthing process involves entering the grey formless landscape, or the catacomb with its dark corridors, to bring lovingly to light what she finds. Simultaneously she uses a traditionally masculine image of exploration and pursuit.

The narrator's experience is mirrored in Mansfield's account of writing 'The Stranger', and hints at the kind of *communitas* she and Woolf may have shared; she describes it in a letter to Murry:

---

[3] Julia Kristeva, *The Kristeva Reader* (Oxford: Basil Blackwell, 1986), 207.

What a QUEER business writing is. I don't know. I dont believe other people are ever as foolishly excited as I am while Im working. How could they be? Writers would have to live in trees. Ive *been* this man *been* this woman. Ive stood for hours on the Auckland Wharf. Ive been out in the stream waiting to be berthed. Ive been a seagull hovering at the stern and a hotel porter whistling through his teeth. It isn't as though one sits and watches the spectacle. That would be thrilling enough, God knows. But one IS the spectacle for the time.[4]

Again this is not androgynous experience but something much closer to Kristeva's formulation that the binary oppositions of the Father's Law should be challenged 'in order that the struggle, the implacable difference, the violence be conceived in the very place where it operates with the maximum intransigence, in other words, in personal and sexual identity itself, so as to make it disintegrate in its very nucleus.'[5] The story's perspective is that of a middle-aged man, John Hammond, whose whole project is to uphold patriarchy's binary oppositions; the stranger of the title is both a man who has died on board at the end of the voyage and Hammond himself as he confronts the foreigner within. The story begins as a crowd waits for a ship to dock; the ship is in liminal space, neither at sea nor in harbour, neither in light nor in darkness; 'the dusk came slowly, spreading like a slow stain over the water.'[6] The sinister implications of the stain have been anticipated in the description of the passengers on the ship as 'little flies walking up and down the dish on the grey crinkled tablecloth' (p. 350). The curiously static comparison of the ocean to a tablecloth enhances the sense of stagnation about the passage. Mr Hammond's authoritative patriarchy expresses itself in his joking suggestion that a signal might be sent to the ship: ' "*Don't hesitate to land. Natives harmless*. Or: *A welcome awaits you. All is forgiven*" ' (p. 351). In retrospect, the reader realizes the significance of the unfunny joke as Mr Hammond is revealed as a colonizer who consistently dominates women: he lifts a little girl on to a high barrel then rushes off and leaves her in danger when someone more important comes along, and he tyrannizes over his wife, the chambermaid, and any other social inferior. His sense of his own significance is such that he

---

[4] KMCL iv. 97, 3 Nov. 1920.   [5] Kristeva, *The Kristeva Reader*, 209.
[6] CS 352.

blames his wife for having left him to visit their daughter in Europe; 'All is forgiven' is what he wants to feel about her return, assuming the power of God the Father. Patriarchal inscription reassures him; he feels that the dangerous inner voyage is over when he sees the labels on her luggage identifying her entirely with her role in relation to him:

'Mrs John Hammond!' He gave a long sigh of content and leaned back, crossing his arms. The strain was over. He felt he could have sat there for ever sighing his relief—the relief at being rid of that horrible tug, pull, grip on his heart. The danger was over. That was the feeling. They were on dry land again.   (pp. 356–7)

The stranger is gradually revealed to the reader through the narrative perspective; the foreigner within is the fearful helpless creature who dreads that his passion for his wife is not reciprocated: 'Would he always have this craving—this pang like hunger, somehow, to make Janey so much part of him that there wasn't any of her to escape? He wanted to blot out everybody, everything' (p. 361). When she tells him that a young first-class passenger died in her arms he enters liminal territory as his fears are confirmed; what is conveyed is that he sees it as a quasi-sexual intimacy:

'He died in my arms,' said Janey.
    The blow was so sudden that Hammond thought he would faint. He couldn't move; he couldn't breathe. He felt all his strength flowing —flowing into the big dark chair, and the big dark chair held him fast, gripped him, forced him to bear it.   (p. 362)

The objects that have symbolized his status to him, the chair where he takes his wife on to his lap, the bed which he has yearned to lie in with her, the fire that he had ordered to demonstrate his power to protect her, have all been made strange and he himself seems to be enclosed in a coffin, in a nightmare world of unfamiliarity that identifies him with the dead stranger:

The fire had gone red. Now it fell in with a sharp sound and the room was colder. Cold crept up his arms. The room was huge, immense, glittering. It filled his whole world. There was the great blind bed, with his coat flung across it like some headless man saying his prayers. There was the luggage, ready to be carried away again, anywhere, tossed into trains, carted on to boats.   (p. 363)

He seems to have become his possessions, and is in control of nothing; the story finishes with his petulant but terrified inner response to his wife's queries: 'Spoilt their evening! Spoilt their being alone together! They would never be alone together again' (p. 364). He is both the helpless, dying stranger and the middle-aged man, in a comfortable hotel and in limbo. The initial image of the grey ship which is neither here nor there becomes a trope for Mr Hammond, clad as he is 'in a grey overcoat, grey silk scarf' (p. 350). At the very moment of sexual desire for possession of his wife his sense of self and of gender is negated; it disintegrates.

The mobility of the narrative voice in these two fictions, and the rhythmic, sensuous language, undermine any suggestion of essential human identity and open up a misty landscape, which forms and dissolves as the reader watches it. The foreigner looms out of the mist, the liminal space beyond borders of definition, and is recognized as part of the self; this perhaps partially explains why both writers recur to colonization and empire. The colony itself is the foreigner within, not a child, not primitive, both the same and different, the double and the stranger. Woolf seems to feel, in the loving letter she writes to Mansfield who is isolated and lonely in France, that affinity which binds them into a public of two; she acknowledges her jealousy in the confidence that it will be understood:

It seems to me very important that women should learn to write. Does it to you?

God knows I don't like them much when they do it—or men either for the matter of that. Mr Beresford gave a lecture upon fiction the other day at the 1917 Club—a deplorable exhibition . . . And then Morgan Forster said that Prelude and The Voyage Out were the best novels of their time, and I said Damn Katherine! Why can't I be the only woman who knows how to write?[7]

---

[7] J. T. Banks (ed.), *Congenial Spirits* (London: Hogarth, 1989), 128, 13 Feb. 1921.

Bibliography

PRIMARY SOURCES

BANKS, JOANNE TRAUTMANN (ed.), *Congenial Spirits: The Selected Letters of Virginia Woolf* (London: Hogarth, 1989).

GORDON, IAN (ed.), *Undiscovered Country: The New Zealand Stories of Katherine Mansfield* (London: Longman, 1974).

HANKIN, CHERRY A. (ed.), *Letters Between Katherine Mansfield and John Middleton Murry* (London: Virago, 1988).

HANKIN, C. A. (ed.), *The Letters of John Middleton Murry to Katherine Mansfield* (London: Constable, 1983).

HANSON, CLARE (ed.), *The Critical Writings of Katherine Mansfield* (London: Macmillan, 1987).

McNEILLIE, ANDREW (ed.), *The Essays of Virginia Woolf* (London: Hogarth, 1987), ii.

MANSFIELD, KATHERINE, *The Aloe* with *Prelude* (Wellington: Port Nicholson, 1982).

—— *The Collected Short Stories* (Harmondsworth: Penguin, 1981).

—— *The Urewera Notebook* (Oxford: Oxford University Press, 1978).

MURRY, JOHN MIDDLETON (ed.), *The Journal of Katherine Mansfield*, Definitive Edition (London: Constable, 1954).

—— (ed.), *The Letters of Katherine Mansfield* (2 vols.; London: Constable, 1928).

NICOLSON, NIGEL, and TRAUTMANN, JOANNE (ed.), *The Letters of Virginia Woolf* (6 vols.; London: Chatto & Windus, 1980–3).

O'SULLIVAN, VINCENT (ed.), *The Poems of Katherine Mansfield* (Oxford: Oxford University Press, 1988).

O'SULLIVAN, VINCENT, and SCOTT, MARGARET (ed.), *The Collected Letters of Katherine Mansfield* (4 vols.; Oxford: Clarendon, 1984–96).

OLIVIER BELL, ANNE, and McNEILLIE, ANDREW (ed.), *The Diary of Virginia Woolf* (5 vols.; Harmondsworth: Penguin, 1979–85).

WOOLF, VIRGINIA, *A Room of One's Own* (London: Hogarth, 1929).

—— *The Captain's Death Bed and Other Essays* (London: Hogarth, 1950).

—— *The Common Reader* (London: Hogarth, 1962).

—— *The Complete Shorter Fiction of Virginia Woolf* (London: Hogarth, 1989).

WOOLF, VIRGINIA, *The Death of the Moth and Other Essays* (London: Hogarth, 1942).
—— *Jacob's Room*, World's Classics (Oxford: Oxford University Press, 1992).
—— *Moments of Being* (St Albans: Triad/Panther, 1978).
—— *Mrs Dalloway*, World's Classics (Oxford: Oxford University Press, 1992).
—— *Three Guineas* (London: Hogarth, 1943).
—— *To the Lighthouse*, World's Classics (Oxford: Oxford University Press, 1992).
—— *The Voyage Out*, World's Classics (Oxford: Oxford University Press, 1992).

SECONDARY SOURCES

ALEXANDER, PETER F., *Leonard and Virginia Woolf: A Literary Partnership* (London: Harvester Wheatsheaf, 1992).
ALPERS, ANTONY, *The Life of Katherine Mansfield* (New York: Viking, 1980).
BARTHES, ROLAND, *Image-Music-Text*, ed. Stephen Heath (London: Fontana, 1977).
BEER, GILLIAN, *Virginia Woolf: The Common Ground* (Edinburgh: Edinburgh University Press, 1996).
BERNIKOW, LOUISE, *Among Women* (New York: Harmony Books, 1980).
BHABHA, HOMI, *The Location of Culture* (London: Routledge, 1994).
BODDY, GILLIAN, *Katherine Mansfield: The Woman and the Writer* (Ringwood: Penguin, 1988).
BOWLBY, RACHEL, *Feminist Destinations and Further Essays on Virginia Woolf* (Edinburgh: Edinburgh University Press, 1997).
—— (ed.), *Virginia Woolf* (Harlow: Longman, 1992).
BURGAN, MARY, *Illness, Gender, and Writing* (London: Johns Hopkins University Press, 1994).
BUTLER, JUDITH, *Gender Trouble: Feminism and the Subversion of Identity* (London: Routledge, 1990).
CARR, EMILY, *The Book of Small* (Toronto: Irwin Publishing, 1986).
DeSALVO, LOUISE, *Virginia Woolf: The Impact of Childhood Sexual Abuse on Her Life and Work* (London: Women's Press, 1989).
DOUGLAS, MARY, *Purity and Danger: An Analysis of Concepts of Pollution and Taboo* (London: Routledge & Kegan Paul, 1966).
DUNBAR, PAMELA, *Radical Mansfield: Double Discourse in Katherine Mansfield's Short Stories* (London: Macmillan, 1997).
DUNN, JANE, *A Very Close Conspiracy: Vanessa Bell and Virginia Woolf* (London: Jonathan Cape, 1990).

EISENSTEIN, Sergei, *Notes of a Film Director* (Moscow: Foreign Languages Publishing House, 1946).

FORMAN, MAURICE BUXTON (ed.), *The Letters of John Keats* (London: Oxford University Press, 1952).

FRY, ROGER, *Vision and Design* (Harmondsworth: Penguin, 1937).

FULBROOK, KATE, *Katherine Mansfield* (Brighton: Harvester, 1986).

GARNETT, ANGELICA, *Deceived with Kindness: A Bloomsbury Childhood* (London: Chatto & Windus, 1984).

GORDON, LYNDALL, *Virginia Woolf: A Writer's Life* (Oxford: Oxford University Press, 1986).

GURR, ANDREW, *Writers in Exile* (Brighton: Harvester, 1981).

HANSON, CLARE, *Virginia Woolf* (London: Macmillan, 1994).

HANSON, CLARE, and GURR, ANDREW, *Katherine Mansfield* (London: Macmillan, 1981).

HAYMAN, RONALD, *Literature and Living: A Consideration of Katherine Mansfield & Virginia Woolf*, Covent Garden Essays, 3 (London: Covent Garden, 1972).

HEILBRUN, CAROLYN G., and HIGONNET, MARGARET R. (eds.), *The Representation of Women in Fiction* (Baltimore: Johns Hopkins University Press, 1983).

HYDE, ROBIN, *The Godwits Fly* (Auckland: Auckland University Press, 1970).

KAPLAN, SYDNEY JANET, *Katherine Mansfield and the Origins of Modernist Fiction* (Ithaca, NY: Cornell University Press, 1991).

KRISTEVA, JULIA, *The Kristeva Reader* (Oxford: Basil Blackwell, 1986).

—— *Powers of Horror* (New York: Columbia University Press, 1982).

—— *Strangers to Ourselves* (London: Harvester Wheatsheaf, 1991).

LEE, HERMIONE, *Virginia Woolf* (London: Chatto & Windus, 1996).

MAJUMDAR, ROBIN, and McLAURIN, ALLEN (eds.), *Virginia Woolf: The Critical Heritage* (London: Routledge & Kegan Paul, 1975).

MARCUS, JANE (ed.), *Virginia Woolf: A Feminist Slant* (Lincoln: University of Nebraska Press, 1983).

—— (ed.), *Virginia Woolf and Bloomsbury: A Centenary Celebration* (London: Macmillan, 1987).

MARSH, JAN, *Bloomsbury Women* (New York: Henry Holt, 1996).

MEISEL, PERRY, *The Absent Father: Virginia Woolf and Walter Pater* (New Haven: Yale University Press, 1980).

MEPHAM, JOHN, *Virginia Woolf: A Literary Life* (London: Macmillan, 1991).

MINOW-PINKNEY, MAKIKO, *Virginia Woolf and the Problem of the Subject* (Brighton: Harvester, 1987).

MORAN, PATRICIA, *Word of Mouth: Body Language in Katherine Mansfield and Virginia Woolf* (London: University Press of Virginia, 1996).

MORTIMER, RAYMOND, *Duncan Grant* (Harmondsworth: Penguin, 1944).

NOBLE, JOAN RUSSELL (ed.), *Recollections of Virginia Woolf* (London: Sphere, 1989).

PILDITCH, JAN (ed.), *The Critical Response to Katherine Mansfield* (Westport, Conn.: Greenwood, 1996).

POOLE, ROGER, *The Unknown Virginia Woolf*, 4th edn. (Cambridge: Cambridge University Press, 1995).

REID, SU (ed.), *New Casebooks: Mrs Dalloway and To the Lighthouse* (London: Macmillan, 1993).

RICE, PHILIP, and WAUGH, PATRICIA (eds.), *Modern Literary Theory*, 2nd edn. (London: Edward Arnold, 1992).

ROBINS, ANNA GRUETZNER, *Modern Art in Britain 1910–1914* (London: Merrell Holberton, 1997).

ROBINSON, ROGER (ed.), *Katherine Mansfield: In from the Margin* (Baton Rouge, La.: Louisiana State University Press, 1994).

ROE, SUE, *Writing and Gender* (Hemel Hempstead: Harvester Wheatsheaf, 1990).

ROSE, PHYLLIS, *Woman of Letters: A Life of Virginia Woolf* (London: Pandora, 1986).

SCOTT, BONNIE KIME (ed.), *The Gender of Modernism: A Critical Anthology* (Bloomington, Ind.: Indiana University Press, 1990).

SÉLLEI, NÓRA, *Katherine Mansfield and Virginia Woolf: A Personal and Professional Bond* (Frankfurt: Peter Lang, 1996).

STANSKY, PETER, *On or About December 1910: Early Bloomsbury and Its Intimate World* (Cambridge, Mass.: Harvard University Press, 1996).

SYMONS, ARTHUR, *Studies in Prose and Verse* (London: J. M. Dent, 1904).

TOMALIN, CLAIRE, *Katherine Mansfield: A Secret Life* (London: Viking, 1987).

TURNER, VICTOR, *The Ritual Process* (New York: Aldine de Gruyter, 1995 (1969)).

TURNER, VICTOR, and TURNER, EDITH, *Image and Pilgrimage in Christian Culture* (Oxford: Basil Blackwell, 1978).

WOOLF, LEONARD, *Autobiography* iii. *Beginning Again* (London: Hogarth, 1964).

Index